WINNING
the
MANDATE

WINNING
the
MANDATE
The Indian Experience

Bidyut Chakrabarty
Sugato Hazra

 SAGE www.sagepublications.com
Los Angeles • London • New Delhi • Singapore • Washington DC

First published in 2016 by

 SAGE Publications India Pvt Ltd
B1/I-1 Mohan Cooperative Industrial Area
Mathura Road, New Delhi 110 044, India
www.sagepub.in

SAGE Publications Inc
2455 Teller Road
Thousand Oaks, California 91320, USA

SAGE Publications Ltd
1 Oliver's Yard, 55 City Road
London EC1Y 1SP, United Kingdom

SAGE Publications Asia-Pacific Pte Ltd
3 Church Street
#10-04 Samsung Hub
Singapore 049483

Published by Vivek Mehra for SAGE Publications India Pvt Ltd, typeset in 10/13 pt Berkeley by PrePSol Enterprises Pvt Ltd, and printed at Chaman Enterprises, New Delhi.

Library of Congress Cataloging-in-Publication Data

Names: Chakrabarty, Bidyut, author. | Hazra, Sugato, author.
Title: Winning the mandate : the Indian experience / Bidyut Chakrabarty, Sugato Hazra.
Description: New Delhi ; Thousand Oaks : SAGE Publications, 2016. | Includes bibliographical references and index.
Identifiers: LCCN 2015041717| ISBN 9789351507444 (hardback : alk. paper) | ISBN 9789351507451 (ebook) | ISBN 9789351507437 (epub)
Subjects: LCSH: India. Parliament. Lok Sabha--Elections, 2014. | Political campaigns–India. | Bharatiya Janata Party. | Modi, Narendra, 1950-
Classification: LCC JQ294 .C45 2016 | DDC 324.954/0532--dc23 LC record available at http://lccn.loc.gov/2015041717

ISBN: 978-93-515-0744-4 (HB)

The SAGE Team: Supriya Das, Guneet Kaur Gulati and Rajinder Kaur

To,

The People of India

Thank you for choosing a SAGE product!
If you have any comment, observation or feedback,
I would like to personally hear from you.
Please write to me at **contactceo@sagepub.in**

Vivek Mehra, Managing Director and CEO,
SAGE Publications India Pvt Ltd, New Delhi

Bulk Sales

SAGE India offers special discounts
for purchase of books in bulk.
We also make available special imprints
and excerpts from our books on demand.

For orders and enquiries, write to us at

Marketing Department
SAGE Publications India Pvt Ltd
B1/I-1, Mohan Cooperative Industrial Area
Mathura Road, Post Bag 7
New Delhi 110044, India

E-mail us at **marketing@sagepub.in**

Get to know more about SAGE

Be invited to SAGE events, get on our mailing list.
Write today to **marketing@sagepub.in**

This book is also available as an e-book.

Contents

List of Abbreviations

AAP	Aam Aadmi Party
ABVP	Akhil Bharatiya Vidyarthi Parishad
AIADMK	All India Anna Dravida Munnetra Kazhagam
AIG	American International Group
AITC	All India Trinamul Congress
BJD	Biju Janata Dal
BJP	Bharatiya Janata Party
BSNL	Bharat Sanchar Nigam Limited
BSP	Bahujan Samaj Party
BWA	Broadband Wireless Access
CAG	Citizens for Accountable Governance
CBI	Central Bureau of Investigation
CII	Confederation of Indian Industry
CPI	Communist Party of India
CSDS	Centre for the Study of Developing Societies
CVC	Central Vigilance Commission
DD	Doordarshan
EC	Election Commission
GPP	Gujarat Parivartan Party
HPC	High Power Committee
IAC	India Against Corruption
IAEA	International Atomic Energy Agency
INC	Indian National Congress
INLD	Indian National Lok Dal
IPKF	Indian Peace Keeping Force
IT	Information Technology
JD(S)	Janata Dal (Socialist)
JD(U)	Janata Dal (United)
JNU	Jawaharlal Nehru University
JP	Jayaprakash Narayan

LJP	Lok Janshakti Party
LoC	Line of Control
MoU	Memoranda of Understanding
NCA	Narmada Control Authority
NCP	Nationalist Congress Party
NDA	National Democratic Alliance
Niti	New Initiatives to Transform India
NOTA	None of the Above
NREGA	National Rural Employment Guarantee Act
NSG	Nuclear Suppliers Group
NSUI	National Students' Union of India
OBCs	Other Backward Classes
OC	Organizing Committee
RJD	Rashtriya Janata Dal
SAD	Shiromani Akali Dal
SC	Scheduled Caste
SHGs	Self-help Groups
SIT	Special Investigating Team
SP	Samajwadi Party
SPG	Special Protection Group
SRCC	Sri Ram College of Commerce
SS	Shiv Sena
SVBPT	Sardar Vallabh Bhai Patel Trust
TDP	Telugu Desam Party
TMC	Trinamul Congress
TRPs	Television Rating Points
UAS	Unified Access Service
UP	Uttar Pradesh
UPA	United Progressive Alliance

Preface and Acknowledgements

Winning the Mandate is our dream project. Seeking to comprehend the electioneering in India, the text engages with the intricate processes that unfold especially during the poll. Each election is different. Hence, there can hardly be a universal model of analysis. Being sensitive to this aspect of election in India, we have paid adequate attention to the contextual–ideological issues that appear to have significantly influenced the election strategies and various modes of campaign. Election manifestos are prepared accordingly by the parties in the fray though the same has lost relevance of late due to competitive populism, replacing, if not undermining, the promises that figure prominently in the widely publicized election manifestos. What, however, remains significant in elections is the local context that significantly influences the minds of the voters. Here comes the importance of election strategies that are usually framed by the local activists. This is perhaps one of the reasons for the success of regional parties in Indian elections, although the 2014 election defies the trend by enabling the Bharatiya Janata Party (BJP, that has national expanse) to secure an absolute majority in parliament. As our study has shown, the massive victory of the party is attributed to the successful application of strategies which were also tuned to the local circumstances. For instance, the landslide win of the BJP candidates in UP in the 2014 Lok Sabha poll cannot be plausibly explained without reference to the Muzaffarnagar communal skirmishes that took place just before the election. The outbreak of communal riots can be said to have polarized the voters to a significant extent, which benefitted the BJP at the cost of the incumbent Samajwadi Party (SP) and its *bête noire,* the Bahujan Samaj Party (BSP). Besides the local contexts, there is no doubt that the personality of the prime ministerial candidate, Narendra Modi, seems to have brought voters together against the erstwhile Congress-led government of the United Progressive Alliance (UPA), which was believed to be corrupt. The argument that the book pursues is about this complex interplay of factors underlining both the local and national contexts. Our explanation of the 2014 poll outcome is thus couched around this argument.

Book writing is a collaborative project. Besides the author, one needs a good and sensitive publishing house to provide a safe home for the text. We are fortunate to have SAGE as our publisher. This book is a sequel to the ones that we have already published with SAGE. This would not have been possible without the support of our colleagues in SAGE. We would like to particularly thank Mr Rudra Narayan Sharma and Ms Elina Mazumdar for their unflinching support during the preparation of the book. The quiet researchers who help collating information are no less important than those who write the book. Jeswin Thomas needs a special mention. Others who have helped in the process include Dipavali, Subhash Chakravarti and Anasuya. We acknowledge their support. We are also grateful to the anonymous referees for their comments that helped us improve the text to a considerable extent. Our successful academic engagement would not have been possible without the support that we have received from our parents, brothers and sisters. Last, but not the least, by allowing us to concentrate on academic feats, our respective spouses have played a role which is not only appreciative, but also deserves a 'Big Thank You'. We cannot thank them enough for their contribution in sustaining our academic zeal and productivity. By being creatively destructive, our kids always remain sources of joy and happiness. We are happy to say that we would not have had what we so far had without our family being so supportive and indulgent of our whims and idiosyncrasies.

Introduction: Is 2014 Election a Game Changer?

On 16th May 2014, India witnessed the result of an intense political campaign hitherto unseen. For those who were vanquished felt that it was the success of a marketing blitzkrieg that actually pollutes a democracy. For those who supported the eventual winner, Narendra Modi-led BJP, it was a great victory. Viewed either way, India's national election for the 16th Lok Sabha in 2014 will remain as a landmark in the annals of political campaign.

The election result was a shock to many, politicians, media persons, psephologists and even political analysts. That Narendra Modi-led BJP would emerge as the largest political party was generally accepted. What stumped most was the scale of the victory. Journalist Rajdeep Sardesai wrote of a dinner hosted by India's telecom baron Sunil Mittal just a day before the election results came on 16th May. Nobody present in the dinner did predict an absolute majority for BJP and a more than 300 seat for BJP-led National Democratic Alliance (NDA). Some in media felt the number for BJP would be 200 or less. Even India's veteran politician and former minister Sharad Pawar predicted a hung parliament with 200 to 220 seats for BJP.[1] More interesting had been the exit poll predictions. None of the channels barring one, a Hindi news channel News 24, predicted much beyond simple majority for the BJP-led NDA coalition. Their estimates ranged between 249 and 289. Only News 24 boldly announced 340 seats for NDA, a figure most felt was mere wishful thinking of a little known psephologist, Today's Chanakya. The exit polls were also far off the mark in guessing the Congress debacle. All were in agreement that the Congress-led UPA would touch 100 with difficulty. Nobody thought that the grand old party of Indian democracy would not even touch the bare minimum to be counted as a recognized opposition party in India's lower house, Lok Sabha. The rules say that to be a recognized opposition party, it has to win minimum 10 per cent of the 543 seats—that is 54 seats. Congress stopped at 44.

The unthinkable did happen. In the 67-year long history of independent India, voters opted for a single non-Congress party headed by a person known for his staunch anti-Congressism. In an India accustomed to fragmented political verdicts and coalition governments, for the first time in 30 years and seven national elections later, a single political party received the mandate to govern the country for five years from 2014. The extent of the victory had been so overwhelming, in an otherwise issueless election, that all supporters and detractors of the winning camp could not but express their disbelief in delight or in despair.

The sentiments were strong since the architect of this victory, Narendra Damodardas Modi, the Gujarat Chief Minister, had been the most hated person for more than 12 years. So strong had been the feeling that even supporters of Modi, known fondly as NaMo, mostly kept a low profile. Only few, known for their erudition and command over English, were bold enough to take up the cudgel in support of him. Journalists from Gujarat noticed that any reports filed which had positive reference to the Gujarat government of NaMo received a harsh caesarean treatment and banished inside, if used at all. But reports, often coloured with acceptable dose of imagination to criticize Modi, found prominent display. Journalists looking for career advancement opted to report accordingly. Modi thus emerged as arguably the most hated politician in rest of India.

There was virtual unanimity of views on him. Think of any polite or not-so-polite abuse that one can hurl at a politician in high position; all have been used on Modi. Even his party colleagues squirmed in his presence worried that this should not get splashed in media. So much had been the antipathy that a political ally and former Chief Minister of Bihar Nitish Kumar went to the extent of cancelling a dinner he was scheduled to hold in honour of visiting BJP leaders in the state capital Patna. During the election campaign, the Chief Minister of West Bengal Mamata Banerjee said that she would not have allowed Modi's chartered flight to land in the state but for the fact that she cared for democratic rights. She kept on mentioning Modi as Mr Riot in her campaign speeches. Reports on Modi abuses did find prominent display.

So strong had been the sentiment against Modi that even on 13th May 2014, just three days before the actual counting of votes was to commence, an MP from the southern state of Andhra Pradesh told journalist Harish Khare that Modi would not win a majority and with support from the former Chief Minister of UP, Mayawati's BSP, a coalition would form the next government in India.[2] There had been free flow of reports, which in media parlance is known as plants. One such report in a leading business paper claimed that Modi's close associate Smriti Irani, who was pitted against the Congress campaign chief Rahul Gandhi, would be disqualified for exceeding the ceiling of expenses. There was no check on the procedures adopted on such matters. Nobody bothered to find it out and the grossly incorrect report was splashed as lead news in that newspaper. There are many such glaring instances of known predisposed reports on Narendra Modi and people close to him.

But the detractors felt that Modi's campaign received favoured treatment in media. Harish Khare wrote,

> It was this singular success in controlling the media—both old and new—to Narendra Modi's prime ministerial project that posed the biggest problem for the Congress campaign. Overwhelming numbers of media players and personnel had simply abandoned the virtue of neutrality, objectivity and even-handedness. The Congress could not impress upon the media its professional obligations. The media's defection—induced and designed—to the Modi corner gave the BJP's prime ministerial candidate a staggering advantage.[3]

This perhaps was an afterthought of Khare who had been the former media advisor of Prime Minister Dr Manmohan Singh in 2009. The fact remains that in an election it is the media that calls the shots by influencing public opinion. It is also an incontrovertible fact that the mainstream media had been reasonably certain that Indians would court disaster by electing a Narendra Modi government. The electorates were expected to pay heed to that. Even if some Indians failed to realize the machinations of the Modi campaign, the views converged that Modi would be so dependent on allies that he would not enjoy an unrestrained authority on his cabinet. Indians, the thinking types, went to bed on 15th assured that their greatest fear would be dispelled on 16th May, the day of the election result. As Khare mentioned, the conclusion of a Congress strategist was that BJP would not cross 200 seats; therefore, Narendra Modi would not be the Prime Minister.[4]

After an arduous five-month long election campaign, on 16th came the deluge. It was a shock to see one NaMo steering a boat instead of Noah. Catastrophe worse than the two world wars would be the fate of

India, lamented some. Good days will come once again (in Hindi: *Achhe din aane wale hain*) said those who voted for him. Eminent economist Jagdish Bhagwati hoped that with Narendra Modi, a votary of growth at the helm, India would avoid the 'Amartya Sen fallacy' of manipulating the social indicators with doles and subsidies and instead would opt for growth. Shorn of the economic nomenclature, what majority of Indians opted for in the election was peace and prosperity. The overwhelming number of young Indians were concerned more of their own future than what detractors of Modi had been crying hoarse—that of secularism, polarization, fascism and so on. They wanted a positive vibe that came from Modi. On Modi's negative vibe, Bhagwati quoted what the English poet Alexander Pope said, 'Everything seems yellow to the jaundiced eye'.[5]

Narendra Modi has been an antithesis of what independent India under its first Prime Minister Jawaharlal Nehru evolved as. There were two aspects of Nehru's thoughts that remained firmly in place long after his death in 1964. One was on economic issues. India turned itself into a state-controlled socialistic economy. His daughter Indira Gandhi took it even further in 1969 and thereafter so as to maintain her grip over the country. Only 24 years ago in 1991, it fell on Narasimha Rao, the first non-Nehru family member from Congress to occupy the post of the Prime Minister for a full five-year term, to dismantle a large part of the licence-control raj of Nehru–Gandhis and liberalize the economy. But liberalization in economic policy notwithstanding, in politics the Nehruvian idea of 'secularism' remained as an acceptable and irrefutable doctrine. Despite the rise of 'fundamentalism' among the Hindus after the movement over the Ram Janmabhoomi temple at Ayodhya in the north Indian state of Uttar Pradesh (UP), the idea of secularism remained firmly ingrained. Even when the Hindu nationalist party BJP came to power in 1996, 1998 and 1999, the government continued to tread along the accepted path. Then Prime Minister Vajpayee, according to some Congress leaders, was the last 'Nehruvian' in BJP. Narendra Modi is different. To follow his idea of India, it is necessary to look back briefly to the issues and views prevalent during the days when India won independence.

It was a conflict between two stalwarts of Congress when the nation won its independence. Sardar Vallabhbhai Patel was the unchallenged leader of Congress, who was the overwhelming choice of the party as India's first Prime Minister. But Mahatma Gandhi intervened and hoisted Jawaharlal

Nehru to lead independent India. Always faithful to Gandhi, Patel accepted the post of the Home Minister and took over as the deputy to the Prime Minister Nehru. Congress then had several conflicting interest groups— broadly the two extreme groups had been those of orthodox Hindu views and the Muslim group that opted to remain in India. Between these spectrums stood the two commanders of the government, Patel and Nehru. Both agreed that unlike Pakistan, which opted to become a Muslim nation, India would not declare itself as a Hindu country. Following the decision of Congress during the country's freedom struggle, India chose to remain secular where all religions had equal positions. This resolve was severely tested during the partition process in 1946–47. Riots broke out between the Hindus and Sikhs on one side and Muslims on the other. During this period, contradictions between Nehru and Patel came to the fore.

Patel was pragmatic, while Nehru was romantic. Nehru's romanticism came, perhaps, because of his modern outlook but espousal of what M.N. Roy called 'medievalism' of Gandhi. Patel was blunt with militant Hindus and sarcastic on undecided Muslims. He appealed to the 'Hindu Mahasabhaites' to join Congress and told them bluntly in a speech in Lucknow (January 1948), 'If you think that you are the only custodians of Hinduism, you are mistaken. Hinduism preaches a broader outlook. I appeal to the RSS not to be rash and tactless. Do not be aggressive'. For the Muslims, his views were plain, 'To Indian Muslims I have only one question. Why did you not open your mouths on the Kashmir issue? Why did you not condemn the action of Pakistan?' After highlighting the vacillation of Muslims, Patel was stern in his message for the community,

> It is your duty now to sail in the same boat and sink or swim together. I want to tell you very frankly that you cannot ride two horses. Select one horse. Those who want to go to Pakistan can go there and live in peace.[6]

Patel was a natural Gandhian, Hindu in faith, and realist in character. He knew Nehru's value in newly independent nation, '...that in the coming election Congress could not do without Nehru's popularity. He also knew that the latter's (Nehru's) international reputation gave him (Patel) the opportunity to consolidate a totalitarian state behind a democratic façade.'[7]

Nehru's opinion on India as a nation and the confusion in a Muslim mind was similar to Patel's. Nehru said:

> Anybody who does not owe allegiance to the state in which he lives can only live there as an alien with no citizenship rights. If Muslims want to live in the Indian Union and owe full allegiance to the state they will be welcomed. Those who want to leave this country are free to go.[8]

But the difference between the two leaders was one of degree. While both Patel and Nehru opted for a secular state, Nehru's hostility towards the Hindus was stronger than Patel's. In the same statement on the question of citizenship of Muslims (October 1947), Nehru stated, 'The call for the establishment of a Hindu state is a reactionary slogan and will bang the door on all future progress'.[9] But a pragmatic Patel was neutral in his approach and opted to handle every situation in a manner beneficial to the country and the Congress party. He acknowledged the presence of strong Hindu sentiment within the Congress. He also knew if the party did not take proper steps, the Hindu Mahasabha would gain strength at the cost of Congress. He refused to antagonize the orthodox elements in Congress and helped Purushottamdas Tandon to win the election as the Congress president in 1950 despite Nehru's opposition. The Nasik Congress illustrated the difference between Patel's pragmatism and Nehru's romanticism. Patel's manipulation too resulted in Tandon getting elected as the Congress President against the will of Nehru. 'The manoeuvre of getting Tandon elected as President regained for the Congress the aggressive Hindu communalism, prejudiced the chances of the rival in the next election, and thus ensured Congress retaining power thereafter.'[10]

While there were disagreements between him and Nehru, this took nearly a point of no return in January 1948 over the issue of paying Pakistan a sum of ₹55 crore (₹550 million). Patel had sent notice to Pakistan linking the payment to a settlement on Kashmir. Nehru differed. He had the then Governor General Lord Mountbatten as his ally. Both persuaded Mahatma Gandhi to intervene and to make Patel agree on payment without a precondition. Events moved at a fast pace thereafter. A Hindu fanatic assassinated Mahatma on 31 January. Patel did not live long enough thereafter and died a few months after the election of Tandon as Congress president in 1950. The secularism of Congress received a makeover, from the down-to-earth Patel style to an idealistic Nehruvian secularism. The latter was more often than not hostile on the majority community. The first such act of Nehru was a crafty removal of Tandon as Congress president in September 1951. Nehru often had differences of opinion with India's first President Dr Rajendra Prasad, a tall leader from the Hindutva camp of Congress. It came to a head when President Prasad accepted an invitation to inaugurate the restored temple at Somnath in Gujarat. Nehru wrote to Prasad that the President should stay away from any religious function. Dr Prasad disagreed and announced in Somnath that he had equal respects for all religions and on occasion would visit all religious places—Church, Mosque, Dargah or Gurudwara.

According to M.N. Roy, a communist and keen political observer, Nehru was split between his modernity and allegiance to Gandhi's 'mediaevalism'. 'The tragedy of Nehru, his failure to unfold his personality to a high degree of creative greatness, was brought about by a conflict of two cultures; the tradition of mediaevalism represented by Gandhi proved much too strong for Nehru's superficial modernism....' Roy felt Nehru's modernism was superficial since he never militated against Gandhi's 'antithetical cultural tradition'.[11] Roy, a former revolutionary, delegate to the congresses of Communist International, Russia's aide to China, could not have appreciated Gandhi's politics which unified India under the Congress Party. But his observations on Nehru's dilemma cannot be winked at as utterly irrelevant.

In course of electoral politics, Nehru too perhaps appreciated the pragmatism of Patel. Roy had a solution to this apparent puzzle in Nehru's character.

> It resulted from the fact that contemporary India does live in two ages: chronologically she lives in the 20th century; but historically, that is to say, in the scale of social evolution and cultural progress, she still languishes in the soporific twilight of the Middle ages.[12]

This paradox of the Indian situation made Nehru create the political theme of secularism. This was Nehru's brilliance as a politician. He knew his popularity lay in his modernity, his acceptance on the global stage and also the fact that he was Gandhi's choice. His modernity and the urge to win international acclaim made him averse towards the Hindu nationalism, but the domestic political compulsion of keeping the party structure intact made Nehru bear with the Hindu chauvinists like Rajendra Prasad. Both the modernists and the traditionalists adopted Nehru's idea of secularism in Indian politics.

Leaders opted to participate in all religious rituals to please their party workers. People in effect became vote banks. It was seen that certain castes opt to vote for fellow caste leaders and, hence, came caste-based politics. It was also noticed that some communities, Muslims in particular, cast votes as dictated and recommended by their religious leaders. Thus, came the aggressive posturing to please the religious leaders who could help in winning additional votes. In the garb of secularism, Indian politics turned into a theatre of the absurd. The trend began with Mrs Indira Gandhi seeking support of Imam Bukhari of Delhi's Jama Masjid before the 1980 elections. This was an effort to win back the Muslim votes that deserted the party in the wake of the family planning drive during 1975–77, the emergency period of Indian administration.

Congress leader and later Indian President Pranab Mukherjee wrote in his autobiography:

> The Congress never ruled by securing the majority of votes in any election; it ruled by securing the majority of the seats. In all general elections when the Congress won a majority of the seats, it did not get more than 43–48 per cent of the total votes polled. The remaining votes were shared by other political parties. Such an outcome is inevitable in a multi- party democracy. The way in which the Congress could secure a majority of seats was by bagging the single largest chunk of minority votes which, however, accounted for less than 51 per cent.[13]

Nehru's secularism stood Congress in good stead.

Narendra Modi broke the trend. He started talking of development in his election campaigns for the Gujarat assembly in 2007, made it stronger in 2012 and then used it in 2014 for the 16th Lok Sabha elections. This break from a well-established trend of Indian politics is the most important deviation in the Modi campaign. The question that remains to be answered is if the trend will persist henceforth. The unprecedented success of Modi might encourage political parties to rethink. But the point to note is that Modi had been and would continue to be a Hindu political leader. So much identified is he with Hinduism that he did not have to overtly espouse the Hindu cause. On the other hand, his gestures to others, Muslims in particular, would make him look a 'secular Hindu' leader, a branding that is natural and most acceptable to Modi's supporters and critics.

Modi knew that Congress was vulnerable due to inept administrative record since 2004. So, he focused his attack on Congress. 'Congress mukt Bharat' (An India without Congress) was his battle cry. This needed to expose the mistakes of the illustrious leaders of the party. Congress, post-independence, effectively had turned into a family-run party. Nehru was the youngest among the top leaders of Congress in 1947. His age was one factor that led Mahatma Gandhi to choose him over the decision of the party to appoint Sardar Patel as India's first Prime Minister. Most of the senior leaders passed away one after another by the time Nehru won the third General elections in 1962. This vacuum helped Nehru to get his daughter Indira elected as Congress president in 1959. The mantle fell on her when Nehru and his successor Lal Bahadur Shastri died within a span of two years. Indira did not tolerate any dissent. She even successfully turned the entire party as her individual fiefdom. Thus, when she was assassinated in October 1984, her son Rajiv Gandhi took over despite some constitutional impropriety. Modi intended to break this family-run party. He reminded the countrymen as to how Patel was denied his due to become the nation's first Prime Minister. He also brought to the fore the contributions of Patel in integrating the princely states under the democratic republic of India. Modi used a symbolism that of constructing a statue of Sardar Patel in the Sardar Sarovar dam on the river Narmada in Gujarat. He sought contributions of iron scraps from farmers for that. It did not matter much if the call yielded tons of iron scraps or not but what it did was important. More than 60 years after India's independence, the country started re-evaluating Nehru and Patel. Due to the sudden interest, books on Patel which had gone out of print, were reprinted and became best sellers. In the process, the country was made aware that for the India of 2014 Patel deserved no less credit than Nehru's. It was a very subtle and clever way of deflating the image of Nehru among the Indians. Modi chose his ammunition shrewdly. At a later stage when election campaign heated up, there was a leak of a report on India's misadventure with China in 1962. The carefully engineered leak made public what the Australian journalist Neville Maxwell while authoring a book on India's China war used as a supporting material, the Henderson Brooks report.

Lt. Gen. Henderson Brooks and Brig. P.S. Bhagat were appointed to enquire the drubbing of the Indian army in the 1962 war against China.

Maxwell was the New Delhi correspondent for *The Times,* London, at the time and had access to the top-secret report. Successive Indian governments refused to make its findings public. Maxwell was convinced that the blame for the war rested with Nehru. Commissioned in the wake of the debacle, the report has never been officially declassified. Even during the 15th Lok Sabha, replying to a question in Parliament, UPA Defence Minister A.K. Antony said that the report could not be released as its contents 'are not only extremely sensitive but are of current operational value'. Later, in response to a request for the report under the Right to Information Act, the army headquarters reiterated this position. The Henderson Brooks' report was sent by the army chief to the Defence Minister in July 1963, who in turn forwarded it to the Prime Minister. The leak of the partial report, about a month before the elections 2014 began, was an embarrassment for Congress and a big blow to the defenders of Nehru's stellar role in India. Modi's theme of 'Congress mukt Bharat' received a boost with this leak.

While Modi deviated from the Nehruvian concept of secularism by not wooing any community, he did not shun all that Nehru did. For instance, in the first ever general election in 1951–52, Nehru created a condition so that the entire opposition, be it the Hindu Mahasabha, Communist Party of India (CPI) or Kripalini's break-away group from Congress, attacked Nehru. This made Nehru a larger hero than he was already. Thus, he could overcome two strong negative sentiments Congress had been passing through. One was due to the riots that broke out with the partition of the country. Second were the factors that arose due to weaknesses and follies in the governance. But Nehru, the dominant personality, was enough to attract Indians accustomed to paying ritualistic obeisance to their feudal lords. Nehru emerged as the new democratic feudal lord of India. Narendra Modi did not have the advantage of circumstances like Nehru's. But the campaign could turn all his opponents hostile to him. They all lost their priorities in their zeal to attack Narendra Modi in person. Like Nehru in 1951, Modi, too, reaped the benefit 63 years later. What is more, Modi kept setting agenda for each day of campaign, trapping his opponents to merely fall for it. Modi, thus, remained the focus of the election agenda with everybody else taking a subservient position.

In effect, Modi shunned Congressism but did not forget to emulate the campaign styles of Nehru and his daughter Indira. In 1951, Nehru emerged as the undisputed democratically elected lord of India. So deep was his authority that he could leave a door open for his daughter Indira to assume the mantle within three years of his death. In 1967, Indira won on the back of the brand of Congress left by Nehru. But in 1971, she eased the old guards and contested alone, seeking votes for herself. In case of Nehru, nobody cared to ask if effectively the election campaign was personality-centric like in the US. Nobody cared to ask in 1971 also. When Narendra Modi turned the campaign 2014 into a presidential type and sought vote in his favour, critics pounced upon him for turning a Westminster-style democracy into a US presidential type contest. But the fact remains that in India that had been a successful mode of campaign initiated by Nehru, followed by Indira and somewhat imitated by Vajpayee. The critical element necessary in such a campaign is a charismatic and strong leader. Not only Narendra Modi had that advantage but also he had the added one of not having any competition, any leader having matching charisma, the advantage that both Nehru and Indira enjoyed earlier. Modi did not hesitate to pick up the successful elements from the Congress campaign and use the same to his advantage.

The most interesting aspect of the successful Modi campaign had been the fact that unlike in the case of Nehru, Indira or even Vajpayee, Modi did not have much backing from the party brand. Congress was a brand when Nehru faced elections in 1951 and thereafter. Indira had the advantage of being the incumbent and repositioning the brand Congress. Vajpayee gained from the BJP brand created largely out of the Ram Mandir (Temple) movement. But Modi took over a rather confused party whose leaders were not strong enough to turn the table against a corruption riddled, confused ruling coalition. Brand BJP was in a moribund state. Modi revived it with his past success in Gujarat, overcame his own negatives arising out of unfortunate riots of 2002 in the state and strengthened the brand to such an extent that the election results shocked his supporters and detractors alike. Rise of Modi is a unique case study in the annals of democratic election campaign. It is a lesson on how elections should be fought in a complex democracy.

How strong had been the Modi campaign would be illustrated by the election results. BJP contested 428 seats and won 282—a success rate of 66 per cent. In contrast, Congress, the only other big national party, contested 464 seats winning just 44—a miserable 9.5 per cent strike rate.

Only four candidates won more than 70 per cent of the votes polled—they all were from BJP. Out of 34 winning candidates with 60 per cent to 70 per cent polling, all 34 had been from BJP. As many as 141 candidates of BJP—half of 282—won polling more than half of the votes cast in their constituencies. Clearly, one cannot say that BJP won majority because of splitting of votes among its opposition.[14]

BJP swept the Hindi-speaking belt. The only state outside the broad Hindi-heartland where BJP could win seats in double digit was Karnataka—the party won 17 out of 28 Lok Sabha seats in the state. In 12 states in the Hindi-heartland (including Delhi, a Union Territory with seven seats) out of 309 seats BJP won 232 seats. Adding 17 from Karnataka, BJP tally was 249 from 13 of 29 states in the country having 337 seats in the lower house Lok Sabha. In contrast, Congress could win just 19 seats from out of these states. As claimed repeatedly by Narendra Modi during the election campaign, Congress tally did not touch double digit in any of the states. The highest tally the party had was nine from Karnataka, a state ruled by the Congress party.

Among the 13 states, Congress and BJP had been in direct contest in 10 states. Barring Bihar, UP and Jharkhand, Congress continued to be a major force in these states where 203 seats were up for election. BJP won 144 and Congress 15 in these 10 states where the electoral contest was in effect between the two political parties, Congress and BJP. Clearly, the Modi campaign could use to the hilt the public dislike for Congress and capture the rival's turf. The three critical Hindi-heartland states—UP, Bihar and Jharkhand—with 134 Lok Sabha seats gave BJP 105 seats. The election outcome of 2014 was similar to that of 1977 when Congress got ousted from the Northern part of the country.

BJP's vote share in other parts of the country improved substantially, but this was not enough for the party to score any major victory in the remaining states. Five states—Kerala, West Bengal, Odisha, Tamil Nadu and Andhra Pradesh (divided into two states after the 2014 elections)—having 164 seats saw only seven BJP win. All these states returned the regional parties or regional allies as in Kerala. In fact in West Bengal, Tamil Nadu and Odisha, the three regional parties in government effectively swept the election to Lok Sabha, leaving just four seats to BJP out of a total of 102 seats. BJP had alliance with as many as 30 political parties. Barring three—Shiv Sena (SS) in Maharashtra, Shiromani Akali

Dal (SAD) in Punjab and Telugu Desam Party (TDP) of bifurcated Andhra Pradesh—all other political parties had mere pockets of influence. Out of these 30, only 14 could win a seat in Lok Sabha. Only SS and TDP won in double digits, 18 and 16 seats, respectively. If BJP and its two alliance partners are excluded, only four other political parties had two-digit tally in Lok Sabha—Congress (44), All India Anna Dravida Munnetra Kazhagam (AIADMK, 37), All India Trinamul Congress (AITC, 34) and BJD (20).

The other interesting fact of the 2014 election is that for the first time in the history of Indian democracy, the ruling party did not have a single Muslim MP in Lok Sabha. BJP had put forward seven Muslim candidates, only one in Bihar, a state from its Hindi heartland stronghold and rest from J&K, West Bengal and Lakshadweep. Not a single Muslim could make it to Lok Sabha from UP. The number of Muslim MPs came down to just 22 (23 if one adds one TMC MP from Arambagh married to a Muslim but who won from a constituency reserved for Scheduled Caste (SC) candidates). In the BJP-led NDA, only one Muslim got elected on the ticket of Lok Janshakti Party (LJP). Later, PDP from J&K joined NDA as a partner of the J&K state government. This raised the number of Muslim MPs of NDA to four. Out of the 23 Muslim MPs, West Bengal sent the largest eight with Bihar, Kerala and J&K, sending four, three and three, respectively. Evidently, while BJP campaign maintained a reasonable impartial tone on religion, the party could not identify many winnable Muslim faces in ticket distribution.

Was the national election result of 2014 a one-off event? It seemed so from the outcome of a few by-elections to different state assemblies immediately after the national election. Out of total 50 assembly seats in different states that went for election in August and September 2014, immediately after the national election, BJP did not fare as well as the party did in Lok Sabha polls. BJP could win 20 out of these 50 seats, losing seven seats it had to rival SP in UP. In Bihar, out of ten assembly, BJP bagged just four, with united opposition Rashtriya Janata Dal (RJD), JD(U) and Congress bagging the remaining six. Had BJP repeated its Lok Sabha election performance, it would have won eight out of ten seats in Bihar. In the southern state of Karnataka, where BJP won 17 Lok Sabha seats in May 2014, the party lost two out of the three seats it contested in the by-elections. In Madhya Pradesh, a central state, the BJP lost one seat of the three it contested, winning the other two. Madhya Pradesh is considered a bastion of the Indian right and the BJP did not lose a single by-election in that state for more than a decade until now. Political analysts noted that these losses, including the surprising loss in Madhya Pradesh, are a signal to the BJP that it should not take its May victory for granted. The message was loud and clear—BJP cannot depend solely on 'Modi magic' to sail through the polls to victory. The results of the elections also suggested that rather than BJP losing votes, the non-BJP parties combined their votes to good effect. In the 2014 general elections, all the non-BJP parties lost badly in Bihar when they fought the elections separately. This prompted the non-BJP parties to come together in order to stop the BJP. BJP's victory was especially threatening to regional, caste-based parties. This saw three such parties SP, JD(U) and RJD joining forces before the Bihar state assembly election in 2015. The results of the by-elections exposed the vulnerability of BJP and the limitations of Modi's appeal.

But the subsequent state assembly elections in four states—Maharashtra, Haryana, Jharkhand and J&K—where the assemblies completed the scheduled tenure, proved otherwise. BJP won three states of Maharashtra, Haryana and Jharkhand on its own. Most interesting was the election outcome in the state of Maharashtra where BJP contested without its long-standing ally SS which is a partner of the BJP-led NDA at the centre. Subsequently SS came back to join BJP in the state cabinet but that was after BJP proved decisively that the party was the leading party even in the state it never won alone earlier. Some interesting features of these elections had been the BJP decision to contest alone without seeking any alliance with state-level parties. No less important was Modi campaigning in these states only on the issue of development. Clearly BJP proved that electorates everywhere wanted a decisive government offering good governance and working for the economic betterment of the state. If the national election 2014 was unique, the subsequent state assembly elections had been no less striking in terms of campaign strategy.

In the states of Maharashtra, Jharkhand, Haryana and J&K, Modi remained the principal campaigner. BJP did not even care to identify any local leader as more equal than others, who would assume the mantle of the state administration. In the troublesome state of J&K, the success was most striking. This had been a case study of how a sympathetic administration could win over a hostile territory with effective governance.

J&K was ravaged by a sudden flood in the month of September 2014—three months before the state assembly election fell due. Prime

Minister Narendra Modi camped in the state, took lead role in flood relief, brought order amidst chaos and won appreciation from mostly hostile residents of the Kashmir valley. In contrast, on the other side of the Line of Control (LoC) in the Pakistan-occupied Kashmir, the administration failed miserably in providing succour. The contrast stood out. Thus, when the assembly election took place, voter turnout in Kashmir valley was a high 65 per cent, the highest in 25 years. India could showcase that the people of J&K took part in the democratic election process proving inter alia that the hostile terrorism seen in the state had largely been an import from the neighbouring country. In terms of electoral outcome also, the vote share of BJP remained the highest. BJP won more votes than any other party—23 per cent of votes polled and won 27 seats with two allies. The regional party PDP came first with 28 seats. The state election result was such that no government could be formed without BJP as a coalition partner. Modi could clearly demonstrate that in a democracy what matters is effective governance, everything else can take a backseat.[15]

Modi's political campaign proved that there cannot be one single formula for electoral victory. While the articulation of messages of development matters, this alone is not enough. In J&K, more than the promises what mattered was the delivery in the time of need. The charisma of Modi served BJP well but the same formula found no place in the party's campaign for the state assembly election in the National Capital Territory of Delhi. Unlike other states, BJP here opted for the police-officer-turned-activist Ms Kiran Bedi as its chief ministerial candidate. Clearly, the urban population of Delhi, mostly young, educated and aspirational would not have fallen head over heels for Modi and his charisma. Delhi would have liked to know who would be the leader in opposition to populist crusader Arvind Kejriwal. His newly formed Aam Aadmi Party (AAP) had surprised many in December 2013 by its electoral performance in Delhi assembly election. That Kejriwal subsequently failed to hang on to the power and frittered away his gains leading to a mid-term poll in Delhi in February 2015 was of less significance. Many predicted that he still could generate support among the less privileged in Delhi. Modi knew he could not have campaigned eyeball to eyeball with Kejriwal. Nor would people of Delhi get much swayed since Modi needed a political boss to run Delhi. Thus came Kiran Bedi as BJP's chief ministerial candidate.

The election scene took a dramatic turn and eventually even BJP could win just 3 out of 70 seats in the state assembly. Arvind Kejriwal's AAP won a record 67 seats winning 54 per cent of the votes. Congress, which governed the city for 15 years between 1998–2013 drew a blank, receiving an insignificant 8 per cent of the votes cast. In the national election 2014 and the subsequent assembly elections, the single most critical point for political campaign that emerges is that if there is one single formula for electoral victory, it is communicating to the people and connecting with them on issues they are bothered about. A political party must have the capacity to change its stance fast enough to catch the imagination of the voters. Focus should be to win even if it means sacrificing long-standing allies or removing squabbling party leadership and importing fresh and popular faces. The second most important factor is planning ahead. Only then can a party top leadership judge would bring them victory. Third and no less important is to grab any opportunity that falls in place in an election bound state. Example is J&K and the flood relief put in place by Modi himself. In the end, BJP did not win any seat in the Muslim majority Kashmir valley but won admiration of people. This increased the party's credibility which helped it to take a shot at government formation in coalition with the local party PDP. BJP under the leadership of Narendra Modi could prove that to win an election, a political party must be focused in its resolve. BJP could do it while its rival parties failed. AAP emulated and used the same in Delhi with disastrous result for Modi's BJP.

India's general election 2014 taught all an elementary lesson on how to win an election in a complex and populous democracy. AAP victory in 2015 proved conclusively that Modi's electoral victory was a result of a well-planned campaign. Viewed from that angle Modi brought in a new style of campaign that savvy leaders will adapt and use in future campaigns in India.

II

The book has two interconnected narratives: on the one hand, it interrogates the 2014 election campaign that Modi and his colleagues in the BJP had undertaken to capitalize on the misgovernance of the erstwhile Congress-steered UPA government; it is also a study, on the other hand, of the election results which are, despite being the outcome of the strenuous and long-drawn election campaign, also dependent on several other contextual factors. As evident, the BJPs' bête noire, the Congress had also undertaken vigorous campaign in 2014 and yet it was not as successful as its major opponent in winning the parliamentary seats. Notwithstanding the critical importance of election campaign for garnering votes, the book thus underlines the fact that the poll outcome is also drawn on the prevalent socio-economic and political context in which the voters make up their minds. For winning votes, election campaign remains critical, but the fact that the outcome of the campaign is not always uniform also suggests that there can hardly be a universal formula. Nonetheless, the nature of the campaign and also the campaign strategies are too important to ignore while explaining the poll outcome. Much of the success in election is contingent on successfully projecting appropriate issues with an appeal to the target group. While devising campaign strategies, the campaign managers concentrate on both national and local issues that are equally important in creating a tangible support base for the party for which a campaign is undertaken. In the 2014 Lok Sabha poll, the misgovernance or the administrative failure of the former UPA government seems to have persuaded the voters in BJP's favour; furthermore, the aggressive Modi and also past track record as the Chief Minister of Gujarat complemented the endeavour of the BJP campaign managers while seeking to garner votes through vigorous election campaign.

The main purpose of this exercise is to comprehend the impact of the election campaign on the 2014 election outcome. Besides the introduction which lays out the context of the 16th Lok Sabha poll, the book seeks to address this query in 12 detailed chapters. As argued in the book, the 2014 election campaign is qualitatively different given the critical role of the leader in securing votes; nonetheless, there are elements of continuity with the past elections. A perusal at the past shows that the remarkable success of the Congress in the fifth Lok Sabha poll, held in 1971, was attributed to the hegemonic presence of Indira Gandhi as a leader who seemed to have cemented a bond with the voters that resulted in votes for the Congress Party. Keeping in view the importance of the past trends in conceptualizing the present, Chapters 1, 2 and 3 dwell on the election campaigns that the contending parties had undertaken to garner votes for their ideologically driven governance agenda. The 2002 Gujarat riot is a watershed in Indian politics and since the pogrom took place when the Prime Minister designate, Narendra Modi was incumbent Chief Minister. He was held responsible and during the campaign, he was even accused of being the *maut-ka-saudagar* (merchant of death) by the Congress Party. How did the BJP campaign managers address these charges is what Chapter 4 deals with. It was a tricky task and the BJP appeared to have taken out the sheen from the opponents' effort by highlighting the track record of the Chief Minister in development and effective governance. The result was obvious: Modi rose like a phoenix despite being continuously charged for his alleged role in the 2002 Gujarat pogrom and appeared to not only have led the election campaign but also guided the BJP to an unprecedented victory. Unlike the BJP campaign in which its frontal organizations, like the RSS, Viswa Hindu Parishad, Bajrang Dal, among other took part, the Congress appeared to have depended a great deal on the top echelon of the organization. As Chapter 5 argues that in spite of drawing on the inputs from the grassroots organization of the party, the Congress had reposed faith on its High Command; it never became effective presumably because the campaign strategies did not appear to reflect what the people wanted the Congress to do. This was reflected in the poll outcome; the Congress lost the 2014 election miserably. Chapter 6 focuses on the administrative failure of the UPA government to combat corruption; it was a handicap that took away much of the goodwill that the Congress had built after having introduced those specific flagship programmes that benefitted a large segment of India's population. In fact, much of the BJP campaign hovered around the charges of corruption which were held true by the outbreak of several financial scams in which the ministers of the incumbent government were reportedly involved. That the 2014 Lok Sabha poll was different was substantiated by emphasizing the fact that it was, for both major contenders in election, the BJP and Congress, a leadership-centric affair, and in the campaign, instead of highlighting socio-economic issues, leaders were projected to garner votes as is shown in Chapter 7. The stronger the leader, the brighter the chances of getting votes, and this was believed by the campaign managers from both the Congress and BJP. It was therefore not surprising, as Chapter 8 illustrates that Modi for the BJP and Rahul Gandhi for the Congress hogged the limelight insofar as the election campaign was concerned. By drawing on the techniques and methods of the campaign that the parties had adopted to secure votes,

Chapter 9 is a stocktaking exercise. The chapter provides a detailed account of the campaign strategies that seemed to have persuaded the voters to vote for a specific political party. One of the major contentions of this chapter is also to highlight the fact that specific issues gained credence in specific socio-economic and political context; given the endemic corruption that crippled the UPA government, the charges of corruption and also misgovernance paid dividends to the BJP, as the election results have shown. The 2014 election campaign was a class by itself since several new e-instruments were utilized for political mobilization. Besides seeking to mobilize voters through the print and visual media, the major contenders resorted to campaign through Twitter, Facebook and WhatsApp, among others. This is what Chapter 10 deals with. In the context of Internet connectivity, these techniques helped build a support base for the parties especially in urban areas. These were new instruments that had gained acceptability as the campaign progressed. Chapter 11 focuses on the outcome of the election campaign; with a threadbare analysis of the poll results, the chapter makes an argument stating that the BJP outsmarted its rivals by its campaign strategies that seemed to have been readily accepted by the voters at large. With its unprecedented victory, the BJP had demonstrated how important it was to have effective campaign strategies to win votes. It is also shown in the chapter that the context is also a critical variable as the BJP juggernaut was stopped in the 2015 Delhi election when it was trounced by the newly created AAP. This also illustrates the triumph of democracy, which creates conditions for alternative ideologies to develop and prosper. On the basis of a thorough analysis of the election campaign preceding the 2014 national poll in India, Chapter 12 pursues two major conceptual points: on the one hand, it suggests that the 16th Lok Sabha poll was a unique event since the campaign was both leadership based and also sought to create and consolidate a support base for the respective parties by drawing upon specific ideological strands. The BJP campaign for a stronger India seemed to have had a bigger appeal to the voters in the light of the growing incidence of scams that the erstwhile UPA government had confronted. Furthermore, by insisting on good governance, the BJP also succeeded in weaning away voters from the Congress which failed to effectively counter the charges of being administratively inept given its track record in governance, especially in its second term (2009–2014). The second important conceptual points relate to the nature of the campaign.

The rise of Modi as the central figure in the election campaign was a clear shift in the campaign strategies that the BJP had adopted. That he became critical in the BJP campaign across the country is also illustrative of his capability as a leader to sway the voters in favour of the BJP and its alliance partners. Given the fact that it was largely a leader-driven campaign, it can be argued that the 2014 Indian national poll had elements of the American presidential election in which the personality of the candidate remains most critical. As the campaign drew to a close, it virtually became a battle between Narendra Modi and Rahul Gandhi, the two aspirants for the top political job in the country; and the election results confirm that Modi became far more successful as a vote catcher than his rival. So, the fundamental point that this chapter offers is about the nature of political communication that is both personality driven and also dependent on the prevalent socio-economic context in which certain specific issues gain immediate acceptance than the rest.

The book is an intervention in an untrodden area of enquiry since political communication did not seem to have received so far adequate scholarly attention. In two ways, the exercise is unique too: on the one hand, by attempting a threadbare analysis of the election campaign that the political parties had undertaken preceding the 2014 election, the book makes a specific comment on how voters are solicited and their supports are confirmed. The book also underlines the point, on the other hand, that the effectiveness of the campaign strategies is contingent on the prevalent socio-economic milieu in which specific ideological appeal succeeds in building an emotional chord with the voters. While highlighting the criticality of the campaign strategies, the book is an endeavour towards conceptualizing the role that the context plays in deciding the fate of the contesting candidates in the election.

In a nutshell, besides providing an account of the campaign strategies in the context of the 2014 India's Lok Sabha poll, the book also dwells on how they are framed and refined by the inputs which the campaign managers receive as they unfold. With this objective in view, the book thus makes two major and one supplementary argument. Of the two major arguments, the first one is linked with the unique nature of 2014 campaign in which ideological issues were presented rather efficiently by specific leaderships, projected by the Congress and BJP, respectively. Along with the importance of the leadership, the book provides the second major argument by highlighting how the contextual issues shape the voters' preferences. The misgovernance and failure of the UPA government to address effectively the charges of corruption and administrative lapses seem to have taken the wind away from the Congress and shifted the balance in favour of the BJP despite the repeated Congress attempts at linking Modi with the 2002 Gujarat pogrom. The text also makes a supplementary argument: Modi's popularity notwithstanding, the BJP failed to make inroads, for instance, in West Bengal where the AITC held the fort by winning 34 seats out of a total of 42 Lok Sabha seats in the state. The BJP had to be content with mere two seats. It was evident again in the 2015 Delhi elections when the BJP had won only three seats in an assembly of 70 members; by winning 67 seats, the new entrant, the AAP stopped the BJP march. This is also a powerful comment on how deep-rooted Indian democracy is: the appeal of Modi did not seem to be as effective in the 2015 Delhi assembly election as it was in the 2014 Lok Sabha poll. Voters exercised their franchise differently and the poll pledges of the AAP swayed the Delhi voters away from the BJP, although it had won all the seven parliamentary seats from Delhi in the 16th Lok Sabha poll. This is a testimony to the fact that democracy in India is not a mere cosmetic design, but a really empowering device for the people always remain the final arbiters in politics.

1

Trends in Election Campaign since Independence

When India went for the first ever general election in 1951, many including Jawaharlal Nehru, the nation's first Prime Minister, were sceptical. There were over 173 million voters, most of them poor, illiterate and rural, without any prior experience of an election. Nobody could predict how these millions would respond, nobody knew what would drive them. There were problems, which even worried Nehru. In other nations, democracy came with the spread of education and economic development. There was a demand from within these countries that the democratic process and the elected government were required to address. In a newly independent India, such political consciousness was barely present, and if it was, then only at a nascent stage. For Nehru, this was a big challenge.

Before the general elections of 1951–52, India had nine Part A states, then known as provinces. These were Assam, Bihar, Bombay, Madhya Pradesh, Madras, Orissa, Punjab, UP and West Bengal. These provinces had an experience of elections but on a restricted franchise, to the Central (later Dominion) and Provincial Legislatures, under the Government of India Act, 1935. Franchise was given on the basis of ownership of property, constituency and voting right linked to religion. India's Election Commission (EC) had reported:

> The qualifications of an elector for the Central and Provincial elections differed from each other and in each Province, again, differing qualifications were prescribed. In every case, the franchise was a very limited one and was related to factors like taxation, property, literacy, community, etc. The result was that only a small percentage of the adult population of the country had the right to vote. Approximately, franchise was enjoyed by only 14 per cent of the population.[1]

Independent India did away with these in favour of universal adult suffrage after the successful conduction of the 'largest' democratic process spread over five months between October 1951 and February 1952.

If Part A states were of concern, Nehru had reasons to feel perturbed over the experience of democracy in the Indian states ruled by the Indian princes. In fact the experience differed widely from state to state. Most of the states had elected or partially elected legislatures. These states were Hyderabad, J&K, Madhya Bharat, Mysore, Patiala and East Punjab states union, Rajasthan, Saurashtra and Travancore–Cochin. The franchise was even more restricted in these states and varied from state to state; in many cases, the rulers used to nominate their representatives. Only the southern state of Travancore was an exception which had adopted adult suffrage.[2]

While it was an administrative challenge for India's Election Commissioner Sukumar Sen to enrol voters and create logistics for people to come out and vote, for Nehru the challenge was greater. For him it was a moral obligation to establish a system that a committee headed by his father Motilal and appointed by the All Parties Conference in 1928 suggested. It recommended among other things a parliamentary and federal structure of government.[3] Jawaharlal Nehru was the acting secretary of the committee.[4] The first general election, thus, had placed a huge burden on Nehru. This was a defining moment in Nehru's life.

The moral responsibility apart, Nehru had to ensure that Congress, as the only broad-based established political party, came to power. This was necessary in order to strengthen the newly liberated nation experimenting with democracy for which it did not have the necessary experience or historical background. But within the Congress party, Purushottamdas Tandon, the elected president, held conservative views which were in conflict with Nehru's line of thought. Nehru used to say that he had the 'greatest affection and respect' for Tandon but had intense dislike for his 'obscurantism', 'communalism' and 'zeal for Hindi' which were 'opposed to the basic principles of the Congress'. Nehru wanted to select candidates who subscribed to his views. He created conditions so that Tandon had to resign and Nehru took over as the president of the party in September 1951, well in time to wear two hats in the first general election. In his first act after wearing the two hats, Nehru dropped the Hindu Marriage Act so as not to turn the conservative Hindus against Congress before the election. Appeasement has been an instrument used by the ruling party from the very first election in India.

The entire election had been a personal triumph for Nehru. He was successful in winning 364 seats in the 489 member Lok Sabha and a total of 2,246 seats in the state legislative assemblies forming government everywhere. His campaign ensured a 44.87 per cent polling with Congress winning 44.99 per cent of the votes cast. Nehru travelled 18,348 miles by air, 5,682 miles by car and 1,612 miles by train. He was the head of the government. The Auditor General ruled that had Nehru travelled by air the cost of security cover would be less. It was decided that when Nehru travelled by special government plane, the party would bear only his air fare. Nehru addressed 305 public meetings and an estimated 30 million people. He was the Prime Minister of the nation. The appeal of his position drew people to his rallies, as did curiosity inspired by elaborate police arrangements ahead of the meetings. Nehru campaigned against the communalists and the communists—the two principal rivals—the Jan Sangh and the CPI, respectively. Nehru's message was simple. Communalists would lead to civil war and communists would destroy democracy. Both were equally dangerous, 'Do you prefer death by drowning or by falling from a precipice'. The election not only positioned Congress as the unchallenged political party of the newly independent nation, but also placed Nehru above any other political leader in the country. He would hold that stature till his death after the third general election.

In the first political campaign in 1951–52, Nehru did not have to worry about funds. Sardar Patel had left enough in the coffer for him to put to use. The second general election saw G.D. Birla taking a lead role in collecting money from fellow industrialists. He could easily exceed the target of ₹1 crore (₹10 million).

How much credit for the first three election victories should be attributed to Nehru? He knew that but for him 'there would have been no stable government in any state or at the centre'. So domineering was Nehru that Lord Mountbatten, years after he left India was concerned over what would happen in case of Nehru's sudden demise. 'After Nehru, who?' Though India adopted a Westminster-type parliamentary democracy in effect, the election campaign and positioning from the first general election onwards had been akin to the US presidential system. One undisputed charismatic leader could sway the election in favour of Congress. Point to be noted is that this was the Congress handpicked by none other than Nehru, despite the presence of strong regional leaders like B.C. Roy, Chief Minister of West Bengal, G.B. Pant of United Provinces and others who could win elections in their respective states on the back of their own popularity.

Nehru was a good orator. His speech delivered at the midnight of India's independence is still considered a great piece of oratorical example. But in oratory, he had a more than competent adversary in the Jan Sangh leader Dr Syama Prasad Mukherjee. In the first election, Mukherjee too had campaigned across India and travelled sometimes using the private aircraft of Ramkrishna Dalmia, the third largest industrialist in India then. But Jan Sangh could win only three seats. Soon after the election, Mukherjee died suddenly. The other interesting sidelight of the first election campaign was the rejection of the opposition to campaign over the All India Radio. They were not happy with the scope of the offer.

The general elections in 1957 and 1962 were a repeat of the Nehru story. The states were reorganized on the basis of linguistic divisions. There were now 13 states and four Union territories. There were 91 general constituencies, which had elected a second member, 76 from SC, and 15 from ST communities. Voters here cast two votes, one for the general candidate and the other for the SC/ST candidate.

Though in the government and in parliament there had been occasions when Nehru had to succumb to pressures, in the electoral field, he was the unchallenged warrior. The only exception perhaps was in the newly created state of Kerala in 1957. Here, the communists (CPI) won nine seats in the Lok Sabha against six of Congress. In the assembly, CPI led by E.M.S. Namboodiripad won 60 of the 114 assembly seats forming the first non-Congress government in India. In fact, it was the first elected communist government in the world. There was immense pressure on Nehru to stop CPI. Nehru's own dislike of the communists was also strong. CPI government lasted just two years when a state-wide agitation over an education bill encouraged the central government to dismiss the Namboodiripad government and impose president's rule.

The setback in Kerala notwithstanding the first three general elections in India were all about Jawaharlal Nehru. There was no other leader to challenge his authority nationally, though some regional leaders enjoyed towering the presence within their states. Media was generally reverential barring some occasional adverse criticism in *The Times of India* and *Hindustan Times*. But even the Nehru magic was steadily losing some of its luster, plagued by corruption charges against ministers, rise of regional and linguistic leaders and the loss of face in the war against China in 1962.

Luckily for Nehru, the war took place after the elections and he did not live long to take the party through the 4th Lok Sabha poll in 1967.

Nehru's death and also the sudden demise of his successor Lal Bahadur Shastri exposed Congress to internal dissentions. Many strong regional leaders left the party. In the centre also there was leadership contest between Nehru's daughter Indira Gandhi who took over as the Prime Minister and Morarji Desai, a strong leader from western India. Indira Gandhi was still searching for a foothold in the party when the 4th Lok Sabha poll took place in 1967.

The result was a shock for Congress. For the first time, Congress campaigned without any charismatic leader at the helm. Still the charm that the party name conjured helped it to win 283 seats out of total 520 seats in Lok Sabha. Its three stalwarts K. Kamraj in Tamil Nadu, S.K. Patil in Bombay and Atulya Ghosh in West Bengal lost elections. Many of their associates lost either Lok Sabha or assembly elections. Congress lost in the state assembly elections in Tamil Nadu, Orissa, West Bengal, UP, Haryana, Punjab, Kerala, Madhya Pradesh and Bihar. In some states, Congress formed coalition governments, in others non-Congress coalitions came in power. That was the beginning of coalition politics and rise of regional parties in India. Tamil Nadu since 1967 is ruled by DMK or its splinter party AIADMK. But in Lok Sabha, still there was none to rival the Congress in the country. Swatantra Party came second, winning 44 seats, Jan Sangh won 35 and the communists (by then split into CPI and Communist Party of India (Marxist) (CPI (M)) could win 42 seats (CPI 23 and CPI (M) 19). State parties won 43 seats.

But Indira Gandhi realized the unavoidable problem the party would have faced had she continued as before. She could sense that the syndicate members were losing popular support and were viewed as retrograde. She realized it was time to present a younger face before the electorate, matching the aspirations of a 20-year old democracy. The signs of restlessness was there in the election result of 1967. Congress lost its hold in several important states. The party's majority in Lok Sabha was rather thin. Indira Gandhi could not precipitate any action by sacrificing the government. She had to succumb to the whims of the 'syndicate'—the working committee, the highest decision-making body of the party—that tethered the administration. Unlike Nehru, Indira did not have any control over the party organization. Syndicate now had an ally in Indira's old foe

Morarji Desai. Their stranglehold over the party saw that when the party president Kamraj retired, a conservative leader S. Nijalingappa got elected as the new party president.

The conflict started on what was to be the next course of the economy—Right or Left. In May 1967, the Congress Working Committee adopted a radical Ten-Point Programme. It recommended social control of banks, nationalization of general insurance, state trading in import and export, ceilings on urban property and income, curb on business monopolies and concentration of economic power, public distribution of foodgrains, rapid implementation of land reforms, provision of house sites to the rural poor and abolition of princely privileges. The right wing of the party notionally accepted the agenda but was determined to stall its implementation. They advocated further dilution of planning, lesser emphasis on public sector, and greater encouragement to and reliance on private enterprise and foreign capital. On foreign policy, they suggested strengthening of political and economic relations with the West in general and the US in particular. Clearly, their idea was to suppress the Left politically. That was the time when the Left was getting stronger day by day due to restlessness of the workers. Within the party, the left-oriented Young Turks needed to be reined in. This desire allowed the syndicate to adopt the ten-point agenda.

For the first time in the 20-year-old history of Indian democracy, the Prime Minister thought of approaching the electorate to put an end to this conflict over leadership. Indira wanted complete command over party and government like her father Nehru. Unknown to her rivals in the party, she started cautiously. After the adoption of the agenda and also the one on abolition of Privy Purse paid to the erstwhile rulers of princely states, Indira Gandhi waited for an opportune time to assert herself. The opportunity came when India's third President Zakir Hussein died suddenly in May 1969. Syndicate chose Neelam Sanjeeva Reddy as the next candidate brushing aside Indira's objection. When the election came, she suggested that Congressmen should vote as per their conscience, which turned the election of India's fourth president into an open contest between the official Congress candidate Reddy and the incumbent Vice President V.V. Giri. A large number of Congress members voted in favour of Giri leading to the defeat of the official Congress candidate Reddy.

Indira Gandhi was now ready for the daring campaign of asserting her control over Congress. First, she stripped Morarji Desai of the finance portfolio and then swiftly she promulgated an ordinance on nationalization of 14 large commercial banks. This made her an instant hero among the people. Mrs Gandhi knew how to use the people power in a democracy. Election of V.V. Giri defeating the official Congress nominee, too, was popular and widely welcomed by media and opinion leaders. Syndicate had to act against Indira for indiscipline and causing defeat to the official Congress nominee. She was expelled from Congress but survived as a Prime Minister. She had the support of 220 members of the Lok Sabha and from the Left. Thus, she could successfully run a minority government supported by the Left.

With the President on her side, Indira brought in the Constitution (24th Amendment) Bill, 1970 to abolish the Privy Purse. Lok Sabha passed it by a majority of 332:154 votes, but the bill fell short of the requisite two-thirds majority in the Rajya Sabha just by one vote—149 in favour with 75 against. Indira Gandhi asked President Giri to derecognize all the rulers. But the ordinance of derecognition was successfully challenged by N.A. Palkhivala before the Supreme Court in the historic Privy Purses case. But in the people's court, Indira Gandhi enjoyed a surging support.

She was now ready for the fifth general election. Lok Sabha was dissolved in December 1970, one year before the term ended. Election took place in February 1971. Congress faction led by Indira bagged 352 of the 518 seats of Lok Sabha and captured 44 per cent of votes polled. Through more than two-year long careful planning, Indira Gandhi reached the electoral success of her charismatic father Jawaharlal Nehru, a feat nobody ever thought could be emulated. Election 1971 was unique in more ways than one. It was then that for the first time in independent India, the Prime Minister planned for an electoral success through carefully trimmed policies. Bank nationalization and abolition of Privy Purse were popular among the electorates who were unconcerned with the fine words of constitution or bank loans sanctioned. That the people of India were devoted to the Nehru–Gandhi family was another lesson from that election. It established the family firmly as the inheritor of the Congress party. Another important point that emerged was that in a poor country a leftward tilt of policy would always have more takers than a market-oriented rightist economic policy. Last but no less important was the aggressive and belligerent campaign style of Indira Gandhi. Her single point message for the common men was, 'I say Garibi Hatao (remove poverty), my rivals say Indira Hatao (remove Indira)'. This brought in the punch line in India's political rhetoric for the first time.[5]

Apart from success in electoral politics, Indira Gandhi excelled in helping East Pakistan to turn into an independent Bangladesh. Not only did her government defeat Pakistan in the war and humiliate the neighbour by taking in 93,000 Pakistani soldiers as prisoners of war, the largest since the Second World War, she also effectively snubbed the US President Richard Nixon's belated effort to support Pakistan by threatening to send the Seventh Fleet to East Pakistan. Indira became a national hero as well as an international politician for the opponents of the US. Effectively, she joined the former Soviet Union in the global cold war that took root post the Second World War.

With success came arrogance. Accustomed as she was to unquestioned use and abuse of power, she felt that she was answerable to none. The use of the government machinery like vehicles, services of officers, etc. in election campaign was illegal, but did not deter both Nehru and his daughter from utilizing the same. Little attention was paid to the misuse and also to the election petition 'no five' filed before Justice Jagmohanlal Sinha in the Allahabad High Court by petitioner Raj Narain against Indira Gandhi, the Prime Minister of India, in 1971. The petition challenged her election to the Lok Sabha in 1971 from the Rae Bareli parliamentary constituency in UP, where Narain contested against her. After four years of hearing, judgement was pronounced on 12 June 1975. Justice Sinha held Indira Gandhi guilty of corrupt practices and her election to the Lok Sabha was declared null and void. She was charged under Section 123(7) of the Representation of the People Act. She was also disqualified from contesting elections for six years.

Within 13 days of judgement, Indira Gandhi imposed Emergency on the nation. The ruling became the primary reason for her hasty action. Subsequently, Gandhi used the opportunity to change the law, which allowed her to rule by decree. She suspended freedom and liberties and brought Indian democracy to a halt. Consequently, in March 1977, Indira Gandhi and her Congress party had to face defeat and Congress was routed in the elections, thus ending its uninterrupted rule over India.

The seed of the election campaign for 1977 was sown in the proclamation of emergency. The latent discomfort of ordinary people against price rise and arrogant state governments in Gujarat and then in

Bihar was taking shape as a national movement under the leadership of the Gandhian Jayaprakash Narayan (JP). Indira Gandhi was finding it difficult to manage the situation. Like she did plan carefully post-1967 on how to ease out the old Congress leaders who had lost touch with people, she herself fell prey to the JP-led 'total revolution'. The events of 1971 and also 1977 clearly indicate the elections are a cumulative effect of the policies of an administration. A campaign cannot be conceived overnight and elections cannot be won that way. For a campaign to be successful, one needs a conducive atmosphere.

The agitation against Congress started in the state of Gujarat. In 1974, the state witnessed the launch of the sociopolitical Nav Nirman Andolan (reinvention or reconstruction movement). The students and the middle class took to the streets to protest against economic crisis and corruption in public life. The movement, confined only in Gujarat, resulted in dissolution of the elected state government. The Nav Nirman Andolan started in Ahmedabad in December 1973, just two years after Indira Gandhi's feat of freeing Bangladesh, when the students of L.D. College of Engineering started protest against 20 per cent hike in hostel food bill. The agitation spread, resulted in clashes with police and state wide strikes, and it drew the middle-class and factory workers. The army had to be called to restore peace. Mrs Gandhi asked the Chief Minister Chimanbhai Patel to resign. Within less than two months after the protest by the students, an elected government had to submit to public pressure. The state assembly was dissolved in the next four weeks and the agitation then shifted its attention to the political action of defeating Congress. In the election of 1975, Congress lost majority and Gujarat saw a coalition of Jan Sangh (now BJP) along with Congress (O)[6] of Morarji Desai winning. But the result came the day Indira Gandhi lost her election petition in the Allahabad High Court.

JP was not involved in the Gujarat movement though he had visited the state. When a similar agitation started in Bihar, JP's home state, he came to lead it. The success of JP in spreading the Bihar agitation to other parts of the country caused concern to the ruling Congress at the centre. Indira Gandhi, too, lost her political astuteness and was in panic of sorts when the court verdict came against her. This was the time when her younger son Sanjay Gandhi started taking interest in politics and administration. Thus, when finally emergency was lifted and election was declared in early 1977, the entire Hindi heartland was waiting to express their disenchantment with Mrs Gandhi. The veterans leading the Janata Party, a coalition of Congressmen ousted by Indira Gandhi, Jan Sangh, Left and other political parties formed the first non-Congress government winning the general election against Indira Gandhi in 1977. Morarji Desai became the Prime Minister hoisted by the architect and rallying point against the ruling Congress.

The common thread in all the elections since 1952 is the towering presence of one leader—barring the election of 1967 when Nehru's baton had just passed on to his daughter Indira who was yet to position herself high above the old guards of Congress. The result in 1967 was disappointing for Congress. Indira realized she had to oust the collective leadership of syndicate and establish herself as the leader whom the people would follow. In 1977, it was JP who had provided this leadership. The others like Morarji, Charan Singh and Jagjivan Ram (who left Congress after election was declared in 1977) had their pockets of influence which were stitched together by JP. India had always opted for a towering personality even when pursuing the Westminster-type parliamentary system. This was clear to Indira who had seen people falling for her father, and she used this characteristic of Indian voters in her successful campaign of 1971. After the loss of 1977, she waited for her time. She knew elections are fought on issues created over the interregnum between two elections. A success in a campaign depends on a durable effort over few years, not an immediate hasty one. Nehru could have done this, so towering was his presence, but after Nehru each leader had to build the persona.

About six months after the election defeat, in August 1977, Indira came to an unknown place called Belchhi that witnessed Bihar's first caste carnage. Her ride atop an elephant, to visit the landless Dalits whose houses were burnt by backward-caste Kurmis, created a nice photo opportunity for the Indian media. She was back as the champion of the people. The elephant ride highlighted the pitiable condition of travel to the place, its slushy roads full at places with waist deep water.

Meanwhile the ruling Janata Party was busy in two activities—squabbling among themselves and fighting Indira Gandhi. The Shah Commission appointed by the government to probe the misdeeds during the Emergency had only archival value. People wanted action on corruption, misgovernance and rising cost of living. But the leaders with regional strong bases and stronger egos did not pay attention to the needs of the electorates.

Most of them had lost touch with reality. In the assembly election that took place in 1977, after the central government dismissed all Congress-ruled state governments, the Janata Party lost West Bengal to the coalition of the Left parties and Tamil Nadu to AIADMK, a breakaway party from DMK, of the film star turned politician M.G. Ramachandran, mentor of the present Chief Minister J. Jayalalitha.

The leaders of Janata Party were ambitious and some of them blinded by casteist prejudices. This stopped Jagajivan Ram, a respected Dalit leader, from becoming the Prime Minister. The leaders had no sense of politics, or even if they did, their judgement was overshadowed by matters of caste. Due to their short sightedness, they made Indira look as a leader being persecuted. First, she was arrested on charges of economic offences. Then, when she entered Lok Sabha winning a by-election from Chikmagalur in the southern state of Karnataka, the government disqualified her and again sent her to prison.

A coalition of opposition, united with a single point: hate-Indira agenda, helped the former Prime Minister to win public sympathy. Indians have a tendency to side with the persecuted. In this case, the victim was a former Prime Minister, a victor of 1971 war, daughter of Nehru, the first Prime Minister. More importantly, it was not easy to prove the charges against her in an Indian court. Certain allegations seemed preposterous that she 'had planned or thought of killing all opposition leaders in jail during the Emergency'. The arrest and long-running trial and also use of intemperate language against her (she was referred to as 'that woman' by some) helped her gain sympathy from many.

The Janata coalition was also crumbling due to its internal contradictions. Finally, in June 1979, Charan Singh and Raj Narain formed their own breakaway party. Singh was promised support from outside by Indira and was appointed as the Prime Minister. Before he could even prove his majority in the house, he lost it and resigned. By then, JP, the man who had stitched together the coalition, had passed away in October 1979. Parliament was dissolved in the winter of 1979.

Though the sympathy was with Indira, after the failed Janata experiment, she took no chances. Before the 1980 elections, Indira approached the then Shahi Imam of Jama Masjid, Syed Abdullah Bukhari and entered into an agreement with him on the basis of a ten-point programme to secure the support of the Muslims. This was perhaps the first ever communalization of Indian elections. Indira needed the endorsement since during the Emergency in 1977, the family planning programmmes were viewed as a direct affront on the Muslims. She had to win them back in 1980.

Indira Gandhi's tenure was cut short when in November 1984, she was shot dead by her two Sikh bodyguards. The event saw her son Rajiv Gandhi, who joined politics and was a member of Lok Sabha after his brother Sanjay died in an air crash, taking over as India's Prime Minister. The term of the seventh Lok Sabha was then nearing completion. The government led by Rajiv's mother had been facing problem with Sikhs in Punjab. The economy, too, was not doing well. Indira Gandhi's charm over the electorate was on a slippery slope. The assassination in 1984 changed it all.

The 37-year old democracy witnessed its second major violent death after the assassination of Mahatma Gandhi in January 1948 by some Hindu fanatics. The entire country turned sympathetic to the charming Rajiv Gandhi. The support for him was so strong that the butchery on the Sikh community that the capital Delhi and some other parts of the nation had witnessed after Indira's assassination was condoned. The election was clinched through an overwhelming sympathy wave, effectively without much effort.

Rajiv had in early 1984 worked with the creative team of the advertising agency rediffusion. Ajit Balakrishnan who was part of the team that conceived the campaign wrote in his blog on the themes they finalized in consultation with Rajiv Gandhi, the then General Secretary of Congress. This was the first known use of a professional agency in an Indian political campaign.

The campaign themes were well researched. It asked the citizens: 'Will Your Grocery List, in the Future, include Acid Bulbs, Iron Rods, Daggers?' The answer was that a strong government was the need of the hour and only Congress could provide it.

Another looked at the separatist movements, and the one in Punjab was high on the list especially after the death of the sitting Prime Minister. 'Would you soon look uneasily at your neighbour just because he belongs to another community?' The message was: Vote for Congress which stood for unity.

The agency research revealed that the industrial growth rate in India was an average 4.9 per cent since 1980 against 1.2 per cent in the US and

0.3 per cent in the UK. The question put before people was to name the country recording higher growth rate than the UK and the US.

The other was on self-sufficiency of food grains reminding Indians about the humiliation of having bread made out of wheat gifted by the US under PL 480 scheme.

The campaign sought to establish the pride, self-sufficiency, growth and security provided by the successive Congress governments. While these were catchy, the groundswell of sympathy wave was strong enough for Rajiv to win 404 seats out of 514 that went for polls and 49.1 per cent of popular votes, a feat better than that of his grandfather Jawaharlal Nehru.[7]

In his tenure, Rajiv was caught in several complicated problems, both domestic and international. Apart from the continuation of the Punjab issue, a new complex ethnic problem arose in neighbouring Sri Lanka. The Tamil minorities in the island nation took up arms against the government there. In order to diffuse the crisis, Rajiv had sent the Indian army to Sri Lanka—Indian Peace Keeping Forces (IPKF). The mission was ill-conceived and turned both the Tamil rebels and the Sri Lankans against India. At home, Rajiv was charged with accepting cut in defence deal—the infamous Bofors scam. Rajiv fell out with his senior minister Viswa Nath Pratap Singh who first held the finance portfolio and then the defence ministry. Rajiv's cousin Arun Nehru, who had quit his corporate job to join him, too fell out. In addition, Rajiv's decision to open the lock of the disputed 'Ram Mandir' at Ayodhya in 1985 inflamed communal passion, and his sharp about-turn in the Supreme Court judgement on Shah Bano case opened up a Pandora's box and his failure to gauge the political risk and take suitable actions sealed his fate.

Rajiv through his naiveté helped the rise of the Hindu chauvinist BJP which had just two seats in 1985 election. In fact the major support base of BJP, the Rashtriya Swayam Sevak Sangh (RSS), a Hindu outfit had worked actively in support of Rajiv in the 1985 parliamentary election. Such support was never available to his mother Indira or grandfather Nehru. But due largely to his lack of understanding of the complexity of Indian democracy, he managed to sacrifice the huge goodwill that came to him unsolicited.

In the annals of political campaign in India, Rajiv Gandhi remains an interesting failure. The nation expected a break from the past under Rajiv. His overtures to the US and rebuilding of Indo–US relation received encouraging response. His attempt to break away from the licence-control raj on economic matters to a more liberal policy was a positive step forward. His choice of teammates—fresh faces like Arun Nehru, Madhav Rao Scindia, P. Chidambaram and others in place of veterans like Pranab Mukherjee had many takers. Rajiv was the first Prime Minister with a loving family. The photogenic Prime Minister's pictures with his Italian wife Sonia did find front-page mentions even without much PR effort. Rajiv was generally viewed as incorruptible till the impression was shattered with the surfacing of the Bofors scandal. Rajiv's political inexperience led to his panic reactions to many cases. He failed to act prudently on the Ayodhya Ram Mandir issue and also the Shah Bano case. This made him vulnerable to the opposition campaign against him on kickbacks in the Bofors gun deal. The involvement of an Italian businessman Quattrochi in the deal made matters worse. Unaware of the consequences, Rajiv presided over the end of Congress hegemony in Indian electoral politics. Since his loss in the election that followed in 1989, when Congress could win 197 seats and sat in the opposition only the second time in the history of independent India, the party has never reached the magic figure of 273 needed for absolute majority in the Lok Sabha. Rajiv paved the way for coalition politics in India. Narendra Modi broke the trend in 2014.

2

Coalition Era Starts

Politics in India changed after the landslide victory of Rajiv Gandhi in 1984. Lack of political experience of Rajiv and his reliance on advisors who saw the issues of common men through a prism of upper-class disdain often led to panic reactions. These redrew the political landscape of the country irretrievably. The painstaking effort of the founding fathers and Rajiv's grandfather Nehru in creating a secular fabric received a minor jolt when Indira Gandhi approached Imam Bukhari before the 1980 election. The assassination of Indira polarized the Hindus against another minority community, the Sikhs. A section of Hindus led and encouraged by Congress leaders in Delhi saw the massacre of Sikhs even before the funeral of the departed Prime Minister took place. An estimated 8,000 Sikhs were killed, 3,000 in the capital Delhi itself. The central government and, then, the nation's Sikh President Zail Singh did not use the forces to stop this unprecedented genocide taking place under their watch. This was perhaps the first one-sided attack and carnage of one of the minority communities in independent India.

Following his mother's assassination, Rajiv received support of the Hindu extremists in his election campaign. Perhaps willy-nilly, he felt that he owed a favour to the majority community. The atmosphere in the north, particularly in the largest state of UP was latently communal with the Hindus asserting themselves. This might have encouraged Rajiv and some of the advisors who were novices in politics to succumb to the demand of the Vishwa Hindu Parishad (VHP) in opening the lock of the disputed Ram Mandir at Ayodhya in 1985. In the annals of India's political campaign, Ram Mandir at Ayodhya has a special significance. Between the Hindus and Muslims, there had been several instances of violence over the right to worship there. Hindus claim that the disputed land had been the birthplace of their Lord Ram, over which, subsequently, the Mughal Emperor Babur had built a mosque. As per records, even in the year 1853, during the rule of Nawab Wajed Ali Shah of Awadh, the Hindu and Muslim communities had clashed over the right to worship at that place.

Under the British rule, there had been instances when the Hindus attempted to construct a temple there and even sought court intervention for that matter. The District Gazetteer of Faizabad district mentioned in 1905 that till 1855 both the Hindus and the Muslims used to worship in the same building. This scene of more or less harmonious co-worship changed post the Sepoy Mutiny of 1857. An outer enclosure was constructed in front of the Masjid and the Hindus were forbidden access to the inner yard. They made their offerings on a platform (*chabootra*), which they had raised in the outer area. There had been a recorded effort in 1883 to construct a temple on this chabootra. But the then Deputy Commissioner prohibited it. A *mahant* (priest in the temple of Ram) filed a suit before the Faizabad Sub-Judge seeking permission to construct a temple on this chabootra. The suit was dismissed. Faizabad District Judge, Colonel J.E.A. Chambiar too, after an inspection of the spot in March 1886, dismissed the appeal. But his observations had planted a seed of discontent that has been watered by communal passions over the years, even to this day. He mentioned in his judgement:

> I found that Masjid built by Emperor Babur stands on the border of the town of Ayodhya. It is most unfortunate that Masjid should have been built on land specially held sacred by the Hindus, but as that event occurred 358 years ago, it is too late now to remedy the grievance. All that can be done is to maintain the parties in status quo. In such a case, as the present one, any innovation would cause more harm and derangement of order than benefit.[1]

Another appeal was filed on 25 May 1886, before the Judicial Commissioner of Awadh, W. Young, who also dismissed the appeal.

There was a communal riot in 1934 when walls around the Masjid and one of its domes were damaged. Under the Act of 1936, the mosque and its appurtenant land, a graveyard known as Ganj-e-Shaheedan Qabristan, were registered as Waqf property. There were also police guards posted at the monument by the then British administration. This continued even after independence. On the midnight of 22 December 1949, when the police guards were asleep, statues of Rama and Sita were secretly smuggled into the mosque and installed there. Afterward, according to the case diary, a crowd of five to six thousand persons, chanting prayers and raising religious slogans, collected around the mosque and tried to enter it.

The then Deputy Prime Minister Vallabhbhai Patel directed the Chief Minister of UP, Govind Ballabh Pant and UP Home Minister Lal Bahadur Shastri to see that the deities were removed. But fearing Hindu retaliation, Patel's order was not carried out. The Sunni Waqf Board and the VHP went to court, and the court declared it a disputed property, so the gate was locked. Congress-led administration did not want to hurt the Hindu sentiment and maintained status quo. The former Congress president and then in the opposition J.B. Kripalani accused in his autobiography that Congress 'communalised the atmosphere' at Ayodhya for political gain. Much before BJP was born, Ayodhya was a symbol of communal campaign in India's electoral politics.[2]

Thus, when in 1984, VHP launched a massive movement for the opening of the locks of the mosque, Rajiv Gandhi did not think of the consequences. In 1985, he ordered the locks on the Ram Janmabhoomi–Babri Masjid in Ayodhya to be removed. With this, he unlocked the open use of communal sentiments in India's electoral politics.

As if opening one of the Pandora's boxes was not enough, Rajiv was ill-advised to open another. His indiscretion would propel a divorce suit to such prominence and foment the Hindu–Muslim divide to such proportions so as to turn it into an issue for heated election campaigns, particularly since 1989. It was beyond imagination.

The Shah Bano case was a simple case of maintenance demanded by a 62-year old Muslim woman and mother of five from Indore in the state of Madhya Pradesh. She was driven out of her 'matrimonial home' by her husband in 1975. In April 1978, she filed a case against her husband, Mohammed Ahmad Khan, asking him for a maintenance amount of ₹500. Meanwhile, Khan in November 1978 gave her an irrevocable *talaq* (divorce) under the Islamic Law. He claimed that Shah Bano was not his responsibility anymore because he had a second marriage permitted under the Islamic Law. But the Supreme Court in its judgement ruled that Shah Bano be given maintenance under Section 125 of Code of Criminal Procedure, which applies to everyone regardless of caste, creed or religion.[3, 4]

Muslims perceived this as an encroachment in the Muslim Personal Law and protested. Rajiv Gandhi felt that by siding with the orthodox views among the Muslims, he would win them over under the Congress fold as well. In 1986, the government passed The Muslim Women (Protection of Rights on Divorce) Act in 1986. It sounds strange but the protection of women's rights act denied Shah Bano her maintenance, nullifying the Supreme Court's judgement in the Shah Bano case. This act upheld the Muslim Personal Law and provided ammunition to the Hindu nationalists who contended that this was a preferential treatment to the Muslims and demanded a uniform civil code.

The election for the 9th Lok Sabha was declared on 17 October 1989. The opposition attacked the Rajiv Gandhi government on the issue of corruption with the alleged kickbacks in the purchase of Bofors gun taking the centre stage.

There was a US$1.3 billion deal between the Swedish arms manufacturer Bofors with the Government of India for the sale of 410 field howitzer guns. It was the biggest arms deal ever in Sweden then. Investigations revealed flouting of rules and bypassing of institutions. The scale of the corruption was far worse than anything that Sweden and India had seen before, and accusing fingers were directed to the then Indian Prime Minister Rajiv Gandhi. It was alleged that the Swedish company paid ₹640 million (US$11 million) in kickbacks to top Indian politicians and key defence officials. The scam came to light when Vishwa Nath Pratap Singh was Rajiv's Defence Minister. Soon thereafter V.P. Singh left Congress and joined Janata Dal. Singh had been preparing the ground from 1988 onwards. The opposition tried hard against splitting anti-Congress votes and provided joint candidates against the ruling Congress. Apart from Bofors scandal, the opposition attacked the government for weak handling of terrorism in Punjab, and failure in Sri Lanka in its ill-planned dispatch of IPKF. Rajiv had signed Indo-Sri Lankan accord and in July 1987 sent Indian forces to end the civil war in Sri Lanka between the rebel Tamil forces and the Sri Lankan army. The rising communal disturbance in India was also a major issue against the Congress. More so because just after the election was announced, there was trouble in Ayodhya.

The ninth of November 1989 is a critical date in the history of world politics. In India, on this day, the first stone of the disputed Ram Janmabhoomi temple was laid in a grand Shilanyas[5] ceremony by VHP. The then Prime Minister granted the permission to lay the stone at the undisputed site. While a wall of communalism received a firm foundation in India, elsewhere in Germany that very day the erstwhile East German (German Democratic Republic) government allowed its citizens to cross the 'Berlin Wall' and visit West Berlin. Communism collapsed in Germany on a day when communalism thrived in India. This was in the middle of an election.

The election results went against Rajiv's Congress. Though his party emerged as the single largest party with 197 seats, it fell about 76 seats short of absolute majority. His principal adversary V.P. Singh-led Janata Dal too could manage to bag 143 seats. But Singh had support from the communists who won 45 seats and BJP which recovered from just two seats in 1984 to 85 seats in 1989. The communal divide created during Rajiv's tenure as the Prime Minister rejuvenated the BJP, which would soon establish itself as the Congress party's principal rival. With the unlocking of the doors of the Ram Mandir, Rajiv unknowingly opened the doors to BJP ascendancy in Indian politics.

But for the BJP, the major electoral support came from four states—Gujarat, Madhya Pradesh, Rajasthan and Maharashtra. The party could win only eight seats from UP where all the actions on the temple–mosque issue were taking place.

Following the shilanyas at Ayodhya, BJP ally VHP had announced that the actual construction of the temple would begin in February 1990. But when V.P. Singh took over as the first PM heading a minority government supported from the outside by the sworn adversaries—BJP and Communists—VHP gave four months' additional time to the new government to work out an amicable solution. This was an impossible task, given the staunch positions adopted by VHP, the Babri Masjid Action Committee and the Babri Masjid Movement Coordination Committee. No solution was possible, though, VHP felt that the government did not even attempt to reach a consensus.

Long after the elapse of the four-month breathing period, in July 1990 (nearly seven months after V.P. Singh took over as the Prime Minister) VHP announced that it would start temple construction on 30 October. However, V.P. Singh had plans to plug VHP's communal agenda, he decided to introduce the caste card against the temple issue. On 7 August, V.P. Singh announced unilaterally that his government would implement the recommendations of the Mandal Commission, giving 27 per cent reservation in government jobs to the so-called Other Backward Classes (OBCs). Apart from dividing the supporters of Ram Janmabhoomi movement, Singh thought that the move would offer him a solid support from the massive OBC vote bank.

But Singh was not oblivious of the effect of the temple movement on electoral politics in India. He had been working out an arrangement. With a formula agreed upon by several ministers and leaders of the BJP, VHP and RSS, V.P. Singh sought to issue an ordinance that ruled to acquire the disputed Ram Janmabhoomi land and hand over a part for temple construction. This received massive objection from the Muslim community who were concerned that their Waqf property would have to be surrendered to the government, and Singh was forced to relent. This did not please the VHP which was also discontent by the fact that nothing on shilanyas found a mention in the ordinance. By then, the BJP had joined the Ram Mandir agitation, throwing its weight behind VHP. BJP president L.K. Advani set out on a Ratha Yatra (road show) from Somnath in Gujarat to Ayodhya. It was planned that he would join in the Kar Seva, the actual bricklaying of the temple, on 30th October. His trip through Gujarat, Maharashtra, Karnataka, Andhra Pradesh, Madhya Pradesh, Rajasthan and Delhi saw massive popular enthusiasm. BJP could unite Hindus under the Ram Mandir issue. Advani resumed the Rath Yatra, moving onward from Delhi to Bihar. V.P. Singh watched helplessly even as his party colleague Mulayam Singh Yadav, the then Chief Minister of UP, put pressure on him to stop Advani. Singh's friend Laloo Prasad Yadav, the then Chief Minister of Bihar, arrested Advani after the Ordinance plan fell through on 23 October 1990.

BJP had its political plan scripted. The party withdrew support from the V.P. Singh government. The ruling Janata Dal fell apart. Dissidents led by Chandra Shekhar and Devi Lal, soon joined by Mulayam Singh Yadav, formed the Janata Dal (Socialist) (JD(S)). Chandra Shekhar worked out an arrangement for a JD(S) minority government supported by Rajiv's Congress. For the first time, a government had to step down for its inability to work out a solution acceptable to the majority Hindu community.

In UP, Mulayam saw an opportunity to come to the limelight and chalk his own course. He pre-emptively arrested all leaders of the Ram Janmabhoomi movement. To stop Kar Sevaks from reaching Ayodhya, he suspended all public transport in the state, blocked roads and imposed curfew in a number of cities. There were house-to-house searches for hiding Kar Sevaks. The state borders were sealed. Hindu Kar Sevaks were put behind bars. The estimated number of arrested people varied widely—from 100,000 to 800,000. Some Muslim Kar Sevaks were also jailed. While Mulayam boasted that not even a bird would fly to Ayodhya, he himself led the dinosaur of communalism into national politics.

As if these steps were not enough, Mulayam in his enthusiasm deployed armed policemen to thwart any move by the temple volunteers to enter the site. On the appointed day of 30th October, thousands of Kar Sevaks stormed through the police barricades, onto the disputed land. They were driven out forcibly, many were arrested and about ten died. On 2nd November, the sevaks returned. When they were navigating the narrow lanes near the Janmabhoomi site, the police opened fire. The death toll was variously reported, from 16 by Mulayam, 30 by the Union Home Ministry and several thousands by local eyewitnesses. The BJP cited 168 and the VHP claimed that it could substantiate a death toll of about 400.

Mulayam's stand did not find favour among the politicians, barring the communist Chief Minister of West Bengal, Jyoti Basu. Even Rajiv Gandhi, who had been supporting the Chandra Sekhar-led government at the Centre had advised caution. But Congress, fearful of a not-so-bright prospect did not press for dismissal of Mulayam government in UP. At that time, politicians of all hues offered sympathy and support for the Ram Janmabhoomi movement.

The 1991 election took place in this backdrop. The dusty town of Ayodhya was on top of the nation's agenda. The BJP, led by Lal Krishna Advani, was on the ascendancy. All other political parties, including Congress were worried about the extent of impact of the Ram Mandir issue on electorates and concerned over the formation of the next government.

The V.P. Singh-led Janata Dal was losing its popularity despite implementing the Mandal Commission report for OBCs.

The 1991 elections were conducted in two phases. In the first, when 211 constituencies went to polls, either the Mandal or Mandir issue ruled voters' agendas. In the interim between the two phases of election, India witnessed its third most sensational political assassination. Rajiv Gandhi at the age of 46 was killed by Tamil terrorists, at Sriperumbudur in Tamil Nadu. It was a scheme plotted by the Tamil Tigers' leader Velupillai Prabhakaran to settle score with Rajiv for his decision to deploy the IPKF in Sri Lanka.

The following phase of election saw a huge sympathy wave, which helped the Congress bag a majority of the seats: it won 244, but still fell short of absolute majority. In the end, Congress formed the government with outside support. For the first time, it elected a non-Gandhi, non-Nehru leader, Narasimha Rao. Yet, despite the sympathy wave for Congress, BJP increased its tally to 120 seats. The party won 51 seats out of 84 in UP and 20 out of 26 seats in Gujarat. Clearly, the Mandir issue had polarized both states.

Economically, the Congress government in 1991 initiated many new measures. For the first time, India embarked on a liberalized economic policy, creating discomfort for the left and also a section of BJP that sought to maintain the status quo for its core support group of traders and small businesses. Politically, Congress faced internal squabbles. Senior leaders like Arjun Singh and N.D. Tiwari formed a separate political party called Indira Congress. Leaders in Tamil Nadu walked out to form a regional party called Tamil Maanila Congress. There was a scandal when a diary owned by a businessman surfaced, revealing that money changed hands against favours granted by various political leaders. The Jain Hawala Diary, high rate of inflation and stagnating economy contributed to Congress winning just 140 seats in 1996 election.

The Jain hawala scandal scalped several leaders before the 1996 election. The big names who were implicated included three Rao cabinet members, Arjun Singh from the breakway Congress (T) party, BJP leader Lal Krishna Advani, Sharad Yadav (leader of the Janata Dal Parliamentary Party), and also the former Congress Prime Minister Rajiv Gandhi. The final list had names of 115 politicians. It caused a major shake up among the political parties. Most significant perhaps was the resignation of L.K. Advani who had led the BJP on the Mandir issue. This was when Atal Bihari Vajpayee took over as the BJP Chief.

Congress Party attempted to campaign on its record on the economy. When Rao took over, the country had hardly any foreign exchange reserve to pay for its essential imports like crude oil. Indian economy was effectively downgraded to the junk status. In its five years under Rao, the economy bounced back and the country recovered from its economic shock. Also, the government could showcase a strong foreign policy record, present its successful handling of the numerous natural and ethnic crises. The international community took a fresh interest in India. Rao could draw attention to Pakistan's involvement in the Mumbai bomb blasts in 1993. He could develop a working relationship with China and also Iran. His Look East Policy saw India coming close to the ASEAN. He had handled the Punjab terrorism issue successfully. But these were not enough to win support from the electorates in 1996 elections. For them, the economic policies of Rao created a disturbance to their set pattern of life dependent on the state largesse.

Janata Dal and the National Front—where the Left were partners—campaigned on maintaining a strong public sector with some commitment to deregulation. It peddled populist measures like more state-run infrastructure projects, subsidized fertilizer and increased education investment away from the economic liberalization initiated by Rao.

BJP had a two pronged campaign plan—one was addressed to the rational and the other was hardcore Hindutva. Its four-point rational campaign centered around probity of public life, self-reliance in the economy, social harmony and greater security. BJP outlined an economic plan for significantly scaling back government intervention and encouraging capital investment and creation. But to address its core constituencies, the party also stressed the role of Hindutva in its vision for India. It promised a more Hindu-orientated state by banning cow slaughter, introducing a uniform civil code and removing the special status of Kashmir. Not surprisingly, the party could win only three regional allies before the election despite a moderate and likeable Atal Bihari Vajpayee as its leader.

But BJP needed more allies if it were to form a government at the centre. In order to attract prospective partners and also silence critics who raised Advani's involvement in the Jain Hawala case, the veteran leader stepped down and handed over the reins of the party to the moderate Vajpayee. This was a shrewd political move on the part of Advani—to sacrifice his own political ambition and take the party closer to power. Yet, it did not work then. Though BJP won 161 seats, the highest among all political parties, it could win only three allies. Along with these allies, BJP could command a support of just 187 members of Lok Sabha, falling short of the magic 273 mark by an unbridgeable 86 seats. Vajpayee as the leader of the largest party in Lok Sabha was called to form the government, but he had to resign after 13 days for failing to win enough support. Since Congress refused to form the government, the third largest party Janata Dal received the call. To head the government, the party first approached the then Chief Minister of West Bengal, Jyoti Basu. But Basu's party CPI (M) felt that with just 52 MPs under the Left bloc, it would not be proper to accept the offer.

Finally, in H.D. Deve Gowda, the Chief Minister of Karnataka, emerged a dark horse to take over as the fifth non-Congress Prime Minister of the country. Congress supported the alliance from outside.

Internal squabbles within the alliance and the new Congress president Sitaram Kesari's decision to withdraw support saw Deve Gowda ousted in one year. I.K. Gujaral then emerged as a choice of the coalition to take over as the Prime Minister. He too lasted for a year. That there would be another election was evident from the time the result for 1996 election was announced.

In the 1998 election, parties campaigned and the people voted for a stable government. BJP-led NDA projected Atal Bihari Vajpayee as their choice of the Prime Minister. NDA could win 254 seats. BJP alone won 182 seats, received support from regional parties like TDP from Andhra Pradesh and AIDMK from Tamil Nadu. Vajpayee had support from 286 MPs and formed the government.

The steps initiated by the Vajpayee government laid the foundation for the next election and also for an election victory for NDA. First was the five nuclear bomb test explosions at Indian army's Pokhran Test Range, following which the Prime Minister Vajpayee declared India a full-fledged nuclear state. There were a variety of sanctions on India as a result. But the country overcame those with the inflow of funds from its non-resident community. Vajpayee also embarked on a mission to ease India's tension with Pakistan. He travelled to Lahore to mark the inauguration of the Delhi–Lahore bus service. The much-publicized event attracted international attention. Vajpayee's stature as a statesman increased manifold.

But the major factor that cemented the Vajpayee government's capability was its handling of the Indo–Pak war that broke out soon after the efforts at peace between both countries. The war caused much international concern because Pakistan, too, had declared itself a nuclear nation close on the heels of India's tests at Pokhran. War between the two nuclear-capable nations and that too at the high altitude of Kargil alarmed the international community.

The war started due to the infiltration of Pakistani soldiers and Kashmiri militants into the Indian side of the LoC, the de facto border. Pakistan claimed that only the Kashmiri insurgents were responsible. The Indian Army, supported by the Indian Air Force, recaptured a majority of the positions on the Indian side of the LOC. Due to immense international pressure, Pakistan finally withdrew from a few remaining posts, handing over control to the Indian forces. The war attracted criticism at home but overall the sentiments in the country stood in favour of the Vajpayee government. The interesting point to note is that Vajpayee government had lost its thin majority in April 1999, before the Kargil war started. The government lost by just one vote in the no confidence motion brought against it in April 1999. The infiltration was detected and full scale war was fought by a caretaker government.

Elections took place in September 1999 after the Kargil war was over. There was no doubt of the return of the Vajpayee government. Apart from the Kargil victory and the peace mission with Pakistan, NDA had the sympathy of the people because of the manner of its loss in the confidence vote, that too by just a single vote. Campaign 1999 was merely a formality. More so since the pre-election coalition put together by BJP-led NDA was strong. In comparison, the Congress president Sonia Gandhi failed to attract allies. BJP retained its 180 seats and with coalition partners won 299 seats to form the government.

The election result of 1999 illustrates certain changes in the preference of the electorates. The Ram Mandir had somewhat lost its lustre. This saw BJP losing its grip over UP. The party won 29 seats against 57 it bagged in 1998 and 52 in 1996. Clearly, BJP did not come back to power in 1999 merely because of its Hindu communal politics.

Second and no less important was the leadership issue. Vajpayee was an acceptable political face for many in the country. His charming style, non-aggressive yet witty oratory and track record in Parliament had made him a leading political leader for long. He was not seen taking aggressive postures on the Ram Mandir issue, though he had defended his party in and outside the parliament. But Vajpayee stood taller than any other right wing Hindutva leader. In 1998, particularly after the disastrous experience of 1996, the country was looking for an acceptable leader to run the government. The economy was not in good shape, inflation was high and growth rate was stagnating. Congress brought in Sonia Gandhi, widow of the late Prime Minister Rajiv Gandhi, as the party president to weather over its leadership crisis. Her Italian origin saw a senior Congress leader, the Maharashtra strongman Sharad Pawar walking out of Congress. In addition, Sonia did not have any experience of electoral politics. She was not even a Member of Parliament in 1998. She contested in 1999 from two seats, one from Bellary, a constituency in Karnataka and the other from Amethi, Rajiv's old constituency. She won both, but retained Bellary. In any case, her effort to form a government in 1998 after the defeat of the Vajpayee government in the floor test did not win her many friends. Mulayam Singh Yadav, the UP strongman, did not offer his support to her. Sonia had a lot to learn before she could hope to lead a government. Clearly, Vajpayee had no challenger in 1999. Sonia sitting in the opposition was quietly bidding for her time. She had an advantage over Rao in 1996. Congress stood united behind her. With so many senior leaders having experience in public life rallying behind her, all she needed was a spark to make a bid for power. For Vajpayee, the infighting within the party was a constant problem. His health was also an issue. Thus, India during the 13th Lok Sabha (1999–2004) was just waiting for yet another political transition to come.

3

The India Shining Campaign and Its Failure

If there had been any landmark election that shaped the politics of the nation, it was the 2004 general election. This was an election when most thought that the competent handling of the Indian economy by the Vajpayee government would lead to a fresh term for the BJP-led NDA coalition. In fact, before the decision to seek peoples' mandate for a fresh five-year term, one year before the term of the 13th Lok Sabha expired, was taken with the expectation that there was a visible sentiment in favour of the ruling NDA.

The campaign 2004 is also important to assess the role of the Gujarat Chief Minister Narendrabhai Damodardas Modi in the Indian electoral politics. To look into the Modi effect on 2014 election, one needs to go back to the Republic Day of 2001 when a massive earthquake hit the state of Gujarat. The two minute that shook the state had its epicentre at 9 kilometres south–southwest of the village of Chobari in Bhachau Taluka of Kutch District of Gujarat. The earthquake of 7.6 and 7.7 magnitude killed around 20,000 people, injured another 167,000 and destroyed nearly 400,000 homes. The shock waves spread 700 kilometres, affecting 21 districts. Bhuj, situated 20 kilometres from the epicentre, was devastated. Also affected had been hundreds of villages in Taluka of Anjar, Bhuj and Bhachau. The quake destroyed around 40 per cent of homes, eight schools, two hospitals and 4 kilometres of roads in Bhuj, in Ahmedabad, Gujarat's commercial capital with a population of 5.6 million, as many as 50 multi-storey buildings collapsed and several hundred people were killed. Total property damage then was estimated at $5.5 billion and rising. In sum, it was destruction all around that left the task of massive rebuilding on the BJP-led government under its veteran Chief Minister Keshubhai Patel.

Keshubhai had been one of the founding members of the BJP in 1980. Prior to that, he started his political career as a worker for the Jan Sangh in 1960s. Jan Sangh had later merged into Janta Party but later was revived as BJP in 1980 after the failure of the Janata Party experience. In his younger days, Keshubhai was praised for the relief work following 1979 Machchhu dam failure that had devastated Morbi. But in 2001, Keshubhai was not at the prime of his health. The earthquake relief work was not smooth and allegation of corruption was rampant. The central government led by Atal Bihari Vajpayee and his close associate the Home Minister Lal Krishna Advani were worried. BJP had been losing people's support at an alarming rate. The party had to act immediately to retrieve the situation and face the state assembly election scheduled in early 2003. The party had just about a year to recover from the slippery slope.

In fact, election was advanced since the incumbent Chief Minister Narendra Modi resigned in July 2002 and recommended the dissolution of the legislative assembly eight months before its term was due to expire. This came within five months of a communal riot in Gujarat. The state was completely polarized at that time. It received some fresh help from two heavily armed attackers who scaled the wall of the Akshardham temple complex on 24 September 2002. This was about two months before the election for the state assembly was scheduled. The terrorists opened fire on about 600 people who were in the temple at the time. They killed 30 persons and wounded more than 80 persons. The state called the National Security Guard (NSG) commandos to intervene. They freed the temple complex after killing both the perpetrators. Modi-led BJP swept back to power in Gujarat with a massive two-thirds majority. The party won 126 seats in the 182-member assembly, improving its tally of 117 in the 1998 election. Congress fared worse than expected, winning 51 seats against 57 it had in the dissolved assembly.

The election results indicated that despite belated efforts, Narendra Modi could not completely erase the negative sentiment of the earthquake-affected regions. Its former Chief Minister and Industries Minister Suresh Mehta lost Mandvi seat in Kutch. In the BJP, stronghold of Saurashtra, where it won 52 of the 58 seats in 1998, the party yielded several seats to the Congress. Saurashtra suffered draught and farmers were turning against the ruling BJP. Same was the sentiment in Kutch region, which was devastated by an earthquake two years ago. There questions over governance figured prominently during the campaign with BJP at the receiving end.

But in the communally sensitive regions, BJP received spontaneous support. In Godhra, where the train carnage changed the course of state politics, BJP candidate and Bajrang Dal leader Haresh Bhatt defeated the sitting Congress MLA Rajendrasinh Patel. BJP made a clean sweep in the tribal-dominated eastern belt of Gujarat, winning all the 12 seats in the region. In Vadodara, another region worst hit by the communal violence, BJP won all the 13 seats. The party did well in central Gujarat, which too was affected by the 2002 riot.

The well-documented fact was that in the election campaign, BJP sought to capitalize on the effect of riot, with the attack on the Swaminarayan temple in September adding the icing on the cake. However, the then Deputy Prime Minister Lal Krishna Advani described the verdict as a defeat of forces that 'spread slander and venom' against the people, administration and police of Gujarat. The election result was presented as the peoples' verdict on the Modi-led government in handling the riot of 2002. While Congress failed to recover its position in the state, there were others waiting outside the state of Gujarat to encash the riot in the political stage outside Gujarat. The assembly election in Gujarat 2002 and the victory of Narendra Modi had been a landmark political judgement influencing the course of politics even today, 14 years after the unfortunate event.

In November–December 2003, there were assembly elections due in three states in the Hindi heartland of India—Rajasthan, Madhya Pradesh and Chhattisgarh. In addition, there was election to the assembly of the National Capital Territory of Delhi. All these states had Congress governments. BJP won all the three major states—winning 50 seats out of 90 in Chhattisgarh, 111 in Rajasthan (out of 200 seats) and 168 in MP (230 seats in total). The election results created an unforeseen enthusiasm among the leaders of BJP. That BJP could win just 20 of 70 seats in Delhi against 47 by the then ruling party in the state of Delhi was conveniently brushed aside. BJP felt that the country in general was supportive of the Vajpayee government and its economic policy.

Election win apart, the Indian economy broke free from its former low level of growth trap. For the first time, the economy recorded more than 7 per cent annual growth rate in GDP. The estimate of growth for the next year was more than 8 per cent, next only to that of China's growth rate. BJP leadership felt the time was opportune for the party to seek peoples' mandate. On the face of it, the government, perhaps for the first time in India, launched a campaign based on its success on the economic front.

NDA's 'India Shining' campaign of 2004 has an instant recall value. No other campaign has been as talked about as the Atal Bihari Vajpayee government's bid to retain power through its sumptuous and flashy ad blitzkrieg and its spectacular failure. The election result which saw BJP winning just seven seats less than its principal rival Congress (it won 138 against 145 of Congress) led to a coalition under Congress to take over the mantle from a reasonably successful Vajpayee government.

The problem that the campaign overlooked was the fact that its audience could not be the impoverished masses. The campaign used the then prevailing mood of optimism over the rising flow of foreign investment into the country. By 23 April, Indian share market saw an inflow of US$4.1 billion, almost two-thirds of the total figure for year 2003. Indian rupee had been the world's third best-performing currency against the dollar and India the best-performing economy after China.

Apart from the economic scorecard, BJP was confident that the Vajpayee charisma and popularity would see it through. The government's successful handling of relation with Pakistan, taming insurgency in J&K and the North-east, and its impressive performance in international issues were thought of as impressive records for the electorate. The BJP also attempted to hard-sell the food security programme, which covered 8–10 crore people, enhanced physical and digital connectivity, rural housing and urban renewal.

BJP flashed statistics to establish that its reforms also had 'pro-people' orientation. The ₹60,000 crore Pradhan Mantri Gram Sadak Yojana provided employment to 500,000 people, 5,300,000 units were built under the Indira Awas Yojana from 1985 to 1999, while 5,400,000 units came up since then till 2003; there had been preferential allotment of land to tribals and what is more important agricultural credit increased from ₹36,860 crore (₹368.60 billion) in 1989–99 to ₹82,000 crore (₹820.00 billion) in 2002–03.

Clearly, BJP wanted to break away from its branding as a temple party with Article 370 and common civil code as other permanent agenda. While attempting this, the party think tank made several mistakes. First and most critical one was the fact that in a country where a large section of the population lived under abject poverty, the very concept of India shining was certainly not a 'feel good factor'. The campaign theme was a distant dream for most of the electorate. Second, by shunning the mandir, common civil code and Article 379, BJP managed to distract the cadres from RSS and VHP in working for its electoral cause. Election needs cadre support to bring the undecided voters to the polling booth. This is one of the most critical parts of any campaign management. BJP had lost the support of its core workers in 2004. Third, and no less important, was the tactical voting by the Muslims. With intense campaign by the left and liberals supported by a large section of NGOs, pictures from Gujarat riots were prominently displayed in many parts of the nation where Muslims formed a sizeable chunk of the electorates. Two contrasting faces stood out, that of Qutubuddin Ansari and Ashok Mochi. Ansari, a tailor was snapped pleading for mercy with folded arms, blood on his shirt, and Mochi, famous as the fiery, wiry Bajrang Dal worker with sword in arms raised in frenzy. The Left from West Bengal even went to the extent of providing shelter to Ansari in the state, away from Gujarat where he was not safe. While BJP attempted to leave its Hindutva image behind, its detractors used it effectively to ensure tactical voting by the Muslims. This saw the non-NDA parties winning seats. Narendra Modi's Gujarat had played a silent role in ensuring defeat of BJP-led NDA in 2004 election. The hands of the 'secular' brigade received an additional support when L.K. Advani, the deputy Prime Minister went on a Bharat Uday Yatra. The theme was to shun the Hindu–Muslim agenda and project the need for building a strong India. But the enthusiasm of the crowd had ebbed considerably by then. The yatra brought to the fore a lurking suspicion of many that Vajpayee would relinquish the post of the Prime Minister and Advani would take over a few months after election victory. BJP leaders did not care to introspect, but the fact remained that Advani had the baggage of Babri Masjid demolition. He never had the kind of popular support that Vajpayee had. Thus, despite a dazzling India Shining campaign, BJP was politically ill-prepared in 2004. This could be seen in forming coalitions in different states. The party had lost several dependable allies—Indian National Lok Dal (INLD) in Haryana, LJP in Bihar and in certain states the ally also had lost its shine like TDP in Andhra Pradesh.

The other important point that contributed to the party's electoral loss was the absence of emotional appeal in the advertising campaign. Originally, it was not created as an election campaign. The idea was the brainchild of Prathap Suthan, then national creative director with the advertising agency Grey Worldwide in India. Media quoted Suthan, 'Honestly, it was not meant to be political but it has turned into the hottest issue in India.' The slogan was part of a ₹65 crore (₹650 million), government-funded campaign to promote India internationally. 'India Shining' was originally the theme for a 60-second video made by the government to highlight the steps it took to boost economic growth. This was aired 9,472 times on television in December 2003 and January 2004, second only to ads for the government's anti-polio campaign. The campaign was stopped by the EC when Congress complained that it would provide unfair advantage to BJP. Little did they know then that the campaign would lead to people's disenchantment and eventual loss of BJP in 2004. Compared to the India Shining message, the Congress slogan that 'Congress hand (its election symbol is hand) is always with the common men' (*Congress ka haath, aam aadmi ka sath*) was better accepted. '"India Shining" is all about pride. It gives us brown-skinned Indians a huge sense of achievement. Look at the middle-class and they tell the story of a resurgent India', Suthan had told media. Little did he know that his 'pride' would bench BJP in the opposition for ten long years.[1]

But it will be unfair on the advertising agency to single the campaign out as the most important negative factor in campaign 2004. The internal problems in the party were responsible in no small way. Clearly, there was undercurrent of rivalry between the two top leaders in BJP. Once the Prime Minister Vajpayee on his return from a foreign tour announced that he was neither tired nor retired to dispel the rumours that he would retire soon. In the second rung of BJP leadership, there was intense rivalry. Leaders like Pramod Mahajan, Venkaiah Naidu, Rajnath Singh, Sushma Swaraj and Arun Jaitley, used to be busy gossiping with journalists on who would be the next candidate for the top post. They all loved leaking stories to Delhi journalists. Their interpersonal rivalry was intense. Once when Advani asked Jaitley and Mahajan to supervise Assam election together, both reportedly refused to work with each other. Finally, Jaitley was asked to look after Tamil Nadu. All these salacious stories hogged the headlines even when BJP was not in power. Meanwhile, Congress had all the time at its disposal to build on its thin election victory of 2004.

During the five years between 2004 and 2009, BJP was busy reconciling with its election loss of 2004. In its desperation, its top leaders turned 180 degrees to present themselves as secular figures. The most ridiculous one was the effort of Lal Krishna Advani in 2005 when he visited Pakistan. Maybe overwhelmed by the surroundings of the mausoleum of Mohammed Ali Jinnah, Advani wrote his tribute to Pakistan's Quaid-e-azam: 'His address to the Constituent Assembly of Pakistan on August 11, 1947, is a classic, forceful espousal of a secular state...' This was on 4 June 2005, one year after the electoral loss. Next, the message was faxed to the party office in Delhi to the spokesperson, Prakash Javadekar. Prakash, predictably, was startled and consulted his party colleagues. Decision was unanimous that this would not be released.

RSS and VHP were furious. Ashok Singhal, the VHP president, demanded Advani's resignation. Praveen Togadia, another VHP leader known for his outbursts, called Advani a traitor. Calling him Lal Mohammed Advani, Togadia told the magazine India Today that, 'Advani rode the Ram Rath to become the leader of Opposition and now he wants to get prime ministership sitting on Jinnah's shoulders'. RSS spokesperson Ram Madhav said, 'This is against the basic ideology of the RSS.' He reiterated the RSS view that Jinnah was responsible for the division and partition of the country. Though the then RSS Chief K.S. Sudershan called this as internal matter of BJP, his next in command and the present RSS Chief Mohan Bhagwat told BJP general secretaries that Advani needed to clarify or resign. Hours after the RSS demand, Advani resigned from the post of party president. But the rivalry within the second generation leaders ensured that Advani could stick to his post till December 2005. Though he did not have much support within the party, leaders like Rajnath, Jaitley, Mahajan, and others did not want to disturb the uncomfortable peace and let Advani continue. This was the time when BJP was completely directionless. Its Chief Ministers in the states of Gujarat, Madhya Pradesh and Chhattisgarh had been facing internal dissension. In parliament, BJP was busy more in disrupting the proceedings than opposing. Even the business leaders were disturbed. Advani had to assure them that BJP would not oppose business-friendly legislations and act as a constructive opposition in the parliament. In a speech at the annual meeting of the Confederation of Indian Industry (CII), a powerful business lobby, Advani said that BJP would support 'any reform that is vital for India's economic progress'.[2]

BJP was in a new phase, the third phase according to Advani. According to the BJP veteran, there had been three phases in the BJP. The first phase began with the Shah Bano case, the first major blunder of the inexperienced Prime Minister Rajiv Gandhi. It lasted even after Rajiv's assassination—the phase was for 11 years from 1985 to 1996. The second phase was when

BJP came to power, first in 1996 just for 13 days, then in 1998 for a year and next in 1999 for a full term truncated by the party's overambitious attempt to prepone the election. This phase lasted for eight years from 1996 to 2004. Then, the phase of indecisiveness began—Advani called it the third phase. This phase began ominously—inability to accept the defeat in 2004, infighting among the second rung leadership, fading away of the most acceptable face of Atal Bihari Vajpayee and Advani's desperation to come back to power and become the second BJP Prime Minister. BJP's election campaign for 2014, too, had its genesis in this forgettable third phase of BJP.[3]

The election for the 15th Lok Sabha in 2009 came when BJP was still struggling to reconcile to its electoral loss of 2004. In between, there had been assembly elections in several states where BJP and its allies were successful. First assembly election that NDA–BJP and its then ally JD(U) won was the eastern state of Bihar. The coalition won 143 seats out of a total of 243 in the state and formed the government. In Punjab, BJP and Akali Dal alliance won the state back from Congress in February 2007. Uttarakhand, too, was bagged by BJP. In December 2007, Narendra Modi swept Gujarat once again. Himachal Pradesh, too, went to BJP. But the most exciting news for BJP was the victory in the southern state of Karnataka in May 2008. Thus in the middle of 2008, BJP and its NDA partners had been in power in nine states against just about five of Congress. That is when came the most prominent victory of the Congress-led UPA.

The issue was the US–India Civil Nuclear Agreement. It had its origin in the 18 July 2005 Joint Statement by the Indian Prime Minister Dr Manmohan Singh and the then US President George W. Bush. India agreed to separate its civil and military nuclear facilities and to place all its civil nuclear facilities under the International Atomic Energy Agency (IAEA) safeguards. In exchange, the US agreed to work towards full civil nuclear cooperation with India. The deal apparently was still born. The UPA government drew its major support from the country's Left which had 62 seats in the Lok Sabha. The Left parties were completely against the deal. Without their approval, it was not possible to get it passed through the Parliament.

But before it did finally reach the road block called the Indian Left, the Indo–US deal took more than three years to come to fruition since it had to go through several complex stages. One was the amendment of the US domestic law, specially the Atomic Energy Act of 1954, a civil–military nuclear Separation Plan in India, an India–IAEA safeguards (inspections) agreement and the grant of an exemption for India by the Nuclear Suppliers Group (NSG), an export-control cartel that had been formed mainly in response to India's first nuclear test in 1974. In its final shape, the deal placed under permanent safeguards those nuclear facilities that India had identified as 'civil' and permitted broad civil nuclear cooperation, while excluding the transfer of 'sensitive' equipment and technologies, including civil enrichment and reprocessing items even under IAEA safeguards.

On 9 July 2008, India formally submitted the safeguards agreement to the IAEA. This came after the Prime Minister of India, Manmohan Singh returned from the 34th G8 summit meeting in Hokkaido, Japan, where he met the US President George W. Bush. For India, time was running out. The term of President Bush was to expire by the end of the year. What his administration offered, the new President was not expected to maintain. So, for Dr Manmohan Singh, it was then or never moment for the deal. Predictably, the benefits of the deal were too high for Dr Singh to ignore. Though his party was not keen to press for the deal since the Left was certain to withdraw support and turn the UPA government into a minority, the Prime Minister was adamant. Media reports suggested that he even threatened to resign if the party did not allow the deal to go ahead. When the government decided to go ahead with the deal, Prakash Karat, the CPI(M) General Secretary announced on 9 July 2008 that the Left Front was withdrawing its support to the government.

The sentiment of the people was mostly in favour of the deal. Though common men in general did not understand the nitty-gritty of the nuclear deal, but most accepted that it was an honourable deal for the future of the country. Manmohan Singh was right in guessing the mood of the nation. BJP, which in ordinary course would have supported the deal decided to play the archetypical opposition and bring in no-confidence motion against the government. This further distracted the core support base of BJP, majority of whom were supportive of the Indo–US Civil Nuclear Deal.

When on 22 July 2008 the UPA government faced its first confidence vote in the Lok Sabha, there were interesting political alignments. First, the Speaker of the House a veteran CPI(M) parliamentarian refused to side with the party whip and decided to continue in his position as Speaker of the Lok Sabha. Second, several smaller parties and a major regional party from UP, the SP, supported the government. The UPA coalition won the confidence vote with 275 votes to the opposition's 256. The victory not only ensured the continuation of the Congress-led government, it also effectively sealed the fate of BJP in the next Parliament election in 2009.

But before the term of the Lok Sabha expired, there were assembly elections due in four states, namely Madhya Pradesh, Chhattisgarh, Rajasthan and the National Capital Territory of Delhi. Of these four states, the three major states barring the capital city of Delhi were ruled by BJP. When the election process was on, terrorists attacked Mumbai, occupied two hotels and inflicted extensive damages to the city of Mumbai. BJP argued that this was the result of a weak government failing to control cross-border terrorism. It was felt that people would exhibit their disgust and vote against Congress in the assembly elections. But the results were not as per BJP's hope. The party failed to make any dent in Delhi and lost Rajasthan. It could retain its hold in the two states of Madhya Pradesh and Chhattisgarh.

The election process exposed the weaknesses in BJP as a political organization. The inner party conflict was acute in Rajasthan where certain caste leaders even left BJP. Narendra Modi was not favoured as a campaigner, particularly in the state of Rajasthan. It was believed that Modi was a divisive figure. His presence would result in Muslims looking away from BJP as an electoral option. The other interesting development the party preferred to wink at was the lack of people's enthusiasm to Advani. His meetings in Rajasthan were sparsely attended. Media was not keen to report on his rallies. On the other hand, the then Chief Minister Vasundhara Raje Scindia managed to attract people to her rallies. But the party lacked cadres to manage election. A large section of RSS workers stayed away. Vasundhara Raje lost the election. In contrast, the Chief Ministers of Madhya Pradesh and Chhattisgarh managed to keep all dissenting voices adequately checked and won their respective assemblies. The inner party conflict in BJP was the maximum in the capital Delhi. The election result, too, reflected its organizational and political weakness. The Congress Chief Minister Sheila Dikshit returned to power for the third consecutive term.

As if the election loss in Rajasthan and near drubbing in Delhi again were not enough, BJP did not even attempt to gear itself up for the Lok Sabha election 2009. The party continued with all its past baggages.

First was declaring Advani as its prime-ministerial candidate. That there was hardly any interest among the electorates on Advani was brushed aside. By projecting their grand old leader, BJP management perhaps bought internal peace, but the option offered was not exciting for its core supporters to campaign enthusiastically. When a party does not have an inspiring leader, the right strategy should not be to project anybody as the claimant for the prime minister's post. Instead by projecting Advani against the incumbent Prime Minister Manmohan Singh, BJP scored a self-goal even before the election started.

The second mistake of the party was its failure to gauge the mood of the nation. The election took place about seven months after the collapse of the Lehman Brothers and the US insurance giant the American International Group (AIG) in September 2008. India was not affected. In fact, a large amount on investible surplus flew into India. The Indian economy did not see any immediate reason to panic nor did the financial brain trust of the nation sense the crisis that might erupt. In short, the general feeling was that everything was hunky-dory. With nothing much to worry over on the surface, the opposition BJP did not have much ammunition to use in the election 2009. BJP trained its gun on corruption citing the use of money in buying crucial votes in the confidence vote of July 2008. But the mood of the nation after the survival of the government was the one of relief. Middle class was happy that the Indo–US Civil Nuclear Deal went through. By drawing attention to the confidence vote, BJP reminded the electorate of the party's short-sightedness during the critical deal.

Third and no less important mistake was Advani's attempt to criticize Manmohan Singh as a weak Prime Minister. This was used when the nation was appreciating Singh's ability to drive the Left out of the coalition and yet win the confidence vote. It was also reported that Singh's firm decision to go ahead with the Indo–US deal did swing even the Congress leadership in his favour. People believed Manmohan Singh was a bold leader and had full sympathy for him. Even normally family-centric Congress realized the same and used photographs of Singh along with Sonia and Rahul Gandhi as their leadership team. Clearly, Advani and his team failed to read the message and attacked Manmohan. The election result illustrated how mistaken was their reading of the scenario. BJP won just 116 seats against 206 of Congress. The UPA-II coalition came back to power with a rejuvenated Congress at the helm.

Advani spoke of three stages of BJP. Two earlier stages, that of Ram Mandir and second one of governance was over by 2004. The third phase of being in the opposition and rebuilding the party for power failed miserably. The primary reason for this failure was lackadaisical leadership of the party in Delhi. This was curious since the party had by then three strong Chief Ministers in the states of Chhattisgarh, Madhya Pradesh and Gujarat. Its ally, JD(U) in Bihar and SAD in Punjab were also firmly on saddle. BJP had also won the southern state of Karnataka apart from Uttarakhand and Himachal Pradesh. Clearly, the central leadership of BJP lacked the necessary ability and determination to recover from the slump it suffered post 2004. The party national leaders had no idea how to revive the fortunes of the party without a symbol like Ram Mandir.

This weakness offered opportunity for a new leader to emerge and take charge. But given the infighting and rivalry among the leaders in New Delhi, the task was onerous. For the Rashtriya Swayamsevak Sangh (RSS), the gradual loss of BJP was a matter of concern. In March, RSS had a new Sarasanghachalak (Chief)—Mohan Bhagwat who was the General Secretary of RSS since the year 2000. Bhagwat wanted to infuse discipline among the Delhi leadership. At his behest, BJP appointed Nitin Gadkari—a relatively junior leader from Nagpur—as the party president in December 2009. Gadkari brought back some discipline within the party, but in due course, he himself became a target of infighting. He had to withdraw his candidature for the second term in January 2013, since there were charges of alleged irregularities in the firm Purti Group promoted by him. Rajnath Singh took over the charge from Gadkari.

When the central leaders were busy fighting each other, the Chief Ministers in the three states of Madhya Pradesh, Chhattisgarh and Gujarat were busy attending the needs of their respective states. Their performances were the only silver lining in otherwise an inept BJP post 2004. The vacuum at the Centre, absence of a charismatic leader who would take ahead the aspirations of party workers, offered opportunity to Narendra Modi to emerge as the tallest national leader in the party.

4

Gujarat Riot and the Incumbent Government

When Narendra Modi received an urgent summon from Prime Minister Vajpayee on 1st October 2001, he was attending the cremation of a news TV cameraman Gopal who died in a helicopter crash the previous day. Gopal of Hindi channel Aaj Tak was with the opposition Congress leader Madhav Rao Scindia when the copter crash killed all the passengers. Modi knew Gopal and attended the funeral. The Prime Minister asked him to come in the evening for an urgent meeting.

When he reached, both Vajpayee and Advani met him. Vajpayee told Modi that he was earmarked to go to Gujarat. Modi was perplexed and wanted to know if he would be in charge of Gujarat only or some other state as well. Slowly, it dawned on him that he was being sent to Gandhinagar to revive the sagging fortune of BJP in the state. For six long years, Modi was outside Gujarat, a persona non grata for the Chief Minister Keshubhai and the state party president Sanjay Joshi. Now he was going back there to replace Keshubhai. Modi took oath on 7 October 2001. Within less than five months on the morning of 27 February 2002, the Sabarmati Express, returning from Ayodhya to Ahmedabad, was stopped near the Godhra railway station. Kar Sevaks who had gone to Ayodhya to take part in a religious ceremony there were returning by the train. Four coaches of the train caught fire, trapping many people inside. In the resulting conflagration, 59 people, including 25 women and 25 children, were burned to death.

The day following the fire riots broke out with mobs resorting to retaliatory attacks on the Muslims. But the response of many—what the then editor of the Hindustan Times, Vir Sanghvi called 'secular establishments'—had been hostile to the newly appointed Chief Minister Modi and his administration. While the incident was well documented that a mob of about 2,000 people stopped the Sabarmati Express shortly after it pulled out of Godhra station, attacked the train with petrol and acid bombs which gutted four bogies and led to the death of 59 persons, some argued that this was a well-planned inside job to incite the Hindus into a communal orgy in Gujarat. The views expressed in different TV channels were that the massacre was a response to the Ayodhya movement, therefore, provoked by the Kar Sevaks themselves. Later on, the UPA-I government appointed an enquiry commission under Justice Umesh Chandra Banerjee who concluded that the Sabarmati Express fire was accidental and started inside the compartment.

When Gujarat was burning, Modi attempted to douse the fire. Chief Minister Modi in a televized speech appealed for restrain. Speaking in Gujarati, he said that though the crime in Godhra was heinous, but he would not tolerate 'ashanti, asangjam and akrosh' (creating disturbance, indiscipline and venting anger). Modi appealed for peace, 'Tit for tat is not a solution. Innocent should not lose life'.[1]

Post-Godhra riot is perhaps the most publicized one in the history of India. In the heat and dust of blames and counter claims, what is lost is how Narendra Modi ended up as the victim number one for the riot. There were certain assumptions that stuck to Modi. First, that he is a Hindu fundamentalist as are all who work in RSS. Second, he is a very shrewd political person who knew that BJP had lost in Gujarat when he came as the Chief Minister and needed some urgent action to reverse the trend. The riot helped. Third and no less important is that he is a loner who can go to any length to reach his goal, a ruthless person. Nobody cared to check if these attributes are justified or not. Within 19 weeks of taking over as the Chief Minister of Gujarat, his first ever experience in government, Modi earned the brand identity that stuck even today, rightly or wrongly.

First, the campaign on Gujarat riot was shrill with Modi as the target. There were good reasons for that. From within BJP, Modi did not have any friend in Gujarat. He was sent from Delhi, a person whom the Gujarat leaders had managed to banish out of Gujarat for six long years. Keshubhai, his predecessor and former tormentor, could not have been pleased. Sanjay Joshi, the then Gujarat state president of BJP had always been an arch-rival. No need to guess that the allegiance of BJP activists was not with Modi. More so since the primary task of the new Chief Minister was to ensure that the earthquake disaster victims receive succour, which was due to them but were evidently being pilfered. In effect, Modi was working against the same vested interests who were part of his political support team. The enemy within found Modi as an exciting target.

Second, the abysmal record of BJP in the state gave hope to the rival Congress leaders who had been out of power effectively from 1990—too long for their comfort. Predictably, they would not have liked a new Chief Minister to come and retrieve the situation for BJP. Also, a defeat for BJP in Gujarat would have weakened the Vajpayee government considerably in New Delhi. The border state of Gujarat was known for smuggling activity mostly handled by Muslim gangsters. They were a major strength for Congress in Gujarat.

Third and no less critical were the liberals, secularists and outright religious fanatics who were not comfortable with the rise of 'Hindu fundamentalist' BJP government in India. They felt that Ram Mandir was a hype that would fade in due course. They had all been waiting for an opportunity to discredit BJP. This group was large and had intellectuals, journalists, commentators, NGOs and religious leaders in their rank. They were unified in one thought, that was to get rid of the 'communal' BJP from power. Modi became a sitting duck in their scheme of things.

Finally and no less important were the officials in Gujarat. It does not need a great introspection to conclude that bureaucracy gains financially from political corruption. If there had been rampant corruption in relief and rehabilitation work after the earthquake, certainly it was in connivance with these officers at various levels of administration. Modi had inherited this baggage when he took over as Chief Minister.

While Modi was presiding over an administrative and political system that had no reason to be supportive to his effort of reaching earthquake relief to the people, all were waiting for a spark to further discredit the former *pracharak* who had no experience of administration. The spark came on 27 February 2002, just a couple of days after Modi won his first election from Rajkot-II assembly constituency in Saurashtra. Given the disenchantment of the people in the constituency, it was not an easy seat for Modi. The former MLA Vajubhai Vala who vacated the seat for Modi was unpopular for his link with builders' lobby. Only incumbency factor saved the day for Modi who won with a considerably reduced margin than what Vala had in 1998. In two other by-elections, BJP lost to Congress. All were waiting for some spark to discredit Narendra Modi who had been earning positive vibes due to his tireless work on earthquake relief. Godhra train burning provided the spark that even today is used liberally to end Narendra Modi's political brand.

Gujarat had always been a hotbed of Hindu–Muslim conflicts. The walled city of Ahmedabad had been notorious for skirmishes between the two communities. The state had, in the past, witnessed major riots. In 1969 when Hitendra Desai of Congress was the Chief Minister, the first major riot took place. It saw death of 660 persons, majority were Muslims. This saw the ghettoization of Muslims in Gujarat. The next major incident was in 1985 which lingered for six months and resulted in death of an estimated 275 persons. Violence between the two communities on minor issues like tumbling of a holy book from a cart or cows passing by were good enough reasons for engaging in skirmishes. Narendra Modi inherited this communal cauldron. The two other major riots in 1969 and 1985 had caused the ouster of the then incumbent Chief Ministers—Hitendra Desai and Madhav Singh Solanki. Naturally, Modi was expected to also follow the same route. More so since the riot in 2002 had many unique features. The most important feature was that the incidents took place when India had several 24 × 7 news channels. Their anchors descended in Gujarat, boom in hand, full of their choicest vocabulary to nail the administration. The riot was the most well-publicized incident in India and still is. The number of people affected was also high. Officially, 262 Hindus and 863 Muslims lost their lives. These include those who died in police firing. Army was deployed in the midnight of 28th February when the Indian Defence Minister was seen with army vehicles marching in Ahmedabad. The riot lasted for 72 hours unlike the previous occasions when it was allowed to simmer for longer. There were good reasons for the same. The central government under BJP's Atal Bihari Vajpayee with Home Minister L.K. Advani, a Hindu fundamentalist leader known for his Babri Masjid demolition incident, could not have risked the riot to continue for long. For Narendra Modi, it was a challenge to bring back order fast enough so as to concentrate on his primary task of reviving BJP fortune in the state.

For the media, the riots provided an unexpected opportunity. The on-the-spot coverage highlighted the inhumanity of such carnages. The fact is nobody loves a riot. The regular faces on TV channels became celebrities of sorts. They all needed a villain of the piece. The behind-the-scene operators from BJP and associate bodies, Congress, Islamic interest groups and babudom would not have made good exhibits. Media zeroed on Narendra Modi who had all the ingredients to emerge as villain number one. He was from RSS, the most hated 'communal' outfit according to many in media and intellectuals. He had been generally a loner, doing his work shunning publicity. The BJP allies found him an easy scapegoat who could have been sacrificed without their image of secular politics taking a hit. The script was loaded against Modi. Even Vajpayee made some allusion that the Chief Minister should follow 'raj dharma' without any discrimination. In his press conference on 4th April 2002, with Modi by his side, Vajpayee offered this advice and provided new ammunition to the detractors of the Chief Minister. The popular belief even today is that Vajpayee wanted to replace Modi but could not do so at the behest of Advani. Venkaiah Naidu who was the party president then told in March 2014[2] to the newspaper *The Indian Express* group's Idea Exchange programme that the collective decision of the party was against Vajpayee's wish. 'Atalji opined that the Gujarat Chief Minister should adhere to raj dharma and step down. But the party collectively decided that he should continue, and that decision prevailed.' Evidently Vajpayee was also making a feeble effort to save his liberal image while accepting the party view since Modi was indispensable for keeping Gujarat with BJP.

The riot thus created the brand Modi. To others he was seen as a ruthless politician who would not hesitate to polarize the people for political end. Clearly, nobody was willing to accept that Modi was not responsible for the burning of the four compartments of the Sabarmati Express on 27th February, howsoever, far fetched that logic might be. The most gratuitous view was that Modi might not have engineered the train carnage but used the incident to extract political mileage. For Narendra Modi, the brand image stuck. His political campaign, even when the messaging was only economic, received a political religious slant when reports were filtered through media.

Narendra Modi acted fast. He attacked land grabbers, law breakers and also smuggling mafia. A large section of the last group was Muslims who received patronage from many politicians, largely from Congress. Modi knew that only popular support would strengthen his vulnerable position. His speech in the assembly in March 2002 was a pointer. In a speech, which was ignored by national media Modi provided the list of arms haul, arrested mafia dons and terrorists. He praised the police for the good work they had initiated and vehemently opposed the critics who had been demoralizing the officers with insinuations. He objected to the tendency of defaming the officials for the Godhra riots and said, 'If you think certain crimes have been committed I am willing to take all those crimes on my head. And if they want to see them hanged, I am willing to be the one to go to the gallows.'

Modi recommended dissolution of the assembly in July 2002, eight months before the completion of its tenure. But India's EC delayed the election date so as to avoid flaring up of communal sentiments due to holding election so soon after the riot in February. The matter turned ugly with Modi holding the view that the EC was biased. There was a constitutional issue also. It was believed that when an assembly is dissolved within six months of its last seating, a new assembly should take office. In case for some unforeseen reasons this cannot happen, then there is a provision of imposing President's rule in the state. Going by this, election should have been completed by 3 October 2002. But the matter went for a reference to India's apex court, the Supreme Court. Meanwhile Modi was under attack by intellectuals and opinion leaders for trying to encash the post-riot sentiment of the Hindus. There was support for the then Chief Election Commissioner James Michael Lyngdoh but Modi did not let go the opportunity to hit out. In a public meeting at Bodeli, near Vadodara, on 20 August 2002, Modi targeted Chief Election Commissioner Lyngdoh for his bias on religious ground. He used to quote Lyngdoh by his full Christian name James Michael Lyngdoh in press conferences, public meetings, etc., to highlight his religious background. Lyngdoh had hit back at Narendra Modi for attacking him on religious grounds saying it was 'quite despicable' and 'gossip of menials' by those who have not heard of atheism. It needed intervention by the Prime Minister Vajpayee to cool the tempers and rein in Modi. Supreme Court ruled that EC had a right to decide on the election date. At the same time, the court opined that the Chief Minister would hold his position for six months from the date of dissolution of the assembly. Thus, Modi could continue when election was finally held and took oath for the second term in December 2002.

The campaign in 2002 assembly election illustrates the character of Narendra Modi. He is a person who could not be cowered by any threat. His readiness to take on Lyngdoh did rattle many and earned admonish from Vajpayee, but the fact remained that even the CEC realized his limit in the fact of attack from a political leader having popular support. It also had shown Modi's ability to fight for his cause alone. He was the star campaigner for his party and won 127 seats against just 51 of Congress. The riots of 2002 might have swept the sentiment against Congress and in favour of Modi, but the people's sentiment turned favourable to Modi for his tireless work. That the administration was now firm could be seen from the fact that the attack of the Akshardham temple in Gandhinagar in September, just weeks before the elections were scheduled did not lead to another round of riots as in February after the Godhra carnage. Clearly, people had faith in the administration of Modi by then. As for Modi, the lesson was that he should view even the independent institutions with some suspicion. For most of them, Modi was a punching bag.

Incidentally, similar situations arose again in 2007 before the assembly election. The EC issued notice for his campaign speech on the slain alleged criminal Sohrabuddin Sheikh. Modi was reportedly angry and wanted to burst out against the EC. It is said that Arun Jaitley restrained him citing that the case was to be heard in the Supreme Court and any outburst would impact the hearing. It was also argued that the EC could debar Modi from contesting election as it did to Balasaheb Thackeray. In any case, the Commission also acted with restrain with Chief Election Commissioner N. Gopalaswami deciding to keep the decision on the 'hate' speech in abeyance.

Realizing that both the national media and a large part of senior bureaucrats were secretly holding negative opinions on him, Narendra Modi plunged himself into the administration of the state. Now that he had the mandate of the people in 2002, he started asserting himself. When he took over in 2001, Modi acted on the advice of his partymen and retained Gordhan Zadaphia as his Home Minister. Modi had misgivings on Zadaphia who later on did play mischief during the 2002 riot. He attempted, from the time he took over from Keshubhai, to create programmes which were transparent with a clear delivery schedule and parameter. This helped him in his effort to reach relief to the earthquake-affected areas. There were several initiatives which helped the state of Gujarat.

One programme he mentions in his speeches is the Lok Kalyan Melas. In effect, this brought the government at the doorstep of people. The senior bureaucrats identified the target beneficiaries after proper scrutiny and then in the presence of ministers including Modi, the beneficiaries collected their cheque or benefits in kind under different social welfare schemes of the government. The open meeting and presence of senior bureaucrats, ministers and media ensured that benefits went to the target persons only. The first such mela was held in February 2002, before the Godhra riot and continues even now in every district of Gujarat. The national media did not care to talk of these schemes. In any case, positive stories do not sell.

Another popular programme of Modi is Kanya Kelavani Programme. Modi set up Mukhyamantri Kanya Kelavani Yojana. Under the scheme every year just before the school admission year starts, senior officials in charge of various districts reach out to the families of children who are at the entry level age for schools. The new school entrant receive in public meeting a school uniform, a school kit and a toy. Girls receive a Narmada Bond of ₹1000 which can be encashed when they complete class seven. Modi donates all gifts he receives to fund the programme. Ordinary citizens too donate to the fund. As a result of the scheme, school drop out rate has fallen and female literacy rate has increased over a period of ten years.

These are just few of the not-so-well publicized programmes. The most prominent one is the biennial Vibrant Gujarat programme. The biennial investors' summit held by the Government of Gujarat brings together business leaders, investors, corporations, thought leaders, and policy and opinion makers. With many high profile Indian businessmen attending the summit, media, too, give due publicity to the event. The first Global Investors' Summit under Modi was held during the Navratri festival in 2003. In this, a total of 76 memoranda of understanding (MOUs) worth US$14 billion were signed. The 2005 summit saw signing of 226 MOUs garnering an investment of US$20 billion, the third summit in 2007 promoted 33 special economic zones of Gujarat. This saw signing of 675 MOUs worth US$152 billion. The Government of Gujarat organized the Fourth Global Investors' Summit on 12–13 January 2009 where 8,662 MOUs to the value of US$241 billion were signed. Such summits apart, Gujarat emerged as the most investor friendly state in India. It attracted high value and high profile investment from various reputed brands. Such investments and the praises showered by top businessmen gave Narendra Modi huge publicity. Rest of the nation, even common men, accept without much debate the success of the Gujarat model of development. Media has helped Modi by leaving out his schemes like education programmes for children or distribution of benefits through Lok Kalyan Melas, etc. This gave Modi an opportunity to talk about the benefits of such simple but innovative delivery systems introduced in the state. When the national media and influencers had been busy demonizing Modi, he was quietly building his brand. This had a durable effect on the election results in the state and now has given him issues to highlight.

But the ghost of 2002 kept on haunting Narendra Modi, thanks to the incessant campaign. The most well-publicized incident was denial of diplomatic visa by the US in 2005. The Asian–Americans hotel owners association invited Modi. A petition was set up and signed by academics requesting that Modi be refused a diplomatic visa, a resolution was submitted by John Conyers and Joseph R. Pitts in the House of Representatives which condemned Modi for inciting religious persecution. Pitts also wrote to the then Secretary of State Condoleezza Rice requesting Modi be refused a visa. Recently, one US official came on an Indian television channel and said that during 2005, the US had been under pressure due to its stand on Afghanistan, Iraq and Iran. Washington had been looking for gestures that would have positioned the US as supportive of Islamic causes. By denying the visa to Narendra Modi, Washington tried to send the message that since he was the Chief Minister when the well-publicized riot took place, the country did not want him there. In fact the US diplomatic mission, too, stayed away from reaching out to Modi though he was rated as the most sought after head of a province for business.

On the issue of accountability of the riot and punishment of the victims there was a never-ending flow of reports. One weekly magazine Tehelka was prominent in exposing wrongdoings in Gujarat. In 2004, it published a hidden camera exposé alleging that BJP legislator Madhu Srivastava bribed Zaheera Sheikh, a witness in the Best Bakery killings trial. In a 2007 expose, it released hidden camera footage of several members of the BJP, VHP and the Bajrang Dal admitting their role in the riots. While the liberal media hailed the expose, several inaccuracies in the statements released diluted the impact of the sting operation. For example, Babu Bajrani and Suresh Richard in the statements said that Narendra Modi visited Naroda Patiya one day after the massacre to thank them. But the official record showed that Naredra Modi didn't visit Naroda Patiya. VHP activist, Ramesh Dave told Tehelka reporter that S.K. Gadhvi, one of the divisional superintendents of Police killed five Muslims in Dariapur area. Gadhvi was only posted in Dariapur one month after the riots. During his tenure, no such incident took place in Dariapur.

In all such campaigns, one critical element was overlooked. There were three hardcore Hindu leaders in BJP, Pravin Togadia, Haren Pandya and Zadaphia, who always used to spew venom against Muslims. The speeches of Pandya used to start with a caution to his audience that if there were any Muslims in the crowd they should better leave before he spoke. In the assembly election 2012, Jagruti Pandya, wife of slain Haren Pandya, contested from her husband's seat Paldi, a Hindu majority well off locality of Ahmedabad. She was representing the Gujarat Parivartan Party (GPP) of the former Chief Minister Keshubhai Patel. The campaign pamphlet asked why the Muslim population in Paldi had been increasing under Modi's watch. Modi cracked down on all communal elements which affected the hardcore VHP, RSS and BJP elements. Some left the party and some like Togadia left Gujarat. This part of brand Modi did not find much mention in the national press. Modi, too, concentrated only in Gujarat. There were many reasons for the same. The cases on the riot had been dragging on and reached the Supreme Court. There were other cases of alleged fake encounters where certain persons were killed. Police claimed that they were criminals or terrorists and died in encounter. The evidences did not indicate that. There were efforts to link Modi to such encounter deaths. His confidant and minister Amit Shah was even arrested. The Supreme Court had appointed in 2008 a Special Investigating Team (SIT) under a former CBI director R.K. Raghavan to investigate and submit report. In March 2011, Modi was summoned by the SIT and questioned for nine long hours about charges made by Zakia Jaffri, wife of former Congress MP Ehsan Jaffri who was killed during the riot. Zakia alleged that it was Narendra Modi who had issued instructions to the police and security establishments to remain inactive and allow a free run to rioters.

In its closure report, SIT concluded that there was no evidence that Modi gave any such instruction. On the contrary, the speeches and public statements of the Chief Minister established his commitments to punish the guilty in the Godhra train burning incident and maintain calm and discipline. But the media still did not budge from its stand that Modi was culpable. NDTV, an English news channel reported, 'But far from proving that Mr Modi could not have given the alleged instruction, the speeches the SIT produces are only likely to fuel suspicions about what might have happened at the February 27, 2002 meeting.'

Earlier in April 2009, SIT had submitted before the Court that Teesta Setalvad, an activist on Gujarat riot, had cooked up cases of violence to spice up the incidents. SIT said that false witnesses were tutored to give evidence about imaginary incidents by Setalvad and other NGOs and charged her of 'cooking up macabre tales of killings'. The court was told that 22 witnesses, who had submitted identical affidavits before various courts relating to riot incidents, were questioned by SIT; it was found that the witnesses had not actually witnessed the incidents, they were tutored and the affidavits were handed over to them by Setalvad. The report was brought to the notice of the bench, consisting of Justices Arijit Pasayat, P. Sathasivam and Aftab Alam. It noted that the much-publicized case of a pregnant Muslim woman Kausar Banu being gangraped by a mob and foetus being removed with sharp weapons, was also cooked up and false.

Gujarat riot cases were a continuous battle, and there were more. The opposition to the Narmada Project was another. Modi wanted to complete the project and bring water to the parched regions of Gujarat. But there were activists like Medha Patkar supported by several prominent personalities like Shabana Azmi, Arundhati Roy who had been opposing the same. There was strong resentment to such movements in Gujarat. The central government was using it as a political tool to disturb Modi. In a meeting of the Narmada Control Authority (NCA) to review the height of the Sardar Sarovar Dam and rehabilitation measures for the oustees, the then Water Resources Minister Saifuddin Soz proposed the lowering of the dam height from 121.92 metres. Modi said that three-fourths of the co-basin states were in favour of retaining the proposed dam height, which had the sanction of the Supreme Court and warned that the Centre would be responsible for any backlash against the attempts to thwart this development scheme and enormous financial loss that the four states would have to suffer. This outburst was a signal to the rest of India that Narendra Modi knew how to assert himself and rally his people with him. In 2006, he was the most prominent Chief Minister despite the constant attack on him for the Gujarat riot.

A clear scenario was emerging. Modi represented the regional aspiration. Near about six crore Gujaratis were with him though not all would vote for him. In fact the trend in election results clearly illustrate that while in assembly election there was no competition for BJP, with the party winning near two-thirds majority since 1998 in Lok Sabha Gujarat had sent more Congressmen than the assembly election results justify. Both in 2004 and 2009, Congress could win 12 and 11 seats, respectively, out of 26 Lok Sabha seats in Gujarat. Both in 1998 and 1999 when the BJP wave was at its highest BJP won 19 and 20 seats from the state. The unavoidable conclusion is that in assembly election more than BJP as a party, Narendra Modi as a person received overwhelming support from the electorates.

What could be the charm of Modi that saw him winning again in 2007? Before the election results were declared, editor of *The Indian Express* Shekhar Gupta wrote that if Modi could win the state assembly election, the stage would be set for an ultimate Modi and Sonia Gandhi battle. This was in the context of the scheduled Lok Sabha election in 2009. Gupta said that though Advani would be the prime-ministerial candidate of BJP, Modi would emerge as the star campaigner. But he was wrong in assessing two factors. First, even within BJP, there were leaders who thought Modi would not win the support that Vajpayee did. They felt that it was better to stick to Advani as their principal campaigner. Second factor that Gupta overlooked then was the reaction of BJP's partner JD(U). By then, the BJP–JD(U) coalition was in place in Bihar. There the Chief Minister Nitish Kumar had been in control, winning lots of accolades for turning around the state. Nitish was acceptable to Muslims who formed a substantial vote share in Bihar. He was careful not to be seen as anti-Muslim, hence shunned Narendra Modi who was accused of inciting the riot in Gujarat. Evidently, Nitish had nurtured the ambition to lead the nation one day as its Prime Minister. Collaboration with Modi, let alone accepting him as a leader, was completely ruled out in Nitish Kumar's scheme. Narendra Modi could sense it well. He did not want to disturb his peer group in BJP or the coalition partner of NDA. He is a patient man as revealed by his stoic acceptance of the barrage of criticisms and accusations for his handling of Gujarat riot. The development in Gujarat since 2002 taught Modi how to administer a communally divided state and how to win an electorate fed on the staple diet of communalism through sheer efficient administration. This was the period which laid the foundation of the Modi campaign in 2014.

5

The Top-driven Congress Campaign for Political Mobilization

Rahul Gandhi had everything in his favour. Born to the Indian National Congress (INC) party president Sonia Gandhi and former Prime Minister Rajiv Gandhi, Rahul had the right pedigree, proper exposure, good looks and ease of entry onto the top of the leadership ladder—everything and more that one needs as background for a career in politics in India.

When he decided to enter the lower house of India's Parliament, he chose his ancestral Lok Sabha constituency of Amethi in the state of UP. Amethi had sent his father Rajiv and later, mother Sonia to Lok Sabha a total of five times since 1981 when his uncle Sanjay Gandhi, then incumbent MP, died in a plane crash, leaving the seat for his elder brother Rajiv to fill. This constituency had shattered the hope of Sanjay Gandhi to enter the Lok Sabha in 1977 when he lost on his debut. Since then, the only occasion when Congress lost the seat was in 1998 to the BJP rival, now Congress MP in the upper house Rajya Sabha, Dr Sanjay Singh. Rahul contested in a seat where 'the family' enjoyed support from nearly two-thirds of electorates year after year.

Amethi also has a history of sending the members of the Nehru–Gandhi family to Lok Sabha on their debut. Sanjay won his first election from here in 1980 (after the defeat of 1977), Rajiv won in 1981, and Rahul's mother Sonia in 1999. Rahul contested from Amethi when Sonia shifted to the neighbouring constituency of Rae Bareilly, a seat earlier held by his grandmother and former Prime Minister Indira Gandhi.

In India's semi-feudalistic political set-up and given the awe in which people hold the Nehru–Gandhi family, all that Rahul needed was to gain political experience so as to handle the responsibility of leading the party and also the government when the time would come. Rahul Gandhi had the requisite ambience—his mother was the party president running the government led by her hand-picked former Finance Minister Dr Manmohan Singh. Rahul had the requisite leadership traits— amenable, charming, gentle and with fresh ideas. During his visits to the constituency, he met the poor villagers who were expecting favours from him. Amethi, 60 kilometres away from Rae Bareilly, was like one of the 600,000 similar villages in India but for the fact that it had the privilege of being represented by the top political family of India.

Rahul had a clear idea of the role he was expected to play. In an interview to a magazine, within one year of his election, he explained how the people from his constituency trusted he would deliver, 'You should see the belief they have in me. Each one thinks I can do things for them. When I see that, I get huge strength and I can actually do it for them.' Armed with confidence, Rahul embarked on his journey for his appointed place in Indian democracy—the office which had been his family's for three generations since India attained independence from the British rule.

Rahul Gandhi was patient. He was mostly active behind the scenes, rejuvenating the party, and meanwhile learning the basics of politics. He was not happy with 'the system', a feeling he readily conveyed to the media, winning appreciation from many. He positioned himself as an agent of change in a corruption-ridden, dynasty-dominated democracy, though he himself was parachuted to the top through his historic family connection. But Rahul was candid. He did not even spare himself. In October 2008, he addressed girl students at a resort near Jim Corbett National Park where he admitted that 'politics' was a closed system in India. He said,

> If I had not come from my family, I wouldn't be here. You can enter the system either through family or friends or money. Without family, friends or money, you cannot enter the system. My father was in politics. My grandmother and great grandfather were in politics. So, it was easy for me to enter politics. This is a problem. I am a symptom of this problem. I want to change it.[1]

It indeed was a welcome start for India's future leader and possibly Prime Minister.

Rahul won the hearts of the people, mostly the young. Here was a person from the family of top Congress leaders who was willing to look at problems afresh and reach for a new age solution. Despite not being accessible to media, despite his silence in Lok Sabha, Rahul Gandhi was certainly the front-runner for the position of India's Prime Minister. His carefully crafted campaign placed him as a person who cares for the poor, the downtrodden. His visits to places like Niyamgiri, Vidarbha or Bundelkhand made headlines.

When in July 2008, Rahul visited the house of Kalavati Bandurkar, in the village Jalka in the Vidarbha region of Maharashtra, it was prominent news but not prominent enough for everybody to take notice. Kalavati's husband had committed suicide in December 2005, hit by crop failure and debt. He left her with a debt of ₹1 lakh (₹100,000). Rahul highlighted her plight in the parliament, in the course of the debate on the Indo–US Civilian Nuclear Deal. His point was that the nuclear deal would bring in electricity to India's remotest corners, which would lead to better livelihood for the countless Kalavati Bandurkars of India. It did touch many a heart.

Rahul was at his emotive best while participating in the debate on no confidence motion against the UPA-I government in July 2008. Though his speech was rudely cut short by the opposition, Rahul managed to position his pitch for energy security through the stories of two poverty-stricken women he had met in Vidarbha. He was confident, his style was informal and it appealed to those watching the proceedings live on TV. It was then that he attempted to speak as an ordinary Indian, 'I was thinking about what I want to say and I came to a simple conclusion. I decided that it is important at this point not to speak as a member of a political party but to speak as an Indian.' He wanted ten minutes to speak but was interrupted due to disruptions. Yet he managed to tell the stories of Sasikala and Kalavati in drought-hit Vidarbha, and their need for electricity.

Rahul is not a forceful orator. He adopted the approach of narrating a story.

> Three days ago, I went to Vidarbha and met a young woman who had three sons. She is a landless labourer and earns ₹60 a day; her husband works in the field and earns ₹90. With their total earning, they ensure that their three children go to a private school. I spent an hour with them. They live in a slum. The eldest son dreams of being a district collector, while the middle one dreams of becoming an engineer. And the youngest wants to do a private job.

Amidst the melee, Rahul went on, 'When I asked Sasikala whether her children would be successful. She said, "absolutely, they will succeed". As I was walking out, I noticed no electricity in the house. I asked the children: how do you study. They pointed to a little brass lamp and they said: we study by that lamp.'

Rahul connected poverty with energy security, 'Energy security reflects itself in the everyday life. It reflects on the industry, reflects itself among all Indians. The point is if we don't secure our energy, our growth will stop.' He hit the bullseye.

This was India's future Prime Minister: modern yet with a compassionate soul. Rahul Gandhi embarked on a dream political campaign—understated yet directed, soft but forceful.

Few months before visiting Vidarbha, Rahul had travelled to the Niyamgiri Hills in Odisha in March 2008. He was then the Congress General Secretary, still learning his ropes in politics. But by that time he had learnt where lay his priorities. He said that he was against mining of Niyamgiri hills at Lanjigarh in Kalahandi district. The region is rich in bauxite deposit where London-listed Vedanta Aluminum wanted to set up an alumina refinery. Rahul won the hearts of the tribals and environmental activists when he declared that he was personally 'against mining at Niyamgiri hills as it would destroy the environment of the area, and affect water sources, livelihood sources and local culture'.

For Rahul Gandhi, this was a well-publicized part of his 'Discovery of India journey'.

On the first day of his tour, he visited a tribal hamlet on the foothills of Niyamgiri and interacted with the members of the Dongaria and Jharania tribes, who had been opposing the proposed extraction of bauxite from Niyamgiri hills for the upcoming alumina refinery. Rahul had clarified that he was not against industrialization, but he sympathized with the concerns of the locals. He did not miss the opportunity of hitting at the opposition-ruled state government for failure to implement centrally sponsored schemes, blamed it for grabbing land of farmers and also diverting water from agriculture to industry. Rahul knew well that in an underdeveloped region, politics of subsidy worked better than the politics of industrial growth. He had learnt from the well conceived but failed 'India Shining' campaign of the previous Atal Bihari Vajpayee government. Rahul took a left-of-centre position like his grandmother Indira Gandhi.

The election to the 15th Lok Sabha in 2009 proved that people in general were happy with the ruling UPA government. The dual centre of powers with Congress President Sonia Gandhi managing the politics and Prime Minister Manmohan Singh handling governance received thumbs up from the people. After four elections, Congress crossed 200 seats mark to reach 206 and with its allies the party attained a comfortable majority in the parliament. What is more, in the largest state of UP where Congress had ceased to be a major power, the party bagged 21 seats matching the tally of two regional parties SP and BSP. Congress tally was double that of arch-rival BJP which had once replaced Congress in the state. It was evident that the charm of Rahul Gandhi worked.

It worked not merely in UP but across the nation. Rahul's photograph was prominent in the campaign material of Congress party. There were three faces—that of the party president Sonia Gandhi, Prime Minister Manmohan Singh and the Party General Secretary Rahul Gandhi. The electorate had no doubt about who the baton would pass to next. The only question was: when?

But there were many doubting Thomases. Rahul did not join the cabinet to gain the much-needed experience in governance. His reticent presence in the 14th Lok Sabha made many wonder if he was mature enough in parliamentary procedures. The critics said that during the first five years in Lok Sabha, Rahul didn't exactly set the house on fire. But he was young—just 39 and had time to gather experience on complex subjects on economy, external affairs and the Constitution. In any case, the election results of 2009 had shown that Rahul had a matured sense on ground reality. He decided to contest alone without opting for building a coalition in the critical state of UP and the result was encouraging. Congress seemed to feel safe under Rahul's leadership. His appeal to the young voters looked certain. The number of seats won in 2009 and the utter failure of veteran Lal Krishna Advani-led BJP to make any impact in the elections indicated that Congress would only improve its tally when the baton would finally get transferred to Rahul.

It was a more confident Rahul that emerged after the election victory in 2009. The Central Government headed by Rahul's Congress rejected environment clearance for the bauxite mining project of Vedanta in August 2010. Rahul Gandhi visited the Niyamgiri hills in a show of solidarity with the tribals who had been opposing the project. Responding to the criticism that the rejection of environment clearance was anti-development, Rahul had said, 'True development takes place by respecting interests of the poor and tribals and not by muffling their voice.' Addressing a tribal rally marking 'Adivasi Adhikar Diwas' (Rights Day) in Jagannathpur village at the foothills of Niyamgiri hills close to Vedanta's alumina refinery, he said he would be their 'soldier' in Delhi and continue their fight. Rahul was at his eloquent best,

> In my religion, all are equal—whether it is rich or poor, Dalits or adivasis. Wherever an individual's voice is being stifled, that is against my religion. This is your victory. It is a victory of your voice, it is a victory of the adivasis.

After the 2009 national election, Rahul's focus was the state assembly election in UP. He was perpetually on a *padyatra* or busy addressing a 'mahapanchayat'. The unexpected performance in 2009 Lok Sabha election enthused the Congress workers. The party office at Mall Avenue in Lucknow was seen brimming with ticket seekers. But party workers in Amethi were somewhat disillusioned. It had become impossible for the common man of Amethi to meet Rahul Gandhi. He had become inaccessible. In Rae Bareilly, Sonia Gandhi had created a structure where her constituency was divided into 16 blocks headed by block presidents, who would meet every alternate Sunday. Around ₹12 lakh (₹1,200,000) was spent in each block from the Member of Parliament Local Area Development Scheme (MPLADS) fund. The block presidents would meet Sonia Gandhi once every two months. Rahul would have done well to emulate such a concept, but he did not.

When Rahul became an MP, he changed the system. He relied on self-help groups (SHGs) to reach out to his constituents. He placed two point persons in Amethi to handle political and developmental work, respectively. Sometimes he brought along foreign guests like Microsoft boss Bill Gates or former British foreign secretary David Miliband to his constituency. This brought him international focus. Often he would make surprise visits and stay overnight at villages. In many cases, it would be at the houses of Dalits—something he began with Kalavati in Vidarbha. He would quote the conversations he had with these people in his rallies and parliamentary speeches.

Rahul Gandhi did his homework. He noticed how the former Chief Minister of UP, Mayawati built up a 'rainbow' coalition of sorts and swept the assembly election in 2007. Rainbow coalition meant winning supports from the upper-caste Brahmins, Dalits and Muslims—a formidable combination for election victory. This was what Congress used to enjoy in the state till 1989 when 'Mandal' and 'Mandir' took over the state. After the success in the Lok Sabha election in 2009, Rahul Gandhi attempted to rebuild the party. On 14th April 2010, birthday of the Dalit icon B.R. Ambedkar, Rahul launched the biggest Congress campaign in UP. His target was the state assembly election scheduled in 2012.

But the task was complex. The state had, some researches pointed out, 66 Dalit castes comprising 21 per cent of UP's population. Jatavs, the largest among them, as per the Census 2001, constituted 56 per cent of the SC population. The Pasis were the next in number, 16 per cent of SCs, with Dhobis, Koris and Balmikis placed in the third constituting another 15 per cent of the SC population. Next were Gonds, Dhanuks and Khatiks with about 5 per cent of SC population.

For Mayawati, the task was easy. She herself belonged to the Jatav community. To woo the others forming the substantial SC community of UP, Mayawati's BSP organized social movements to bring different Dalit castes together. Rahul had some welcome signals from the 2009 election performance of his party. Congress won 4 per cent of Jatav votes doubling the 2 per cent vote share in 2007 assembly election. It also improved its non-Jatav tally from 5 per cent to 16 per cent.

The success was the result of painstaking effort of Rahul. He kept up regular visits to the houses of villagers to know in person their problems and to redress the same. He visited a Jatav family in March 2008, in an Etawah village, whose five members had been killed by dacoits. Next month, he visited Ghisauli village in Jhansi. Rahul was open to criticism. When he heard that Dalits felt against the fleeting visits, which they viewed as more a media opportunity than an assistance, Rahul returned to Jhansi a week afterward and took a delegation of 300 Dalits to the district commissioner to demand fair wages under the National Rural Employment Guarantee Act (NREGA). He even had meal with a Dalit woman, Shanti Devi.

In May 2008, Rahul took the villagers of Banpurwa by surprise when he went straight to a meeting of a women's self-help group. Rahul chatted with them for two hours and then asked one Rekha Pasi for dinner.

When in October the same year Rahul Gandhi was denied permission to address students at a university in Kanpur, he went to rural schools. He singled out the backbenchers, who were Dalits, for interaction. In a speech delivered before the visit ended, he said, 'People from different sections of the society are being exploited as vote banks. If the trend continues, it will become a major challenge for the country.' Rahul had understood the need to address poor as a uniform community without segregating them as different castes. He said in one of his speeches, 'This glorious state has suffered over the past two decades essentially on account of the politics of caste and religion'. While addressing the Congress' student wing National Students' Union of India (NSUI) workers at the Jawaharlal Nehru University (JNU) sometime in September 2009, Rahul said he went to meet poor people in villages and it was the media that labelled them Dalits or adivasis. He repeated in Thiruvananthapuram, 'I ask my office to arrange for my visit to a poor man's home in the poorest village. You see him as a Dalit. I see him as a poor person.' Rahul knew the value of his efforts even though these were part of a clearly planned communication exercise.

A high-profile visit was organized in January 2009 when Rahul Gandhi accompanied the then British foreign secretary David Miliband to a Dalit village in Amethi to show him the 'strength' of India. The day happened to be the state's Chief Minister Mayawati's birthday. Miliband and Rahul spent a night in a Dalit woman's hut at Simara village in UP. The visit had come as a complete surprise to the villagers. The village SHGs were at a meeting when at around 10:30 PM, the motorcade of Rahul Gandhi arrived, and Rahul interacted with the members of the SHGs. Shivkumari, the chosen host for Rahul's customary meal, had nothing to offer her high-profile guests. The Rajiv Gandhi Charitable Trust made the arrangements of food, mattresses and pillows.

At some point Rahul Gandhi's 'core team' decided to recruit a Dalit member. Ranjan Chaudhary, a Pasi by caste, and an Indian Institute of Management graduate who left his job abroad to return to UP politics, was the chosen candidate. The task he was set was to 'analyze' Rae Bareilly and Amethi. His sister Reena Chaudhary had been a Lok Sabha member from Mohanlalganj in 1999 as an SP legislator but had lost the election on a Congress ticket in 2004.

Rahul continued with his mission of reaching out to the Dalit homes and villages. In September 2009, Rahul reached a predominantly Dalit village in Shravasti district and stayed overnight.

Following their young leader, the top leadership of the UP state Congress decided to strengthen the outreach programme. On

Mahatma Gandhi's birthday (2nd October) in 2009, the UP Congress leaders decided to mark the day by emulating Rahul and spending a night in a Dalit house in various parts of the state. Party workers arranged for cooks and plates, mosquito nets and mattresses. Unfortunately, the other leaders failed Rahul by not continuing with the visits.

On 14 April 2010, the birth anniversary of Ambedkar, Rahul Gandhi started a massive 'rath yatra' programme as part of a push to rebuild the party cadre at all levels. But this was not successful since very few Dalits attended the Congress functions for they were busy with their own Ambedkar Jayanti celebrations. Yet Rahul persisted with his outreach programmmes.

However, the difference was that unlike Mayawati, Rahul Gandhi could not openly hold caste gatherings. It would have alienated his support base among the urban youth in JNU and elsewhere, the sort of audiences Mayawati did not target. More important, Rahul could not compete with the caste-based leaders given his upbringing. He could project himself as a sympathetic leader but could not become a part of the lives of the target group. Rahul's class came as a barrier between him and his effort to build durable relations with the poor.

The result in the 2012 assembly election in UP proved disheartening. Congress improved its tally from 22 in 2007 to 38 in 2012, but the success of the 2009 parliament election could not be repeated. What was even more striking had been the electoral loss of Chief Minister Mayawati's BSP. The tally of BSP came down sharply from 206 to just 80, while its arch-rival Mulayam Singh Yadav's Samajvadi Party captured power with 224 seats. The signals were clear: the electorates are fickle. They had no permanent loyalty to any party or its leader.

For Rahul, the 2012 assembly election loss was a great blow. Till then the young leader had been enjoying success—Congress was on a come back trail. Had he managed to hold on to the results of 2009 Lok Sabha poll and captured the assembly segments his party won, there would not have been any issue. There are two distinct features of the assembly election outcome.

First, electorates have a mind of their own. They are not permanently loyal to any political party. Clearly, one could not treat the Muslims, Dalits and other castes as vote banks for a single leader. Partially, certain sections, like Jatavs, continued with their chosen party and leader affiliation but even among them, there had been some who opted to vote outside, breaking away from the traditional loyalty factor. Second and no less important was the sense that voting behaviour differs between an assembly election and the national parliamentary election. In local elections where there is choice, electorates opt for strong local leaders, not a distant national leader.

Rahul Gandhi proved a failure in UP, all his ground research was rendered futile, after all he led the party campaign in UP. Rahul attempted to learn how the BSP first cornered the Dalit vote and then saw its grip slacken. He spent time listening intently to an academic paper presentation on the subject. He tried to understand how Mayawati's hold on the Dalit vote was weakening due to the treatment of the community only as a vote bank, without commensurate development gains.

Visiting villages, meeting villagers, spending nights to familiarize himself with their issues had been one part of Rahul's mission to understand the nation. He also attempted to meet cross section of people when travelling and chose the railway for that. First in September 2009, it began as a part of the austerity drive of the government and the party. He travelled to Ludhiana in the northern state of Punjab in a second class chair car. Unfortunately on his return journey, there was trouble. Miscreants stoned the moving train, damaging a few windows in some compartments. Though stoning is not unusual and was not directed at the VIP passenger, Rahul's Special Protection Groups (SPGs) ordered the train to skip the scheduled stop at Panipat station. This led to resentment among passengers and adverse publicity in media.

His next well-publicized train travel in Mumbai in February 2010 went as per the script. He took a local train from Andheri to Dadar and then from Dadar to Ghatkopar. Many compared Rahul's train journey with his grandmother Indira Gandhi's visit to the state of Tamil Nadu in 1965 amidst anti-Hindi agitation there. Mumbai at that time was having heated exchanges on Marathi and migrants' issue where the belligerent SS had taken a strong stand against the migrants.

Rahul's decision to travel by train was an impromptu one. It was reported that after addressing college students at Bhaidas Hall, he made a sudden stop at an ATM to withdraw money and headed to Andheri station to buy a first-class ticket to take the local. His earlier scheduled itinerary included being driven to Juhu airport and boarding a helicopter to get to Ghatkopar. The local party SS's Uddhav Thackeray was not happy. But Rahul won accolades from Mumbaikars. A local newspaper reported, 'Young girls went ecstatic meeting Gandhi. One girl squealed at Ghatkopar, "I saw him, I saw him" and the only buzz around the station was "Rahulji, Rahulji". Gandhi obliged, turning to wave and smile.'

Rahul was matured. He did not mention the then ongoing migrant issue, but in a brief speech to Congress youth party cadre in Ghatkopar, said, 'I get inspiration from the city and Mumbaikars whenever I have visited the city.'

Next in October 2010, Rahul Gandhi ventured into a 36-hour-long train journey by ordinary sleeper class from Gorakhpur to Mumbai. The travel was not publicized but was released only after ten days of his travel. Rahul's mission was to acquaint himself with the problems of the people who migrate to the metropolis in search of livelihood. He landed at Gorakhpur from a special plane from Bihar and then boarded the 2,451 Gorakhpur–Lokmanya Tilak Superfast Express. He travelled in the sleeper class during the 36-hour-long journey.

Later in an interaction (on 4 April 2013) with the members of India's largest industry body, the CII, he recounted his journey, 'I spent a large part of the 36-hour journey moving across the train and talking to travellers—youngsters, weary families, and migrants moving from the dust of Gorakhpur to the glitter of Mumbai. Took us 36 hours. It is called an Express!' Rahul showed he cared for those youngsters who are forced to migrate far away in search of livelihood. He was concerned of the inadequate infrastructure. He was transparent, not at all hesitant to criticize the Indian Railways controlled by the government his party presided over.

With his focus on UP, Rahul could not remain just a spectator on the agitation by farmers in Delhi's neighbourhood, Noida. Farmers were restive over the forceful acquisition of village land by the building mafia which they claimed was in connivance with the then Chief Minister Mayawati's party BSP. On 11 May 2011, Rahul, riding pillion on a bike, managed to enter the Bhatta–Parsaul villages, giving the district administration a slip and challenging Mayawati administration. Here, the villagers were protesting against the acquisition of land by the state government and the protests had turned violent. A few days later, Rahul went to meet the Prime Minister Manmohan Singh to apprise him of the situation. After the meeting, he told reporters:

> The issue here is a more fundamental one with regard to these villages in
> particular and a large number of villages in UP down the Agra highway,
> where state repression is being used, where people are being murdered...
> quite severe atrocities are taking place there.... There is a set of 74 (mounds
> of) ashes there with dead bodies inside. Everybody in the village knows
> it. We can give you pictures. Women have been raped, people have been
> thrashed. Houses have been destroyed.

These were serious allegations, but were not backed up by evidence.

Unlike his previous attempts, Rahul did not come to the fore when the
Lokpal agitation started with the social activist Anna Hazare sitting on a
much-publicized fast-demanding legislation on Lokpal in April 2011. He
participated in the Lokpal debate in Lok Sabha later in August the same
year. But what he said there is nothing much to recall. Rahul failed to live
up to his nuclear debate promise.

A bold step that Rahul took was on the government's proposed ordinance on allowing politicians convicted of criminal offences to continue
in the parliament. When the bill went for approval by President Pranab
Mukherjee, Rahul barged into a press meet of the party's media cell chief
and general secretary Ajay Maken. And in the presence of the entire Delhi
media, he tore up the ordinance. He said the ordinance passed by the
Union Cabinet to protect convicted legislators from complete disqualifica-
tion was 'complete nonsense'.

India's Supreme Court had ruled on 10 July 2013 that an MP or an
MLA, if convicted by a court in a criminal offence with a jail sentence of
two years or more, would be immediately disqualified. On 24 September,
the Union Cabinet cleared the Representation of the People (Amendment
and Validation) Ordinance, 2013 to negate the Supreme Court ruling. This
ordinance would have allowed convicted MPs and MLAs to continue in office on the condition that their appeal would be admitted by a higher court
within a period of 90 days and their conviction stayed. Rahul Gandhi felt that
this was incorrect and said, 'I'll tell you what my opinion on the ordinance
is. It's complete nonsense. It should be torn up and thrown away. That is
my personal opinion'. The episode embarrassed the Prime Minister who was
in the US at that time. Rahul did violate the process of communication but
received accolades for his sudden outburst. Some suggested, 'Rahul has his
heart in the right place'. They felt that there was nothing wrong in calling
rubbish, a rubbish. That Rahul ensured 'victory of the people'.

To be fair to Rahul, one must admit that he had been talking about transparency in the party. He claimed to have made the Youth Congress and the NSUI fully elected bodies. He was involved in the RTI. He had been aware how the writ of RTI was needed to be extended to include the political parties. Rahul also wanted the party members to choose the candidates in the party. He even attempted to initiate the step in selected constituencies in the 2014 election.

Rahul said in his only exclusive TV interview:

> I have an aim, I have a clear aim in my mind and the aim is that I do not like what I see in Indian politics, it is something that is inside my heart. It is like in our mythology when they talk about Arjun, he only sees one thing, he does not see anything else... that the system in this country needs to change, I don't see anything else and I am blind to everything else. I am blind because I saw people I love destroyed by the system. I am blind because the system everyday is unfair to our people...[2]

Rahul added, 'I am here basically for one thing, I see tremendous energy in this country, I see more energy in this country than any other country, I see billions of youngsters and I see this energy is trapped'. Unfortunately, such ideals cannot be positioned when the country is in the middle of an acrimonious election debate. Despite the right intention and a strong background with the advantage of starting from the top, Rahul, too, acted at a snail's pace. In ten years, what he could not articulate he attempted to highlight the same in a one-hour long interview. In the end, Rahul Gandhi remained a prisoner of the painfully slow system that moves India, even the nation's grand old political party.[3]

6

India Against Corruption, a Campaign Builds Up

When Narendra Modi was consolidating his position in the state of Gujarat, the Congress-led Central Government in New Delhi was busy devising new ways of expanding the Central Government's effectiveness. One by-product of this effort, as revealed by subsequent developments, was to favour certain entities close to the power. The other agenda was to raise funds. In an economy where demand is more than the supply, there is always a scope of earning rent by those who are in a position to dole out favours. Since India's telecom sector had seen a boom, particularly after the New Telecom Policy of 1999 announced by the Vajpayee government, the sector became the first target for exploitation by unscrupulous elements. The conditions were ripe too since the queue for new licences in the sector was long. Big money bags were knocking at the door for fresh set of licences so as to enter the lucrative sector.

There was some deep-rooted corruption hidden in the telecom licences given by the UPA government, which was concealed from the public glare. This came to light when one NGO, Telecom Watchdog, filed a complaint before India's Central Vigilance Commission (CVC) on the illegalities in the allocation process. But when such complaints were initiated, India had already re-elected Congress-led UPA government under the leadership of Dr Manmohan Singh for the second consecutive term in 2009. In the election, UPA government received a moral boosting verdict. Congress increased its tally substantially from 145 to 206. This was the first time since 1991 a party could cross 200 seats mark in the Lok Sabha. In 1991, Congress won 226 seats after the assassination of its leader Rajiv Gandhi. In contrast, BJP fared poorly, its number of seats went down to 116 from 138 in the previous Lok Sabha.

The 2G scam refers to the illegal manner of granting licences for use of the second-generation wireless telephone technology. In India 2G mobile phones started operation in the mid-1990s, flourished under the Vajpayee government between 1999–2004. The licences were restricted to four per telecom circles with one reserved for the state-owned operator Bharat Sanchar Nigam Limited (BSNL). In view of the appreciation of capital value of the operators, many others who missed the bus during the Vajpayee government had been looking for options to enter the lucrative business. Those who were in a position to offer the key to the entry gate, too, wanted to earn 'rent' from the new licences. The 2G-spectrum scam involved politicians and government officials illegally undercharging mobile telephony companies for frequency allocation licences. According to the telecom policy of India, when a licence is allotted to an operator, some start-up spectrum is bundled along with it. In 2008, 122 new 2G Unified Access Service (UAS) licences were given to telecom companies at a price arrived at in 2001 and on a first-come-first-serve basis. India's Comptroller and Auditor General estimated that the undercharging between the money collected and the money which the law mandated to be collected was as much as ₹176,645 crore (₹1766.45 billion). The calculation was based on the spectrum charges the exchequer received during the selling of 3G and Broadband Wireless Access (BWA) spectrum in 2010.

There were several glaring irregularities involved in the deal. For the Telecom Minister A. Raja, a Lok Sabha member from the alliance partner DMK (a regional party from the southern state of Tamil Nadu), the allocation of licences was an opportunity. Within three months of taking over the charge of the crucial ministry, his department initiated the process of allotment of 2G spectrum for telecom along with UAS licences. On the cut-off date of 1 October 2007, the Department of Telecom (DOT) received 575 applications for 46 UAS licences. Curiously, the cut-off date was advanced on 10th January 2008 by a few days to 25th September, and the licences were issued on the same day to those applicants who could complete the formalities including arrange the deposit fee between 3:30 PM and 4:30 PM. In short, the arbitrary announcements and decisions were too glaring for anyone to miss. Yet the opposition BJP did not notice it, busy as it was in its internal squabbles. If the ruling coalition could escape detection of a large-scale fraudulent process of issuing telecom licences, the credit should go to the central leadership of the principal opposition party.

Due to media attention, the government was forced to act on the scam. According to the *Time* magazine, the telecom scam was the second most conspicuous abuse of power next to only Watergate scandal. This was in 2011. Public opinion had turned from being negative to hostile to the government for inaction over the brazen abuse of power. The government had to act and arrest minister Raja, political leader and MP M.K. Kanimozi, daughter of DMK Party Chief M.K. Karunanidhi, Telecom Secretary Siddharth Behuria, Raja's private secretary R.K. Chandolia and a number of businessmen in February 2011. On 20 February 2012, the Supreme Court of India delivered a judgement on a PIL directly related to the 2G spectrum scam. Declaring the allotment of spectrum as 'unconstitutional and arbitrary', the court quashed all 122 licences issued in 2008 by the then Minister for Communications and IT, A. Raja. The judgement was a slap on the government but there was no problem for it to survive, so weak was the opposition BJP.

The unravelling of the 2G scam was just the beginning of the avalanche of troubles waiting for the UPA government. When the 2G scam was getting unravelled, the government received another shock from the Supreme Court. In a major blow to the Centre, in March 2011, SC quashed the appointment of P.J. Thomas as India's Central Vigilance Commissioner. Responding to a writ petition filed by the Centre for Public Interest Litigation, India's former Chief Election Commissioner, J.M. Lyngdoh, and others, SC took the decision. Mr Thomas was appointed CVC pursuant to a recommendation made by a High Power Committee (HPC) headed by the Prime Minister Manmohan Singh. Sushma Swaraj, of BJP and the Leader of the Opposition in the Lok Sabha who was an HPC member, disagreed with the decision. The other member was Home Minister P. Chidambaram who sided with the Prime Minister. India's then Chief Justice Kapadia, who wrote the judgement, held invalid the HPC's decision, as of that date Thomas was accused in the Kerala palmolein case pending in the Court of the Special Judge, Thiruvananthapuram under the Prevention of Corruption Act, 1988.

There were two other well-publicized cases of corruption. It came to light that the massive expenditure for building and refurbishing the infrastructure in Delhi for organizing the Common Wealth Games in 2010 had massive leakages. The day after the conclusion of the games, the government announced formation of a special committee to probe the allegations of corruption and mismanagement against the Organizing Committee (OC). This probe was in addition to investigation by the Directorate General of Income Tax, the Central Bureau of Investigation

(CBI), the Enforcement Directorate and the CVC investigations. When India Against Corruption (IAC) planned the fast by Anna Hazare over the Lok Pal Bill, the CWG case was at its peak. In fact Suresh Kalmadi, a Congress MP and the Chairman of the CWG OC was arrested on 25th April, just few weeks after Anna broke his much-publicized fast.

CWG was a scam in the national capital Delhi, and Adarsh Housing Society Scam was another from the film and financial capital Mumbai. The Adarsh Housing Society is a posh, 31-storey building constructed on prime real estate in Colaba, Mumbai. This was meant for the welfare of war widows and personnel of India's Ministry of Defence. But over a period of several years, politicians, bureaucrats and military officers conspired to bend several rules concerning land ownership, zoning, floor space index and membership. They deprived the war widows and got themselves flats allotted in this cooperative society at rates much lower than the market rate. The Adarsh scam was unearthed in November 2010. The then Chief Minister of Maharashtra, Ashok Chavan, had to resign. Thus, when the agitation over the Lok Pal Bill started, the opinion of common men had completely been adversarial to the political masters of the nation.

The country had been losing faith in the government and also the entire political system for failing to check nepotism. This was when the Arab Spring movement had caught the imagination of the world. In early 2011, after the successful uprising in Tunisia against the former leader Zine El Abidine Ben Ali, similar anti-government protests were launched in Egypt, Yemen and many other Arab countries. India, too, had its anti-corruption movement under the leadership of activists who formed an alliance India Against Corruption (IAC). IAC took up the issue of enactment of an anti-corruption watchdog called Lok Pal, an idea first mooted in the 1960s by the then Law Minister Ashok Sen. Despite several attempts, this could not be enacted and a new version was under process under the UPA government. IAC used the stalled Lok Pal Bill as a symbol and used the social activist from Maharashtra Anna Hazare to lead the movement. The members of IAC, which included Lawyer Prashant Bhusan, Activist Arvind Kejriwal, former Police Officer Kiran Bedi and former Lok Ayukta of Karnataka Justice Santosh Hegde, planned their moves carefully. They avoided any clash with India's most popular sport cricket. The date of hunger strike was fixed on 5 April 2011, a couple of days after the Cricket World Cup final.

Anna Hazare launched his 'fast unto death' movement on 5 April 2011 in the capital Delhi to press for a Lok Pal law at the Centre to combat corruption. Hazare dismissed the government version of the law and said, 'Like SC and Election Commission, an independent body called Jan Lok Pal should be set up at the Centre and a Jan Lokayukta should be set up in each state to receive complaints of corruption, investigate them within six months and prosecute the guilty.' Resolving not to return to Maharashtra till the government took concrete action, Hazare said a joint committee comprising civil society members and government officials should be set up to draft the law. Anna had earlier written letters to the Congress President Sonia Gandhi, Prime Minister Manmohan Singh and the BJP leader L.K. Advani.

The launch of the Lok Pal movement illustrates how the same brush painted the government and the opposition. Clearly, it took the shape of no confidence against the entire political class and the legislative system. There was no moral strength among the leaders then to point out the unconstitutionality of the movement of IAC so bereft of any moral stand against corruption and nepotism. It was evident that the next parliament election due in three years from 2011 would have corruption as its principal theme. It was also not certain that for how long would the government last under the popular uprising. Indian media, particularly TV channels found the movement an ideal bait to attract audiences and earn high television rating points (TRPs).

The fast started on 5th April despite several efforts of the government to dissuade Anna. The government engaged a sub-group of ministers to frame a bill acceptable to the activist. But he received encouragement from his supporters to begin his fast. Many others from across the country joined him in the fast. Religious leaders and organizations like Sri Sri Ravishankar, Baba Ramdev, Vincent Concessao and Jamiat-Ulema-i-Hind supported Anna. An estimated 7.5 crore people supported the demand for a better Lok Pal Bill than the one drafted by the government. The growing popular support saw the resignation of the senior minister and Maharashtra strongman Sharad Pawar resigning from the ministers' panel on Lok Pal Bill. Pawar was cited as an example of corrupt minister, therefore unfit to suggest anti-corruption legislation. Hazare also had a dig at Kapil Sibal who took over as the Minister for Telecom. Sibal had mentioned that there was zero loss to the exchequer due to allocation of 2G licence.

Anna's protest took place at Jantar Mantar in New Delhi, just outside an old and ill-maintained building owned by the Sardar Vallabh Bhai Patel Trust (SVBPT) at 7 Jantar Mantar Road. This was the first official head quarter of the INC party when the office shifted from Allahabad to Delhi some time in 1948. When Indira Gandhi split the Congress in 1969, she lost the control of the building. Anna was seen presiding over an event, sitting just outside this historical building that weakened the Congress-led government considerably and laid the foundation of its electoral loss in 2014.

Success of the Lok Pal movement laid the foundation of a political party with the sole objective of fighting corruption. In April 2011, few thought that the latent idea will finally fructify and turn reasonably successful. More so since there had been a lot of confusion among the civil society activists. First, there was lack of uniform views and voices among those supporting Anna. Swami Agnivesh was a suspect to the core group of IAC led by Arvind Kejriwal. Second, the activists who were members of the National Advisory Council (NAC) led by Sonia Gandhi, too, attempted to join the IAC move against the Lok Pal Bill. Aruna Roy and Harsh Mandar, two members of NAC, had differing views on Anna's fast. They felt that he should have waited till NAC submitted its report on the draft bill. The members of IAC had other ideas. They did not want others, let alone the Congress president's NAC, to go one up on them. Amidst confusion, the fast started, received popular support and finally the government had to strike a deal for Anna to break his fast. The Lok Pal movement was successful because of the overwhelming disenchantment of people with the political establishment and activism of electronic media which did dramatize the events to keep interests alive. The IAC brain trust turned the event into a nationwide opinion against the government. They used the same technique again few months later in August.

In August, this was a 12-day long fast, which Anna broke on a Sunday. It became a huge spectacle for India's TV viewers. The gestures of IAC members were stronger than what they displayed in April. This was expected given the public support they could generate then. Also the corruption cases—CWG, 2G, Adarsh, and so on—were still dominating the media headlines. The government was also more careful unlike in April. The effort was not to allow another sit in fast. In their lopsided zeal, the government made the first mistake that of arresting Anna with his supporters and taking them to Delhi's Tihar jail. The publicity gave the much-needed curtain-raiser boost to the second fast of Anna.

The Lok Pal movements of April and August in Delhi illustrated the role of emotion over logic in any discourse, more so in political discourse. It substituted one man for the people and in effect the constitution of the country, which stood the test of time. Economist and left ideologue Prabhat Patnaik called it antithetical to democracy in an article on 24 August 2011 published in the Hindu.

The substitution of one man for the people, and the reduction of the people's role merely to being supporters and cheerleaders for one man's actions, is adversative to democracy. Now that the heat and dust of that movement is far behind us, one may look at the events objectively and see how political campaign changed in India post-Lok Pal fasts. First, the government's flip-flops exposed the weakness and incompetence. Second, the indecisiveness of the political class, be they in the government or in the opposition, was badly exposed. Third, the failure of the political class despite their correct logical views to impress the people, more so through media, demonstrated that politicians as a class had lost credibility and was not attractive to those who had been watching the developments at Delhi's Ramlila Maidan. For media, viewership is what matters. Politicians when scorned and spurned made better stories than when peddling right views. Thus, politicians Uma Bharti, Omprakash Chautala, Gopinath Munde and Anant Kumar of BJP and the Congress ministers P. Chidambaram and Kapil Sibal, who attempted to visit Jantar Mantar in April and at Ramlila Maidan, were heckled and booed.

There were only few sane voices then. Writer Arundhati Roy was the one who called the legislation as a dangerous piece of work. She saw through the movement that it was the brainchild of Arvind Kejriwal and Manish Sisodia who had obtained funds from Ford Foundation to engineer such a campaign and Anna was 'picked up and propped up as the saint for the masses'. But there were few takers of sane voices at that time. Clearly, emotion had taken over logic supported in no small measure by media.

In parliament, some members highlighted the parliament's supremacy in a democracy but few heeded that. The political leadership was also at their wit's end. Then BJP President Nitin Gadkari, for instance, moved from one end of the poll to the other in less than two weeks. First, he said that the government had the right to bring a legislation before the House. Later, he issued a statement that his party would march behind Anna's leadership. Congress, too, did the same. First, it abused him for sheltering corruption and next extolled him for his idealism. Team Anna also shifted its stance from an unexceptionable one of right to protest and place views before public to accept Anna's bill or he would continue with the fast and mayhem would follow. What prevailed over was the message that the messiah decide what was good for people. That it was a serious concern and a threat to our democratic system did not have many takers at that juncture. Few like Rahul Gandhi did point out in the parliament, 'Witnessing the events of the last few days it would appear that the enactment of a single Bill will usher in a corruption-free society. I have serious doubts about this belief.' But nobody cared to listen, so strong was the hysteria.

The Anna movement was a smart piece of campaign by the members of IAC. They monopolized the electronic media so much that Arundhati Roy questioned their judgement. She felt that if the TRP had been the primary force behind TV beaming Anna's fast then when such events are not there would they opt for pornography! But Roy was blinded by what was visible. The crusaders had ruled Indian cyberspace during his fast. Evidently the young were attracted as a result of such smart campaign. During the agitation, the search engine Google produced 29 million results when a query was made by entering Anna Hazare's name. In contrast, Sonia Gandhi's name yielded a little below 9 million results. Even many such mentions were in relation to Congress stand on the Anna movement. The Facebook page on Anna had 364,000 likes against UPA chairperson Sonia Gandhi's page having a mere 57,291 likes. Another account 'Support Anna Hazare fast against Corruption' attracted 145,000 likes. Interestingly, the 'I hate Anna Hazare' page had just 4,137 likes. On You Tube, two videos Anna in Tihar jail compound and another on Anna's fast were the second and fourth most viewed videos during the month in Indian news and politics category. SMS containing Anna Hazare were voluminous which shot up the day Anna broke his 12-day long fast. Twitter, too, was full of Anna Hazare supporters. For 24 × 7 TV channels, there was no option but to follow the lead seen on the social media to remain in the reckoning.

The Anna Hazare movement highlighted certain essential ingredients of political communication, not all of these were newly discovered. The primary issue neglected by the leaders in Delhi was that democracy essentially meant a participatory role for the people in shaping the affairs of society. People had a right to protest, demonstrate and agitate on issues apart from electing members for legislative assemblies and parliament periodically. But in 2011 India, there were hardly any leader, be it in the government or in the opposition, who could enthuse the people. This vacuum helped Anna Hazare movement to succeed. Second, the credibility of the leader was critical. Anna had taken the Gandhian route of protesting against the corrupt systems from his village Raleigan Siddhi and had a clean image of public service. The brain behind the show, Arvind Kejriwal and his friends, used his credibility to hoist themselves to the political sphere. This was evident when after the April fast, Arvind Kejriwal made a statement dissociating the movement from BJP or any outfits sympathetic to the BJP cause. Anna's background caught attention of the people and was strong enough for the movement.

Apart from the leadership issues, the IAC movement illustrated how media could be used to create hysteria among the people across the vast country. Even a small gathering at Jantar Mantar, which barely could hold few thousands, became a nationwide movement due to clever handling of the media. Both the BJP or Congress needed to learn from Kejriwal. This, apart from the smart use of social media, was a pointer. No less important was the message that people wanted a change. Corruption had been one major issue, but more important was the aspirations of the youth and the PR campaign of IAC attracted them. It was neo-satyagraha of Gandhi. Out came the Gandhi cap in a new avatar—a white cap with 'I am Anna' written on it. Creating an atmosphere of festivity—jubilant over the new India they had been fighting for. They all were there as a support to the messiah—Anna in this case. People were there as spectators, fillers in the drama where only Anna, the messiah, was the lead actor. The people participated in large numbers, with great enthusiasm, cheering, singing and praying for him. This made nice television spectacle and good news point. The crowd was there not to understand the nuances of the Lok Pal Bill or the weaknesses of the government draft. Neither was that their concern nor did the leaders surrounding the messiah care to explain it to them. The idea is to whip up enthusiasm and this, the organizers of the Anna movement did efficiently. Media feel prey to them. The purpose was not to debate or discuss but to force the government and political establishments overwhelm with the demonstration of popular support. Those who could not be at Jantar Mantar physically opted for Facebook,

Twitter and SMS. The agitation thus crossed the physical boundary of the Jantar Mantar road and spread all over.

The advantage that the Anna movement had was that in 2011 India, there were not many skilful orators who could inform people as well as hold their attention and had the requisite charisma. Nehru was the undisputed leader having mesmerizing hold over his audience. Indira Gandhi did acquire the skill in due course. Her son Rajiv Gandhi did not require the skill in his first election swept as he was by the sympathy wave. Atal Bihari Vajpayee had the ability, which worked in BJP's favour. In the states there had been such leaders, and Jyoti Basu was one such leader. Their speeches conveyed information, analysis of issues relevant for the target audience, used to rebut the statements of the opponents and helped people to decide on right or wrong on a topic.

The political overtone of the Anna movement could be seen on several occasions. Anna broke his fast by sipping tender coconut water and honey. Two little girls—Simran who was a Dalit and Ikrah, a Muslim, offered this to Anna. The IAC think tank did not wink at the caste and communal issue of Indian politics. Earlier in April and again in August, Arvind Kejriwal emphasized that the movement was secular in nature. In April, he was specific and said, 'this movement has nothing to do with BJP or RSS, as is being alleged. It has no alignment with any political party'. Kejriwal also rebutted Anna's praise for the Gujarat Chief Minister Narendra Modi and Bihar Chief Minister, then NDA partner, Nitish Kumar. Two messages were clear. That India was losing patience with the political leadership in Delhi. Most of them were viewed as responsible for corruption if not corrupt themselves. Second, the political leadership needed to reinvent themselves if they had been looking to win elections. Anna movement was a wake-up call. Realizing it no leader wanted to be seen on the wrong side of the Anna movement despite there being several anomalies in their demands and legality.

A postscript of the Anna movement was the formation of a political party by Arvind Kejriwal. It was a not-so-hidden agenda for the savvy observers. The movement since inception was politically correct. In November 2012, he turned the movement into a political outfit called AAP. This was a natural transition since after the Lok Pal agitation, the movement could not find any new rallying point to attract similar wide attention. An opportunity came in December 2012 when a girl was brutally raped in a moving bus and was thrown on the Delhi road to die.

The perpetrators were arrested but after this incident, the city burst into protests. The volunteers of AAP were active in the spontaneous agitation, which again left the political parties high and dry. Kejriwal and his supporters built up a base through their work in the slum clusters, protesting against the rising costs of electricity and water and police atrocities. Their relentless activism created a strong base for the fledgling party in Delhi. Such social activism apart, the party brought to light corruptions in high places through well-planned press conferences. In a series of such moves, the party attacked Robert Vadra, the son-in-law of the Congress President Sonia Gandhi, who, it was alleged, made huge gain through land deals with the real estate giant DLF, Mukesh Ambani, India's richest industrialist on gas price, GMR on Delhi airport. These attacks, the first time in Indian politics, provided Kejriwal a huge media attention. But more than that, such attacks changed the character of political campaign in India. Now, no political party or no political leader could hope to escape unnoticed on rumours of favouritism. The 2014 election illustrates the newfound no-holds-barred campaign of political parties on crony capitalism. Even a large corporation like Adani had to come to media and explain their side of the story on allegations hurled.

The fledgling party AAP won 28 of the 70 seats in the Delhi assembly election in December 2013. The success came in about a year of forming the party. Congress lost badly with its Chief Minister for 15 years, Shiela Dikshit losing her seat to Kejriwal. The party could manage to win just 8 seats. BJP won the largest number of seats—32—but fell short of absolute majority to form a government. Congress offered support and Kejriwal became Delhi's Chief Minister. This catapulted him among the topmost sought-after politician in India, at least in media. His presence in the larger electoral contests also contributed to the changes that we see in the campaign 2014.

Kejriwal is an activist. He could attract activists from different corners of the country. Thus, in the 2014 election, he had no shortage of willing and credible candidates. Opposition to corruption being his main theme, Kejriwal had no conflict with anyone willing to join his party. Since he maintained equal distance with both BJP and Congress, his party could be a third alternative in India's two national party-centric politics. First, there were only a few aberrations. Primary of these was Kejriwal's decision to form the government in Delhi with support of Congress. Second, his mysterious silence over the Vadra land deals after raising the same in October 2012. This led his opposition to claim that he acted at the behest of Congress. Third, his stringent criticism of large corporates like Mukesh Ambani scared many other business giants. Predictably, AAP failed to raise adequate funds to contest the election 2014. Fourth, he failed to maintain his rapport with media as he did earlier. In many of his interviews, he was seen losing his cool and charging the interviewers with bias. More importantly, his gimmicks to attract media attention were too frequent. Arvind Kejriwal as an activist directed his guns to the lead campaigner in the national elections—Narendra Modi. Pitted against such a formidable adversary, he committed several tactical mistakes. The most important one was his decision to challenge Narendra Modi in the temple town of Varanasi. But such aberrations notwithstanding nobody can deny Kejriwal the credit of influencing the campaign, both in style and content, during the general elections 2014.

The major impact of Kejriwal's anti-corruption movement was on the opposition BJP. The success of the movement exposed the weakness of the party. It did not have a single leader who had charisma to change the course of debate away from Lok Pal in 2011. Its two leaders in the parliament, Sushma Swaraj and Arun Jaitely exhibited their debating skills in the house, but they did not have the skill which Vajpayee or Jyoti Basu had to set the agenda. This vacuum helped Narendra Modi to assume the charge of BJP poll campaign first and then get projected as its prime-ministerial candidate.

The influence of Kejriwal was seen on Rahul Gandhi, the Congress Vice President also. He started talking of corruption, change in the party and governance and a new Congress dedicated for the youth. If in the end he faltered, there were many other factors for his failure.

The Kejriwal effect was strongest on media. First, the euphoria over the IAC movement led the TV channels to think what attracts eyeball. Their focus changed accordingly. Second and no less important was the success of the social media. True social media was increasingly turning popular for few years since 2005, but the success of the Anna campaign was a wake-up call for the political parties.

One likes him or not, the fact that Kejriwal rewrote the rules of political campaign cannot be denied.[1] Kejriwal also learnt from his mistakes in 2014. After cutting a sorry figure in the general election, he came back to Delhi, focused on the weak points, took lesson from Modi campaign and relaunched himself with a record-breaking win in the assembly election of Delhi in February 2015.

7

The Leadership-centric Election Campaign

Arvind Kejriwal rose through a well-planned fast track movement. For Narendra Modi, the steps were steeper. Despite the Apex Court clean chit, his detractors kept on passing their own judgements on the Gujarat riot 2002. His three successive election victories could not cut much ice with them. But not all were as blind. Shekhar Gupta, Editor of *The Indian Express*, speculated even before the counting of votes in Gujarat assembly election 2007 that it was contest between Modi and Sonia Gandhi. A victory, he felt, would turn Modi a contender for the country's top post. What Gupta perhaps had in mind were the national elections 2009. But Modi was in no hurry though there had been not insignificant numbers from within BJP who wanted to see him in the national politics. During the 2009 election campaign in BJP's then prime-ministerial candidate L.K. Advani's constituency of Gandhinagar, certain BJP leaders declared openly that Gujarat would offer the nation two prime ministers—Advani now and thereafter Modi.

There were two issues that Modi camp had to overcome. The usual one was the Gujarat riot of 2002 and the alleged complicity of the Modi-led administration. The other was acceptance of Modi by BJP leadership and its allies.

Even when RSS top brass were planning to anoint Narendra Modi as BJP's Prime-ministerial candidate, not all senior functionaries of the Sangh felt that Modi would be the right choice.[1] In fact Manmohan Vaidya, who is in charge of all RSS three publications, was among those who did not endorse the choice of Modi. Vaidya is also its national '*prachar pramukh*' (head of publicity). When *Panchjanya* and *Organiser*, the Hindi and English weeklies of RSS adopted the editorial line which was supportive of Modi even when RSS leadership did not take any public stand, Vaidya decided to act. He removed both the editors of the weeklies and replaced them with junior staff. This was a clear message that Modi was not the choice at least not till April 2013. Interesting point to note is that Modi had already launched his town hall-type campaign by then. He had at least two very successful sessions with the students of Sri Ram College of Commerce (SRCC) and ladies of FICCI in Delhi. Yet Modi was not the choice of all who mattered.

The unsatisfied ambition of BJP stalwart Lal Krishna Advani and his hope to take yet another shot at the prime minister's post in 2014 was a major stumbling block for Narendra Modi. Advani was Modi's mentor when he was sent to Gujarat as Chief Minister. But for 2014, they emerged as roadblock for each other. Thus, when in September 2011 the two-day national executive of the BJP began in Delhi, all eyes were on what shape the possible leadership tussle takes. The signal was clear when the Chief Minister of Gujarat, Narendra Modi skipped the national executive committee meeting. It was evident that the talks of differences between him and Advani were not mere idle gossip. One factor that contributed to the absence of Modi was Advani's effort to launch yet another yatra on good governance in October and that too from Patna, a state ruled by Modi's critic and BJP alliance partner Nitish Kumar, the Chief Minister of Bihar.

The campaign had to be carefully planned so as to obfuscate both the issues. The success of the Modi campaign in 2014 had been in overcoming both odds with ease. Meanwhile in 2011 a third obstacle came on the way, the anti-corruption movement of Arvind Kejriwal. This became instant darling of the media. Looking back at the IAC movement helped Modi campaign in no small measure. The movement exposed the weaknesses of the entire political class in Delhi. It affected the image of BJP leadership of Advani, Jaitley and Sushma as well. The mood of the people turned in favour of change. The existing leadership of BJP would have meant opting for status quo. Meanwhile, there was assembly election in Karnataka, a state ruled by BJP. The party was in disarray there due to corruption scandals and infighting. BJP was certain to lose the election. Thus, when the election result revealed that BJP won just 40 out of 223 seats (against 110 held earlier), there was not much shock. Modi who was busy in attending select town hall-type meetings did not even take any prominent role as a campaigner. Modi supporters in the party were also waiting for the Karnataka result to blow over.[2] By the time BJP had its two-day national executive meet in Goa on 7th June 2013, the party was gearing up to bring in Modi as the face of its campaign for 2014. The detrators from within led by Advani were also flexing their muscles in opposition. Advani wanted to appoint an election committee for the three major state assembly elections

(Rajasthan, MP and Chhattisgarh) scheduled in December 2013. In order to win a section of RSS, he suggested that the former party president Nitin Gadkari should lead it. Among the senior BJP leaders who stayed away from the national executive were Advani, Jaswant Singh, Yashwant Sinha, Uma Bharti and actor turned politician Shatrughan Sinha. Those who took the lead role in anointing Modi had been the young and emerging leaders like Manohar Parikkar, Chief Minister of Goa and also established leaders like Gadkari, Jaitley and Rajnath Singh.[3] The national executive members and the party cadres were enthusiastic in anointing Modi as BJP's campaign face. Sushma Swaraj was viewed as a competition but did not enjoy support from within other than that of Advani. So strong was the support of the party cadres that there was even demonstration in front of Advani's house in Delhi for skipping the crucial meet to delay Modi's annointation. Effectively, Goa in June 2013 was similar to the national convention held in the US after the party primaries to announce their choice of presidential candidate. Modi was the choice due to overwhelming support from party workers including those in sister organizations like RSS.

There was more to come. The long time alliance partner and Chief Minister of Bihar Nitish Kumar was provoked by the decision at the BJP national executive and broke away from the coalition with BJP in Bihar. Advani resigned to withdraw the same later. He again used the similar card when in September 2013 BJP upgraded Modi as its prime-ministerial candidate from the head of its campaign committee. In a rally in Bhopal organized in support of the MP Chief Minister Shivraj Singh Chauhan's re-election bid, Advani did not even acknowledge Modi when the latter touched his feet in respect. These made good copies for media.

Thus, Modi campaign was pitted against many formidable adverse factors in media. First was the baggage of 2002 and media's steadfast refusal to take a relook at the events. So overwhelming was the sentiment that the Gujarat-based scribes, too, turned biased willy-nilly. They observed that as they had played up a report with allegations of atrocities and suffering of a certain community, their reports found prominent slots. This helped them in moving up the professional ladder. Thus, reports from and on Gujarat continued to remain coloured. How would Modi campaign overcome this fortress of aversion?

Second and no less important was the overt leaning of mainstream media towards the ruling UPA government. Most journalists in the top had exhibited this trait since the time NDA lost election in 2004. Many among these newspersons had close rapport with politicians working in Delhi, not all of them were part of the ruling coalition. It was evident that no leader, barring few, in BJP or NDA was enthused by the prospect of Modi emerging as a prospective Prime Minister. The third problem of the Modi campaign was of more recent origin, that of April 2011 vintage. The success of business during the anti-corruption campaign converted many in media as die hard supporters of Kejriwal. The Modi campaign would have found it difficult to enter the media horizon during its honeymoon with the anti-corruption crusaders. To begin with, Modi-campaign started on a weak wicket.

There were issues of logistics also. The long period of lay off from the peoples' movement, BJP leaders had lost their charm over its cadres. The infighting was intense. Barring three effective Chief Ministers, in Gujarat, Madhya Pradesh and Chhattisgarh, the squabbling did not allow any breathing space to the local leaders. Thus, Karnataka, Himachal Pradesh and Uttarakhand were lost. In UP, the party had been barely in existence. In Bihar, though it was strong, but remained subservient to the powerful JD(U) Chief Minister Nitish Kumar. BJP even had to swallow his insult in June 2010 when a furious Nitish cancelled a dinner he was throwing for the visiting BJP leaders in Patna. The Modi campaign had the onerous task of revitalizing its party machinery, injecting self-confidence in them and creating winning cadre base to meet the regional as well as UPA challenges. The ingredients were there with a scam-a-day revelations in Delhi, the unchecked price rise and peoples' discomfort therefrom and also the confused leadership of the UPA government in Delhi. It needed to stitch it together, offer alternative suggestions and win the electorate. Facts were not sufficient for an election campaign. It needs the spice of emotion.

Emotion, prima facie, was loaded against Modi. Wasn't he as the Chief Minister of West Bengal, Mamata Banerjee called him, the butcher of Gujarat or as Sonia Gandhi said in 2007, 'the maut-ka-saudagar'? The entire branding of Modi was on this line. Did he require a rebranding? Was such a rebranding possible despite the Supreme Court judgement and a gap of 12 years between then and now? But on the positive side had been the track record of the Chief Minister of Gujarat—the growth rate of the state, the efficient administration and what is more peace among the communities. The question was if the electorates would listen to logic, see through the statistics and come running to cast their votes in favour? The past experience of any campaign, be it in India or in the US and other democracies, had been that emotions guide voting behaviour in particular and all types of behaviour in general. The challenge before the Modi campaign was to turn the negative emotional connect of Gujarat 2002 to a positive one through projection of the developments during the next 12 years. In a huge, diverse and complex country like India, the task was even more critical. How can Modi overcome the constant negative projection of him in other parts, say Nagaland, West Bengal, Bihar, Kerala or Tamil Nadu. People of these regions are so far removed from an average Gujarati that it was a challenge to conceive even a homogeneous campaign around Modi. More critical had been the appeal of BJP as a political entity or its absence in many parts of the nation.

In an election generally there are four issues that guide the voting behaviour of an average voter. First, she will like to know if the candidate shared the values that mattered to her most. Second was the trust factor, will the leader represent her faithfully. This has another problem in a Westminster-type democracy. Electorates elect a representative who in turn elects the Prime Minister. On many occasions, the representatives go missing from the constituency after election. The Modi campaign had to ensure that people have a feeling that by casting vote for the candidate, they actually are voting for the leader. Third factor is if the leader has the requisite integrity, competence and leadership ability to meet the aspirations of the people. Finally is the issue of special interest—in case of Modi, the question is if the two communities will manage to live peacefully. Point to note is that nobody loves a riot.

Apart from these obvious issues, the Modi campaign had to face the paucity of time. Only after Gujarat assembly election in December 2012, Modi could come to stake a claim for national leadership. In contrast Rahul Gandhi, the Congress heir apparent, had been active since 2004. Arvind Kejriwal, a new kid on the bloc, came with a professional campaign in 2011, catching the imagination of certain section. Time constraint was onerous when seen together with the intense opposition that the campaign would face, nationally and regionally. In addition, the challenge was massive—with 814 million voters, to reach a large section of them was near impossible. Next was the challenge of creating enough emotion among the people who had an overdose of unfulfilled political promises. The majority near about 65 per cent of Indian voters was below 35 years of age. Most of them had little sympathy for the Ram Mandir or uniform civil code. They wanted to hear messages of hope that will be within their grasp in the next five years. This was an advantage for the Modi campaign. But the question was how to reach out to them since media was overwhelmingly negative on the Chief Minister of Gujarat.

The solution to this predicament was novel. Modi fell back on the tools of yesteryears—that of stump oratory—rallies as Indians call it. This was audacious. It was near inhuman to traverse the country and talk to the people. Modi demonstrated his undaunting spirit and stamina. In a matter of one year, he had been addressing people—in rallies, seminars and party meetings. He addressed 437 public rallies and covered an estimated three lakh (0.3 million) kilometre criss-crossing the country, if we take his first rally on 15 September 2013, at Rewari in Haryana. He addressed public meetings in 25 states besides 1,350 innovative 3D rallies. The 3D rallies had been a unique experiment used first time by Modi during the Gujarat assembly election in 2012.

Stump oratory had gone out of fashion in most developed countries where TV became the medium to reach to people. Adlai Stevenson, the Democrat challenger of General Dwight D. Eisenhower relied on stump oratory and expected network television to telecast his speeches. Stevenson was a good orator with humour to boot. And due to his campaign style in 1952 and again in 1956, he is now derisively mentioned as the dinosaur of the television age. Stevenson felt that TV would beam his speeches. But one person talking with camera fixed on his face did not find viewers who were glued to serials like I love Lucy.[4] Unlike Stevenson, Modi had one small advantage. Since in India people come for rallies out of curiosity. Still his campaign had two major issues. First, how to attract the attention of people and entice them to come in large numbers to his rallies. The second was how to make the hostile TV channels beam the speeches. Here, Modi's oratorical skill and ability to connect with people helped.

The show started on 15th September 2013 with an ex-servicemen's rally in Rewari in Haryana and continued till the evening of 10th May 2014. But before that on 6th February 2013, he spoke to a captive audience of the students of Delhi's SRCC. He connected with the young students instantly. There was no political message but in a speech tailored to the aspirations of the students, he could hold their attention. That was Modi's first address to young that was televized live despite media's aversion for him. It was clear that as long as Modi could hold the attention of the audience and make them respond to him spontaneously, even media would not ignore him. Television is a medium of entertainment. It would follow a politician as long as he could provide entertainment even through propaganda. Modi narrated short anecdotes, like the one on the banana farmers from near the Maharashtra–Gujarat border. A delegation from them came to meet him and asked for pebbled road so that they could transport bananas without damage to the fruit and export the same. The message was on the increased aspiration of people, and the hidden message was that Modi delivered what they wanted. The entire speech was full of many such anecdotes based on Modi's experience in Gujarat enthralling the students. Even before he launched his election campaign, he gave a curtain raiser on what was in store.

According to experts in political communication, people will hear when the leader talks of something they are concerned of. This is a necessity for television audience. In case of rallies, those who come they would wait, enjoy or bear with the surroundings and stay put even if the speeches are banal. Modi knew well enough that he could not afford to repulse the audience. Word-of-mouth campaign was necessary to attract people for the series of campaigns he had planned. So, there was a team of analytics, researchers connecting with their on-ground research team providing inputs to the leader. For example, in SRCC, he spoke of how Japan had been marketing the forthcoming Olympics the country would organize. When he linked with the chaotic Common Wealth Games organized in Delhi, the students were thunderous in applause. The Modi campaign was relieved. They had a charismatic leader who could instantly connect to his audience.

In contrast, the Rahul campaign was handicapped. A major problem was that he was found missing at material juncture. When Uttarakhand suffered due to a cloud burst in June 2013, Rahul Gandhi was away celebrating his birthday in some undisclosed destination. A serious politician would have cut short the fun and marked his presence in the disaster-management efforts. But even when he was available and spoke at rallies, he was at best incoherent. In a rally in Rajasthan, he wanted to make some point on exploitation of labour in road projects by the opposition. His anecdotes in the speeches were not interesting. He could never hold the attention of his audience while speaking. He also had the habit of asking counter questions as he did in his interview with India's leading TV news channel Times Now in January 2014. Once in October 2013, he sought to argue that due to their social disadvantages, Dalits needed to work much harder to improve their circumstance just as the velocity needed to escape Jupiter's gravitational pull is much higher compared to Earth. The escape velocity created huge volumes of jokes on social media that embarrassed the Rahul campaign.

Rahul's speeches could never be interactive as Modi's were. Despite a head start in PR campaign, Rahul could not catch people's imagination due to his lack of oratorical skill, knowledge and experience. His speeches were of about 15 minutes or so while Modi could easily keep the audience engaged for more than even an hour. This was one of the most critical reasons for the success of the Modi campaign. Another major problem for Rahul campaign had been the complete absence of chain of command. An example was when India's official broadcaster Doordarshan (DD) sent a request for an interview, there was no response from his team. Modi's team responded and completed the recording of the interview in three days. DD has the largest footprint in the country. Rahul missed the opportunity.

But during the election time, there are pressures on the channels. They also have a limited budget. It would have been rather ambitious for the Modi campaign to expect that all rallies would receive equal priority in the channels. What if the channels decided for some reason or other not to oblige? The solution was in technology. The IT team of Modi campaign arranged professional coverage for all rallies. The feed was directed to websites like Niti Central for people to watch live streaming. Within a few hours, the feed was made available for viewing on YouTube. Many news channels also found the live feeds of the rallies useful. People were curious to hear Modi. The responses were positive. By showing the freely available professionally produced feeds, the news channels could attract viewers. The plan worked and even the rival Congress initiated the process of providing free feed to the channels.

The contrast between the rallies of Rahul Gandhi and Modi was clearly visible on 27 October 2013. That day, Modi was addressing a rally in Patna, the den of his former ally turned foe Nitish Kumar. Rahul Gandhi had a rally in Delhi. Some channels even started showing both the rallies together splitting the window into two. They had to drop Rahul and telecast only Modi's Patna rally after a little while. Rahul could not hold his audience who started leaving. His speech was short. Ability to hold the attention of the audience and make the speech entertaining was a point hopelessly missing in Rahul. Apart from the anti-incumbency to the UPA government, this weakness of the star campaigner of Congress also contributed to the party losing its steam midway into the campaign.

The knack of Modi to speak extempore and raise issues spontaneously eclipsed all others during the gruelling election campaign 2014. In his rally in Delhi in September 2013, Modi raised two issues and linked those together to attack the Congress Vice President. This was in the context of a news item, which revealed that the Prime Minister of Pakistan, Nawaz Sharif in a banquet made fun of Indian Prime Minister Manmohan Singh and said that Singh whines like a village woman. Just a couple of days before that Rahul had called an Ordinance passed by the Congress Core Committee and the Union Cabinet was nonsense and tore the same before media in Delhi's Press Club. Modi linked the two insults to the Prime Minister and blamed the Congress first family of Gandhis for the same. Modi also started derisively calling Rahul Shehzada. Sarcasm sticks, and sticks deeper, when hurled by a forceful orator. Within less than two weeks of Modi launching campaign, Rahul had to scurry for cover.

The most important moment for the Modi campaign came as a gift from the terrorists in Patna on 27 October 2013. In a huge venue at Patna's Gandhi Maidan, BJP planned a rally and called it *Hunkar* rally. The security was lax. Some terrorists planted bombs in the rally site. These started exploding when the rally started. The intention perhaps was to disrupt the rally and create a stampede so that BJP's future rallies find few enthusiastic spectators. The BJP top brass present in the rally had shown remarkable maturity. They diverted the attention of the people away from the blasts calling those car tyre burst. Modi delivered his arguably the most notable line—poor Muslim and poor Hindu has one common enemy and that is poverty. There was no mention of terror. The rally was a huge success. Reports of bomb blasts hogged the headlines after the rally was over. The nonchalant way Modi delivered his speech and kept the audience enthralled was evident. This exhibited the cool leadership capability to even his detractors.

This was the Daisy and the little girl moment for the Modi campaign. The only difference with the famous advertisement of President Lyndon B. Johnson in 1964 was that the bombs in the rallies were part of a planned terror attack not a planned advertisement.[5]

The Johnson campaign in 1964 had planned the controversial political advertisement that was aired only once on television on 7 September 1964. This was considered a factor in Johnson's landslide victory over Barry Goldwater and an important turning point in political and advertising history. The advertisement showed a little girl tearing the petals of a daisy and counting 1, 2, 3,... By the time she reaches 7, reverse counting for a nuclear bomb explosion starts. The camera zooms into the eye of the girl and the screen is filled with the blast scene. Johnson's voice is heard, 'We must either love each other, or we must die'. Recall what Modi said—poor Hindu and poor Muslim should not fight each other but fight poverty together. It was said on the spur of the moment. But the message was delivered. Like the Johnson campaign, the Patna Hunkar rally blast positioned Modi campaign at a level that was much higher than all other competing voices in 2013–14.

Modi also used effectively his oratorical skill in creating an emotional attachment with the audience. A parallel with former US President Bill Clinton's campaign in 1992 will not be out of place. In a simple television advertisement, Clinton's message was direct, his humble background, living with grandparents with a tight budget, working hard and reaching the high with determination. He was the embodiment of the American dream. Mixed with suitable visuals, it was a great story told, connecting instantly with the people who had then been struggling in an economy under pressure. Later, President Barak Obama, too, could use his humble origin to move his voters. Modi, too, told his story that of struggling as a child, having no money to go for a recruitment camp for soldiers, assisting his father in his tea stall and selling tea in train compartments. He did not hide the fact that his mother used to help other households in domestic chores. Even he mentioned his lower caste background to connect with a large section of the electorate. Then, like Clinton, Modi sold the dream of Indian democracy, particularly his party BJP, putting emphasis on the fact that despite his humble background, his party chose him to be its prime-ministerial candidate. With the narrative, he connected with the average Indians, and at the same time dismissed the family-centric policy of rival Congress and its leaders Rahul and Sonia Gandhi who came just because of the Nehru family connection. The Modi campaign was lucky that their task was to position a person who had all the ingredients to win the hearts and votes through his speeches.

That patriotism is a critical element in drawing people under one umbrella needs no iteration. Narendra Modi did remember that 27 January 2014 was the 51st anniversary of the hugely popular patriotic song rendered by India's most well-known singer Lata Mangeshkar. The song was created in remembrance of the soldiers who sacrificed their lives in the Indo–China war in 1962. 'Ae Mere Vatan Ke Logon' was sung in the presence of India's then Prime Minister Nehru and his immediate family members. The commemorative meeting on the 51st anniversary of the first rendering of the song was organized in the Mahalaxmi Race Course in Mumbai. Organized under the banner of Shreshtha Bharat Divas celebrations, it gave Modi an opportunity to talk on patriotism of Indian soldiers. Octogenarian Lata Mangeshkar sang the song in the function. Modi not only positioned himself among the patriotic Indians and Indian armed forces, but also won tacit approval of the legendary singer Lata Mangeshkar.

The inability of the Gandhis—be it Sonia Gandhi or her son Rahul—cost Congress dear. Despite the spread of television, India still loves rallies. They come to see their leaders talk and join in the festivities. Even if they get to watch television, it will not be for political rallies. For them the speeches are monotonous sound mostly irrelevant for their life. Unless someone like Modi turns these speeches into an interactive spontaneous drama linking to their modest requirement in life connecting to their daily problems, they will not be swayed by it. Arvind Kejriwal, the activist turned politician from Delhi was the only other person who could connect to people in his rallies. But Kejriwal is not a good orator. He lacks the voice, theatrics and presence of Modi. The other weakness of Kejriwal is that he does not spread the message of hope and, hence, fails to connect with the emotion of a larger audience. In fact, in a way he contributed to Modi's rise. His constant mention of corruption matched with Modi's thunder on the ruling Congress. To an ordinary person, his speeches would sound as a prelude to what Modi propagated. Since he did not have any message of hope, in the end the common man would move towards Modi. Kejriwal's constant battering of industrialists such as Mukesh Ambani or Gautam Adani did not find many takers since these were unknown names linked to a complicated concept called crony capitalism. In Delhi, Kejriwal could build an instant rapport with the people, particularly the migrant workers who suffer from rent seekers of various kinds, local police, the political muscle man of the locality, the jhuggi owners, and so on. For them, Kejriwal looked a saviour and they voted for him. But in a national election that too in regions unknown, Kejriwal could not connect with the people. At best, he was a well-meaning outsider who did not seem to have the capacity to bail them out from the rent seekers thriving on them. Kejriwal style of politics is effective in a small geography like in Delhi where he could make a difference with his brand of activism.

Modi thus had a virtual unchallenged field for himself. All he had to do was to multiply his strength through technology, manpower and party resources. This was another aspect where the Modi campaign excelled. This was no easy task. In India's political campaign, volunteers come to earn some quick pocket money. Unless supervised effectively, they are not of much significance. The Modi campaign had to engage suitable supervisory system. This is where the campaign scored over any other rival matching even with those in states governed by regional parties.

Many will be tempted to compare the Modi campaign with the US Presidential campaign. Like the US primaries, Modi, too, moved up the party ladder step by step. First, he sealed his victory in the 2012 state assembly election. Next, he ventured out of the state—first was the meeting with the students of SRCC, and then in April 2013 a discourse on good governance before the FICCI Ladies Organisation. In between his participation in the India Today conclave and Network 18 Think Tank initiatives saw him occupying prominent position among the politicians. Modi did not lose much time after he was made BJP's prime-ministerial candidate. Beginning with the rally at Rewari, he was on the roads since then with brief interludes in between.

To support him, there was a team of professionals. A team of engineers and statisticians who analyzed data of election result trend, socio-economic factors and demography; checked data collected from their own opinion polls; used real-time inputs from different teams and broke the data booth wise. The analytics team provided suggestions on the campaign theme, how the theme was working, when this should be changed based on which Modi kept on changing his tone. An example perhaps was Modi campaign in West Bengal, a state where at the height of Vajpayee regime there were two MPs. The party even now does not have any base in the state. On his first visit, Modi addressed a rally of modest size. The candidates for the poll were all locals with some modest celebrities. Except in the hill constituency of Darjeeling, none of the BJP candidates seemed formidable. Slowly, the scenario started changing. Modi's rising acceptance elsewhere had a positive effect in West Bengal. Mamata Banerjee, the Chief Minister heading a regional party called Trinamul Congress (TMC) made several tactical mistakes, major one being trying to rope in Anna Hazare to prop her as a possible prime-ministerial candidate. When the same failed and election date came nearer, Mamata faced the heat from a chit fund scam. A chit fund called Sharada had flourishing operation in the state with direct support from TMC MPs and leaders. Mamata's declining graph and Modi's rising one encouraged BJP campaign in the state. On his subsequent visits, Modi upped the ante against Mamata. There was another reason as well. West Bengal was witnessing a four-cornered contest among TMC, Left Front, Congress and BJP. Realizing that BJP's increasing vote share would hurt the electoral prospect of TMC candidates, Mamata went aggressive against Modi. A quid pro quo was Modi also raised his campaign pitch.

Analytics need constant feedback. In political communication, this involves continued opinion polls and in a phased election like India's exit polls to judge the campaign success. If there were visible changes in Modi's speeches, content and use of media, the analytics team's report based on ground level data caused the shift. Modi's sudden shift to emphasize on his lower caste birth just before the 8th phase of election on 7 May had in all probability been a result of such analysis. In the last two phases, on 7th and 12th May, elections were mostly in the eastern part of UP and parts of Bihar where caste mattered most. Modi's constant display of his backward caste origin even led to India's formidable caste-based leader Mayawati, a Dalit leader and former Chief Minister of UP to come out and arrange a press conference. But Mayawati, too, is not an orator. The Chief Minister of Bihar, Nitish Kumar, another backward caste leader, had been wearing his caste credential for too long to display it again and match Modi's.

Modi also had a chosen team of experts drawn from the field of journalism, economics, foreign policy experts, and so on, to brainstorm on issues and provide him inputs. Members of the team used to travel to Gandhinagar and meet Modi. Even in the middle of hectic election campaign, Modi assembled the team to receive suggestions. The Citizens for Accountable Governance is one such think tank for Modi. A brainchild of Prashant Kishore, a former UN Mission Chief in Africa had been supporting Modi for three years.

Rahul's campaign had also assembled young advisors and brought in relatively younger faces from within the party to work with him. Ajay Maken, a Lok Sabha member from the New Delhi constituency, left his ministerial post to lead the media cell. Jairam Ramesh, another articulate minister, also joined the team but due to important responsibilities like bifurcation of the southern state of Andhra Pradesh did not leave the cabinet. The team had engaged experts to assess the people's expectations. Some professors from Delhi University and JNU were roped in. The team had innovative ideas. It decided that candidates for the party would be selected through primaries like in the US, local party members would select the candidate. Certain seats were identified to begin the experiment. One such seat happened to be Vadodara in Gujarat where Narendra Rawat, a city-based Dalit leader, was chosen through such 'primary'. But when Congress found that Narendra Modi chose Vadodara as his constituency from Gujarat, the party changed Rawat and opted for its General Secretary Madhusudan Mistry. Mistry was till then looking after the Congress election campaign in UP. By replacing Rawat, a Dalit, the party began on a negative note in Vadodara and gave opportunity to Modi to point out Congress antipathy to the lower caste. Clearly, the plan and activities of Rahul's war room had been a blind copy of the US system without adapting the same to the Indian condition. The other major problem of Rahul's team had been infighting. The leaders constantly competed against each other to win Rahul's attention. They were too keen to pass on the responsibility of any failure to competing colleagues. Ajay Maken lost favour allegedly due to his incompetent handling of media. It was a continuous seesaw among the team members. No campaign can be successful amidst such chaos.

8

The Election Campaign and the Manifesto and Subtle Articulation of Political Messages

While Narendra Modi emerged as the crowd puller in certain sections of the nation, he was persona non grata in many others. When Modi visited Kolkata in West Bengal, there was demonstration against him arranged by the city's intellectuals. Bihar Chief Minister had also expressed his reluctance to share the stage with Modi. When Lok Sabha election for 2009 was held, Modi was still confined to Gujarat. But there, he was now the unchallenged popular leader. The state assembly election in 2007 had sounded the warning bell on Modi's emergence as the tallest leader in the state.

The Gujarat assembly election results came out on Sunday, 23 December 2007. Defying all predictions, Modi won a stunning electoral victory by coming back to power with near two-thirds majority. Under his leadership, BJP won 117 seats out of the total 182 state seats and Congress won 62 seats, gaining three more seats from the previous year. BJP was ahead of Congress in all the regions except central Gujarat. The three seat gain of Congress led media, which was hostile to Modi as before, to conclude that Congress appeared to have regained the ground that it had ceded after the post-Godhra riots of 2002. They were quick to admit that the recovery had been far from what would have helped it pose a serious challenge to the BJP for the power in Gandhinagar. The BJP's net loss was ten seats; the net gain of the Congress and its ally, the Nationalist Congress Party (NCP) was seven seats.

The result was not what many anticipated. The odds were against Modi as late as in September 2007. Saurashtra, accounting for 54 seats, had risen in revolt against Modi. Farmers had gathered in Rajkot, denouncing Modi for leaving them to rot. Rivals were happy seeing the underclass, in their tattered clothing turning up in hordes to listen to Sonia Gandhi. The numbers, formed by Gujarat's poor, Dalits, Adivasis and Muslims, seemed to favour her. Add to this, Modi's internal problems. RSS leaders were not happy. Members of VHP and Bajrang Dal too were sulking. They had lost their clout under Modi's strong-arm administration.

On record, they claimed and anti-Modi media persons lapped those up that Modi had crossed the line on a fundamental Sangh belief: '*vyakti se paksh mahan, paksh se desh mahan*' (party is greater than person, country is greater than party). Since Modi emerged as an autonomous power centre, sections of the administration—from ministers and bureaucrats to lower level staff, police personnel and teachers who were important part of the election machinery—were alienated. Opponents felt that these sections would sabotage Modi's prospect in the election.

The problem started when Modi embarked on a large-scale drive to improve infrastructure. He gave free hand to municipal commissioners to widen roads, pull down unauthorized structures and clear encroachments. Such illegal structures had been there for long with none of the governments daring to pull these down. In 2006–07, some time before the assembly elections were due, Modi government paid special attention to this task. In cities like Ahmedabad, Vadodara and Surat, mandirs and mazars built on public land and other buildings were removed. This led to riot in Vadodara where the municipal council decided to remove the dargah of Syed Chishti Rashiduddin, a medieval Sufi saint. The incident resulted in six to eight people being killed and 42 injured, 16 of these were from police shooting. Then, Home Minister, Amit Shah had brought in para-military forces beforehand to control the mob. When the Gujarat High Court looked into the incidents suo moto, it decided that 'encroachments on public roads cannot be tolerated'.

Fundamentalists were not happy. VHP called Modi modern-day Mahmud of Ghazni, a ruler from Afghanistan who had conquered the temple town of Somnath and plundered the rich temple of the Hindu god Shiva. There were many who would have loved to see Modi biting dust in 2007 assembly election.

The acrimonious campaign showed Narendra Modi's incredible chemistry with the voters, evident in all his rallies. In 2007 in Gujarat, people attending Modi rallies wore Modi masks, waved his posters and roared in approval as he made his jokes about Sonia and Congress.

The Gujarat assembly election of 2007 was unique. Gone was the high-pitched contest between 'Hindu communalism' and 'Congress secularism'. It turned out as a war of votes between the Congress President, Sonia Gandhi and Narendra Modi. Congress targeted its vote banks carefully, of Kshatriya, *adivasi*, *harijan* and Muslims, adopted a right strategy and selected candidates with the right caste and community identity. The election turned out as a referendum on Modi's economic agenda, which did not contain any populist component. Modi became one of the first Indian leaders who made no such promises that cannot be fulfilled. The experts said that there was Modi charisma but no undercurrent in his favour. But he swept the election despite the dogged effort by all sections opposing Modi, be they from RSS, VHP, Bajrang Dal, Keshubhai cronies, NGOs espousing Muslim causes, media wishing his downfall and finally all led by Sonia Gandhi herself. What was the magic wand that Modi had?

There was no doubt that since the formation of the state of Gujarat, there never was a leader in Gujarat who had been as popular as Modi. All previous leaders had been leading some castes or sections. Madhav Singh Solanki, for example, had charmed the poor and Kashatriyas, with his influence limited to Congress pockets. Chimanbhai Patel was, largely, a Patel leader. So was Keshubhai. Unlike any other leader, Modi simplified his communication with the people in one single word—development. The cynics among political class had to accept that this message clicked with people. The subtext of the message was that under Modi rule, one could make money without any political, communal or social disturbances. No wonder that top industrialists fell for Modi. So did the common men who even went to the extent of crediting Modi for every good thing happening in Gujarat. Rediff.com, a news portal, quoted the middle-class voters, 'Modi shuknaiyal che' (Modi's rule is auspicious).

Modi's overpowering presence turned the election into one man issue—for or against Modi. Everybody else became irrelevant, including Sonia Gandhi. In fact she contributed to this polarization by calling Modi 'maut-ka-saudagar'. This is a case study on how opponents of a charismatic leader should be careful while attacking such a domineering personality. Modi's response on the issue was sharp. It resulted in a notice served on him by India's EC. Modi's response to the notice explains the incident. It also brings to light the running battle Modi was having with Indian media. The complaint according to Modi was based on false media reports. His response to the Commission was:

> The basis of the complaint appears to be a report dated 5th December 2007 of *The Times of India* by one Shri Prashant Dayal. The relevant extract in *The Times of India* reads as under: Modi: 'You tell what should be done

to Sohrabuddin?' People at the rally: Kill him, kill him. Modi: 'Well, that is what I did. And I did what was necessary'. ...This last sentence is not reflected in the CD as having been used by me.[1]

Modi also explained the reason for his response and took the opportunity to reiterate a complaint lodged by BJP on a speech delivered by Sonia Gandhi. He wrote to EC:

> On 1st December 2007, AICC President Mrs Sonia Gandhi visited Gujarat and referred to me by suggesting those who are ruling Gujarat are 'liars, dishonest and merchants of fear and death' (maut-ke-saudagar)... My speech, therefore, has to be read entirely in this context. It was a political response to Mrs Sonia Gandhi referring to me as those who rule the Gujarat as a 'maut-ke-saudagar'. Surely it cannot be policy of the Election Commission first to ignore the violation of the Code of Conduct in her statement and then censor my political response to that statement. I have gone through my speech on the CD supplied. It is merely a response to Mrs Sonia Gandhi calling me 'maut-ka-saudagar'.[2]

While media relished using Sonia Gandhi's statement on Modi and published it prominently, in electoral politics this provided huge ammunition to Narendra Modi to beat back any anti-incumbency he had after ruling Gujarat for six long years. It was Sonia Gandhi who reminded Gujarat of the communal divide providing Narendra Modi an opportunity to press two points close to his heart—pride of Gujarat and anti-Hindu stance of Congress president. Development apart, this speech did cost Sonia's Congress dear in Gujarat 2007. It offered Modi an opportunity to refer to the soft attitude of Congress government on terrorism:

> I responded that the 'maut-ka-saudagar' are all those who attacked parliament. It is the Congress party which is delaying the execution of the guilty accused. I have made a reference to the Sohrabuddin's case and mentioned the allegations against him. I have accused the Congress of suggesting that I have engineered a fake encounter.[3]

Modi was caustic on media and said that the alleged comments attributed to him were 'journalistic inventions intended to engineer a "Hate Modi" campaign and not evidenced in the CD supplied by the EC. My criticism in the media was concocted and engineered by this "Hate Modi"

Campaign.' The response to the EC notice clearly illustrates Modi's strained relationship with Indian national media. In all his campaigns, he was careful to note this point and use the media 'bias' to his advantage. This was handled in a well planned manner in campaign 2014.

Post his election victory, some researchers paid a closer attention to what Modi did that won him so much support in an otherwise issueless election. Some identified polarization as the main factor for Modi's success. Others talked of industrialization. Few mentioned the development of infrastructure like port. What most winked at was the fact that Gujarat's agricultural performance had been by far the best in India. Between 2000–01 and 2007–08, agricultural value added grew at a phenomenal 9.6 per cent per year, more than double that of India's agricultural growth rate, and even much faster than Punjab's farm growth in the green revolution heyday. Indeed, 9.6 per cent agricultural growth is among the fastest rates recorded anywhere in the world. That drives home the magnitude of Gujarat's performance. None in media cared to mention that millions of happy farmers in Gujarat contributed to Modi's victory. This growth came when Sardar Sarovar Project was incomplete. But semi-arid and arid farms of Gujarat still could irrigate their crop by building check dams, village tanks and bori-bunds which are built with gunny sacks stuffed with mud. Modi's response to the Congress slogan 'chak de, chak de Gujarat' in 2007 was 'check dam, check dam Gujarat'. Interestingly, this move was not Modi's innovation. He simply increased the scale of building check dams, which had been in place even under the previous Keshubhai government. These played a big role in the agricultural growth of Saurashtra and Kutch. Better water availability increased milk and livestock production. Modi also put emphasis on drip irrigation offering subsidies and loans, and also fast-tracking and simplifying procedures. A leader simply cannot win votes through oratorical skills unless the claims are supported by some visible results.

Politically, Congress in Gujarat 2007 was way behind BJP. It was so busy destabilizing Modi that it chose many who defected from BJP and gave them tickets. Probably, they defected since they would not have received BJP tickets. By turning Modi-baiter, they could bag Congress ticket, but in the process Congress invited ire of voters. Modi government in his first term could provide electricity in all homes of Gujarat. The electricity charges had been steep, but it was available. Farmers could get stable supply for eight hours. Stable electricity without voltage fluctuation meant longer life for their pump sets. The supply system of drinking water too improved. A large number of villagers were happy that they had a tap in their homes for the first time in their family history. While the quality of new roads in the interiors was questionable, the fact remained that villages were connected by roads. There might have been corruption at the higher level but Modi ensured that at the lower level and panchayat level ordinary people got computerized copies of their land ownership. E-government has been a pet subject of Modi and its help in systemizing land records did make an impact on young people. Thus, Modi managed to sell dreams while the opposition campaign relied on scare mongering. In any election campaign, when the theme touches people's emotion, it becomes successful. Thus, Congress campaign in Gujarat 2007 proved inadequate to dethrone Modi from Gandhinagar. Even Muslims support-ing Congress felt safer under Modi though they would have not voted for him. 'We have peace without justice under Modi's rule. We have opted for peace', said one to media.

Narendra Modi, despite his political success in Gujarat continued to be a persona non grata in states outside Gujarat. The assembly election of December 2008 saw the BJP Chief Minister of Rajasthan Vasundhara Raje Scindia lukewarm to Modi's presence in the campaign for her re-election. In fact, so touchy was Vasundhara over the Hindutva agenda of the hardcore BJP that many in the state BJP office remained distant to the campaign. Narendra Modi came and spoke in a few rallies near the border of Rajasthan and Gujarat. He never was allowed to take any important campaign role. Vasundhara was concerned that the balance of the efficient administration she ran for five years would get disturbed by the hardcore Hindutva image of Modi. In the end, Vasundhara lost, partly due to her inability to appease all sections within the party and partly due to her effort to run a one-person campaign led by her. The assembly election in Rajasthan that took place about six months before the national election 2009 illustrated that time was not ripe for Modi's ascendancy in BJP.

When there was reluctance to endorse him within the party, it was natural that the allies of BJP, too, would hesitate to accept Modi. Prominent among them was the NDA Chief Minister of Bihar Nitish Kumar. He seemed to be touchy over his secular image which he felt depended on him maintaining distance with Narendra Modi. When Gujarat election in

2007 was at a critical stage and Modi was being attacked by Sonia Gandhi and UPA leaders, Nitish Kumar too had joined in the chorus. This was in the context of reported statement of Modi over the encounter killing of Sohrabuddin. Nitish campaigned for JD(U) candidates in Gujarat. During such campaigning Nitish alleged, 'The Gujarat chief minister has deviated from the path of development and has been ignoring the cause of tribals and Dalits.' Though Nitish congratulated Modi after his election victory in 2007, he was careful in not identifying him as a friendly soul to Modi. In fact, JD(U) politicians felt that it was appropriate for Nitish to show dislike for Modi. This helped Muslims in Bihar to understand that though the party was in coalition with BJP, it maintained its 'secular' credential.

This secular credential seemed to have been seriously affected when some businessmen in Bihar placed an advertisement welcoming Narendra Modi in Bihar to attend the BJP national executive meeting in Patna. The advertisement had a photograph of Modi and Nitish campaigning together holding each other's hands. Nitish was mad seeing the advertisement. He cancelled the dinner he was to host for the BJP leaders that evening. This was in June 2010. BJP swallowed the insult for the sake of its coalition, but the message was clear that there could be no peace between Modi and Nitish. For Nitish, what mattered was Modi's image of 2002 riots. It mattered little to him that he was the Railway Minister when the Sabarmati Express was burned and that he did not even visit the site. In India's vote bank politics, Modi was untouchable. Later when there was contribution from the Gujarat government for relief of the flood victims in Bihar, Nitish returned the money thinking that it smelled of Hindutva. In any meetings of India's national development council or where all Chief Ministers of the country attended, Nitish never acknowledged Modi's presence. The polarization between Nitish and Modi was complete.

The hostility of Nitish, then an ally of BJP, towards Narendra Modi brings to the fore the well-accepted principle of Indian politics. If any leader had ambition to occupy the top post in the country, the leader must have a 'secular' credential. By secular, it meant that the leader had to be acceptable to the Muslims in India. This code perhaps led to the successful Hindu communal leader of BJP L.K. Advani trying to buy peace through his comments on Pakistan founder Mohammed Ali Jinnah. This had seen political leaders throwing lavish Iftar Parties during the holy month of Ramzan. Detractors of such exhibitionisms call this appeasement.

But given the electoral arithmetic, appeasement seemed unavoidable for any campaign.

For Narendra Modi, the way his image shaped due to the post-Godhra riots, it was not possible to attempt an image makeover. Not that Gujarat administration under Modi was overtly biased towards the Hindu fundamentalists who had been strong in the state much before Modi came as the Chief Minister. In fact, due to Modi's presence some of them turned hostile to him and his government.

It is said that Modi and Togadia shared a warm relation in 2002. Journalist Aditi Phadnis wrote that Togadia was heard boasting in 2002 that 'Narendrabhai is riding the horse, but the reins are in my hand.' Togadia was even keen to form an alternate organization to look after the interest of Hindus since he felt that the Gujarat BJP under Modi BJP had become a 'B-team of the Congress'. VHP tried to launch a movement around the trishul—encouraging Hindus to carry a miniature trishul like a Sikh kirpan. It failed since Modi did not find the idea exciting and people of Gujarat, too, cold-shouldered it. So, Togadia went to Rajasthan to popularize it. Modi knew how VHP workers earned their living. They flaunted their connection in the state government and trade the same against a fee. Under Modi, all such middlemen were cut out from government transactions. The desperation of VHP was evident when before assembly election in 2007, Togadia said at a press conference that the VHP would not support the BJP in the elections. While in Gujarat VHP became a firm, implacable enemy, outside the state even political allies like Nitish or party colleagues like Vasundhara were overtly or covertly reluctant to rub shoulders with him. This was a tragedy of Narendra Modi which he needed to overcome had he wished to take a prominent position in the national politics. The election of 2009 was not the opportune time for Modi to make any such effort.

After the SIT report and exoneration from courts, Modi embarked on a journey across Gujarat called Sadbhavana Mission. Modi interacted with people and observed one-day fast in each district. It was Modi's attempt to unify Gujarat under one theme that of friendliness. Modi turned emotional and wrote, 'The pride and satisfaction of an election victory dwarfs in comparison to the fulfillment of seeing people treat each other with utmost respect and deep regard'. It was a demonstration of peace and unity in Gujarat. Modi was happy that 'the world has to take note of the fact that Gujarat's atmosphere of unity, peace and brotherhood is the main reason behind our rapid progress'. He also took a dig at his detractors and pointed out:

> ...we have our nation being dominated by the poison of caste, religion based vote-bank politics that has deeply disappointed and broken the trust of every Indian. The 'Divide and Rule' philosophy adopted by the Centre has caused irreparable damage to the image of our great nation.[4]

In contrast, Modi's Gujarat adopted the path of peace, unity and brotherhood. He was proud that 'Gujarat has shunned vote-bank politics and adopted the politics of development'. Clearly, Modi was setting the context of his foray outside the state for a larger political role. The campaign was suitably planned.

Representatives from all states and 'well-wishers' from many political parties were present at the Sadbhavana fast held at Ahmedabad from 17–19 September 2011. At least one member from 70 to 75 per cent of the families in Gujarat participated during the 36 Sadbhavana fasts. Over 50 lakh people from 18,000 villages were present, which was cited as the scale and public participation in the Sadbhavana Mission. Modi shook hands and met personally over 15 lakh people. Narendra Modi knew instinctively the value of scale in any public event. If an event has to be organized, it should be so arranged that people are compelled to take note. The entire Sadbhavana Mission was planned accordingly.

Modi decided to observe fasts. Along with him, thousands of Gujaratis voluntarily joined the fast. Over 4.5 lakh people including 1.5 lakh women observed fasts and gave moral support to the Sadbhavana Mission. During the Sadbhavana Mission, hundreds of *padyatris* arrived to the venue of fast from various holy places. Over one lakh people, especially the youth joined the mission as padyatris. Sadbhavana Marches (*Prabhat Pheris*) were organized in thousands of villages despite cold weather and saw a participation of over 16 lakh people, thus spreading the message of Sadbhavana across the state.

Sadbhavana Mission was not merely a political campaign. During its course, about 40,000 Tithi Bhojans were organized in villages through which around 42 lakh poor children were provided with nutritious meals. More than six lakh kilograms of foodgrains were distributed to poor families in rural areas. Rupees four crore was donated to Kanya Kelavani Nidhi to promote girl child education in the state. It touched social issues also. Like citizens pledging to contribute for the welfare of society, young people denouncing social evils like dowry and infanticide. Mere political agenda would not have ensured participation of people. Modi knew it well. The Sadbhavana Mission was a new style of campaign for the assembly election in 2012.

The term coined by certain channels during the assembly election in 2007—Moditva replacing Hindutva—was perhaps the hint. Modi assiduously reached out to his people through social sector missions. This helped Modi to emerge much larger than the party. Other leaders in BJP surrendered since they could all remain in power under the umbrella provided by Modi. The election to the Gujarat state assembly in 2012 should be assessed from this perspective.

For media persons who returned to Gujarat after the 2007 election, the state capital twin city of Ahmedabad and Gandhinagar was a new experience. Some saw the wider gulf between the rich and the poor. Some saw examples of shining Gujarat. Many could not help wondering at the beautified Sabarmati Riverfront. For TV news, the beautiful spot offered a good backdrop to record their programmes or at least PTCs. Rewards of having Modi as Chief Minister were many, uninterrupted power supply, adequate water, pucca roads, houses, strife and fear-free environment. Here was a leader who exemplified the Gujarat identity. Modi was considered as God's gift to Gujarat. There were many who did not join in this Modi-mania but indulged in Modi-bashing. Prominent among them had been the supporters of Keshubhai. But even they knew nobody would defeat Modi.

Why, in 2012, did people treat Modi's victory as a given? One reason was that the Congress in Gujarat was in abject surrender. Congress won nearly a 40 per cent share of the vote in Gujarat at the 2012 assembly elections despite it being both structurally and psychologically eclipsed locally by Modi's BJP. At his office in Ahmedabad, its leader Arjun Modhwadia told Patric French forlornly that Narendra Modi had 'captured the mind of the people' through his mysteriously effective use of the media. Congress did not have any idea on how to counter Modi. The old style leaders of Congress only complained that Modi had turned the contest like a presidential form of election. Modi's speeches all over Gujarat claiming that only he was a saviour and a bold administrator did find many admirers with critics wondering how to match it. Then, Congress leaders had no answer to Modi's charge on their central leaders. They bitterly complained, 'He makes these vulgar speeches saying Rahul Gandhi is a shehzada or a calf. You never hear such language from Mrs Sonia Gandhi. They come from a reputable family'.

Congress politics in Gujarat became purely reactive. They simply followed the agenda set by Modi. Clearly, they did not know how to appeal to the popular sentiments of people, how to inspire them, connect with the young and create a wave of support. This was the state of affairs of the Gujarat Congress in 2012. One wonders what did the party do when it seemed that Modi might emerge as the main leader of the opposition BJP in the parliament election for 2014.

Modi knew how to reach to his audience. He also knew that he would not manage to reach the entire state. He, therefore, opted for technology and initiated 3D broadcasts of his speeches. The initiative said to have entered the Guinness Book of World Records—the record for most simultaneous shows of 'the Pepper's Ghost Illusion' (a technology). The record was held by Raj Kasu Reddy and Mani Shankar of NChant 3D, which telecast a 55-minute speech by Mr Modi live to 53 locations across Gujarat on 10 December 2012. Modi lost no time in mentioning the same in his blog. Here was a politician who knew how to reach to his people and communicate to them infusing aspiration and hope, at the same time, run down his opponents with sharp and choicest phrases.

Narendra Modi rewrote the grammar of political campaign in his test tube called Gujarat. The very character of the people in the state also suited Modi-style campaign. He spoke of development. An average Gujarati knew the value of money, therefore of development. They were also fed on the staple diet of communalism given the staunch orthodox nature of an average person from Gujarat. The riot of 2002 alerted Modi to the perils of using communalism as an ingredient for electoral politics. From his Ram Mandir experience, he knew that the sign of a religious symbol couldn't be sustained for long. More important on a personal level also, it seemed Modi was not comfortable with that brand of politics. He had to ride the tiger once in 2002. Though still he is blamed for the riot, the fact that he distanced from the communal brand of politics at the first opportunity illustrates that he did not enjoy his ride on the tiger.

Modi thus considerably toned down his rhetoric increasing his emphasis on the language of growth and development. Over the three assembly elections—in 2002, 2007 and 2012—a new brand of politics emerged which many derisively called Moditva. But still Modi was far removed from the elements a national leader requires. He talked loudly on the Gujarati pride, not of Indian pride. He did not need to talk of nationalism because he was in combat with the central government for which the parochial touch was good enough. Modi kept himself confined within his core strength. Thus, when he did not find welcome mats for electioneering outside Gujarat, be it Bihar in 2005 or Rajasthan in 2008, he did not bother. For him, these were the learning sessions on how his possible rivals had been addressing issues, how successful such methods were and how the same could be improved. Nobody can fault Modi for his impatience.

The fact that Modi was inspirational for Gujarat only could be seen in the Lok Sabha results of 2004 and 2009. Despite Modi and his ability to captivate the voters in Gujarat, Congress could win 12 and 11 seats, respectively out of 26 Lok Sabha seats from the state. Clearly, people of Gujarat were not ready to vote for BJP to rule in Delhi. This also illustrates that the additional seats in the assembly election for BJP came because of people's support for Modi as a leader. Even in Modi's Gujarat, voting pattern for assembly and the Lok Sabha polls differed due to different options of leaders before the electorate.

For Narendra Modi, victory in 2012 election was a foregone conclusion. What demonstrated maturity of Modi as a leader was his gesture immediately after the results were out. After paying respect to his mother, Modi went to the residence of his staunch critic and predecessor Keshubhai Patel. There in the full glare of the TV camera, Modi touched Keshubhai's feet and sought his blessing. Keshubhai's GPP had campaigned bitterly against Modi and ate into some of his votes though its vote share was not enough to harm Modi's election sweep. By seeking Keshubhai's blessings, Modi delivered his key message. First message was that no amount of Modi bashing can hurt his electoral prospect in the state. Second and perhaps most symbolic was that after three successive electoral victories, a record in Gujarat, Narendra Modi would now look for a larger platform to use his skills. Keshubhai could realize that there was no point in opposing Modi anymore, certainly not on the plank of the Hindutva agenda. Modi had outgrown the same and was now aiming for a larger canvas. Defeat in an election happens to any politician, Keshubhai was no exception. But Modi's visit to seek his blessing was a crushing blow to the elderly politician of Gujarat. He resigned his assembly seat due to poor health. His party decided to merge with BJP. Narendra Modi's victory over the hardcore Hindutva element in Gujarat was complete.

This victory and thereafter the exoneration from the courts on his responsibility in the Gujarat riots led Modi to write in his blog that truth alone triumphs—*Satyameva Jayate*. But that is a different narrative.

9

Assessing the Election Campaign

Quintus Tullius Cicero wrote a short pamphlet 'How to win an election' for his brother Marcus in the summer of 64 BC. Marcus was a gifted orator, had a distinguished record of military service and possessed a brilliant mind. But he was not of noble birth. And nobody other than a noble had won the election for consul in a class-conscious Roman republic. Quintus wrote the pamphlet, the first known manual on electioneering, to help his elder brother.[1] Those were for different times, for a different set of people and in a culture alien to India 2014. But certain salient points mentioned in the pamphlet are still pertinent for campaigning in an election. More so, it fit into the Narendra Modi campaign in 2014.

Quintus warned his brother, 'since you are seeking the most important position in Rome and since you have so many potential enemies, you can't afford to make any mistakes'. Substitute Rome for New Delhi and the name of the campaigner gets automatically substituted as Narendra Modi in place of Marcus Cicero. Like Marcus, India's Modi had to remember the warning of Quintus, 'You must conduct a flawless campaign with the greatest thoughtfulness, industry and care.'[2] Narendra Modi was careful yet there was one slip up. In an interview with Reuters, Modi said and PTI reported on 12 July 2013

> Another thing, … any person if we are driving a car, we are a driver, and someone else is driving a car and we're sitting behind, even then if a puppy comes under the wheel, will that be painful or not? Of course, it is. If I'm a chief minister or not, I'm a human being. If something bad happens anywhere, it is natural to be sad.[3]

Prima facie there was nothing wrong in the simile but proved grossly incorrect for the Chief Minister of Gujarat who was accused of providing tacit encouragement of riots in 2002 riots which saw a large number of Muslims getting killed. It was irrelevant for his detractors that there had been not a shred of evidence against him and the nation's highest court exonerated him from any kind of suspicion. The interview created a storm accusing Modi of comparing Muslims with puppies.

Running for an elected office according to the oldest guide on election campaign, could be broadly divided into two kinds of activities. First was to secure the support of friends. Modi had an advantage. Barring just few colleagues in Gujarat, he did not have many who could help him in the electoral battle. He had to therefore focus on the second kind of activity, that of winning over the general public. Even the divinity had to concede to Modi on this point. He won hearts of the common men across the country. How could he do it? Even in 64 BC, Quintus knew that communication skills are the key. Narendra Modi had proved beyond any shred of doubt that he is the best communicator the world has seen in many years. Many, particularly the Americans, addicted as they are to list anything American, on top of a chart they love to create, would place out the communications skills of their Presidents Obama and Bill Clinton higher than that of Modi's. But they must remember that US electorate is much more homogeneous than those in India. Modi has won through his communication skills, votes from Ladakh in the Karakoram mountains in the north to Kanyakumari in the southern tip of India, the desert of Bhuj in the west to Nagaland in the east. He could even swing substantial votes in states relatively hostile to his party BJP—Kerala in the south and West Bengal in the east.

Even before the final outcome of election 2014 came in May, there had been a curtain raiser of sorts during the assembly elections in December 2013. Ashok Gehlot, the vanquished Congress Chief Minister of Rajasthan, had no qualms in accepting that Modi factor caused the landslide for BJP in his state. But why did the Narendra Modi factor work? Jyotiraditya Scindia, the important young leader and minister of Congress provided the answer. 'Communication is the key to any election, at any level', said Scindia. The unavoidable conclusion is that Modi has communicated better than others in the end of 2013 assembly elections.

What are the messages the electorates delivered? First and most clear message is for Congress and its two most prominent leaders, the mother and son duo of Sonia and Rahul Gandhi. In the later phase of the national election 2014, Modi called the Central Government as *ma–bete ki sarkar* (government of the mother and son). The people of all hues are not swayed by their 'charisma'. The rub off effect of this dislike has seen the drubbing of Congress candidates in all the four states and the Lok Sabha election.

Second, the reason for the anger of electorates is the complete absence of governance of the Manmohan Singh government. Prices had been soaring; everyday some corruption cases were hogging the limelight; the harassment of the common men was a routine. There was complete aversion of the ordinary people for Congress.

Third and no less key message had been that voters were not begging for subsidized schemes but demanding opportunities for earning their livelihoods. Gone are the days when mere promises of sops or even schemes could placate the suffering millions. They now know well enough how much of such money is consumed by the scheme managers—politicians, bureaucrats and ordinary babus. Congress leader Rahul Gandhi while talking on the benefits of such schemes actually kept on insulting the self-respects of the forgotten millions.

Fourth and final, the elitism of Congress campaign and politics received thumbs down from the majority of the electorates.

Communication is an art. In the assembly elections in December 2013, a curtain raiser for the elections 2014, the Modi effect was seen on the results. So bad was the drubbing that the Congress 'high-command' of mother and son had to acknowledge it. 'We failed to carry our message to the people', said Sonia Gandhi in December 2013. The message on 16 May 2014 after the loss in the Lok Sabha elections had been the same though differently worded and accompanied by Congress Vice President Rahul Gandhi with a mysterious grin. Clearly, Narendra Modi could deliver the key message. That is Modi effect.

Two more advices of Quintus are important. One was to know the weakness of the opponents and exploit the same. The other is to give people hope.

On the issue of weaknesses of his opponents, Modi began targeting the ruling Congress party. A major point of attack was the stranglehold of a particular family on the party and the government. While Manmohan Singh had been the Prime Minister, he was in effect executing the orders from the Gandhi family. Modi coined the term 'ma–bete ka sarkar' to convey this arrangement to the ordinary Indians. He also used the epithet Shehzada for Rahul Gandhi. Predictably, the opponents of Modi were disturbed. They could follow the sarcasm but had no answer to this. Raja of rage is what they called Modi. One TV anchor asked, 'Why are Modi's speeches laden with so much invective?' There had been many examples.

Modi poured scorn on Mamata Banerjee's paintings. He called the Congress Finance Minister P. Chidambaram as the recounting minister. This referred to Chidambaram's narrow election victory and the refusal to recount by the election officials at Shivganga, his constituency. On Mamata's paintings, the question that was asked why there surfaced buyers of her paintings after she became the state Chief Minister. It might be impolite but the facts were incontrovertible. Modi repeatedly derided the Gandhi family as the mother–son government. He had vented his rage against 2G, CWG, Damaadji and Shehzada. He also mocked the 'baap–beta' (father Mulayam and son Akhilesh Yadav) government of UP. He has asserted that 'the country does not want a deaf, dumb and handicapped government'. Detractors viewed the remark as insulting to people with disabilities. He called journalists 'news traders'. He called Arvind Kejriwal AK 49, dubbed the Defence Minister as another AK, similar to an AK 47, which is helping Pakistan. He said that he would make arrangements for JDS leader Deve Gowda to stay in an old age home. In return, horrendous and unacceptable monikers like 'butcher' and 'chaiwallah' were continuously flung at Modi. In fact Mani Shankar Aiyar, a Congress member, helped Modi when he said in January 2014 during the Congress session in Delhi referring to Modi selling tea in trains as a kid that since Modi would never be the PM if he desired to sell tea in the Congress session, Mani Shankar would help. Modi responded that he had his kettles ready in case people did not vote for him but what would happen to those who did nothing other than remain in power and enjoy privileges.

Calling names for known follies is one matter but hurling abuse and filing charges on unsubstantiated gossips had been a tactic often used against Modi. There was a charge that Modi had tapped phones of a young woman and asked his sleuths to shadow her. The girl's father said that this was done at his behest for protection of his daughter. Even the girl in question endorsed the statement and filed no complaint. Despite that taking cognizance of the fact, the Congress Cabinet decided to engage a judicial commission. But no retired judge came forward to head such a commission. During the election campaign time and again, nearly all rivals of Modi used that allegation and attacked Modi alleging his personal frailties. In addition there had been efforts to malign Modi on his marriage that took place when he was 17 years old. He left home thereafter and never went back. His wife Jasodaben taught in a school and was living with her brother post-retirement. There had been several efforts to stalk Jasodaben and create some sensational negative reports on Modi. During 2014 election, Modi filled up his nomination form mentioning Jasodaben as his wife. Earlier in assembly elections, he used to leave the column blank. Senior leaders including Congress president Sonia Gandhi's daughter Priyanka Vadra used these two to paint Modi as a misogynist. Modi bore with these insults. In an interview with the national television Doordarshan, he said that since Priyanka had been campaigning for her mother Sonia and brother Rahul, she had been making harsh comments and he would not bear any grudge for that. Even this comment was distorted. It was reported as if Modi had said that Priyanka was like his daughter. Prompt rebuttal came from Priyanka with an air of arrogant dismissal that she was Rajiv Gandhi's daughter. There was no apology even after the real statement of Modi came to light.

Modi's detractors said that his unsophisticated humour won audience approval, but did not meet the test of civility. His comments come laden with invective and are bitterly harsh on everyone without exception. Such insults on his opponents according to Modi-baiters, raised an unbreachable wall between speaker and listener. Particularly harsh had been the women journalists and women rivals like Mamata Banerjee, herself known for her foul language. Since Modi can't control his mouth, how can he control the country, asked Mamata.

Indian politics adopts a queer principle. There is a *Laxman Rekha* in political discourse. Nobody is expected to cross the same. Particularly revolting is attack on the Nehru–Gandhi family. One is expected not to criticize the members of family in course of delivering political messages. Narendra Modi breached the convention of offering a meaningless ritualistic obeisance to a particular family. Indian politics has accepted that the family members have a right to rule without the subjects having any right to question. They have a right to travel abroad for celebrating birthdays and when on holiday receive the SPG protection at taxpayers' money but the hapless taxpayer has no right to know where do they travel. The ruling party president goes abroad reportedly for treatment but the taxpayer has no business to know where did the leader go, what is the ailment. What is more Modi crossed the Laxman Rekha since he had the audacity to mention in public meeting that if the party president was unwell the vice president should take over.

This was defamatory as Congress spokesman claimed on TV. Offensive perhaps it was, at least for the parasites living off the benevolence of the family. But how can the same be viewed as defamatory is beyond any rational thought. True, Narendra Modi has been crossing with impunity the Rubicon of civility accepted in the political discourse of the country so far. He has even broken free from what the former BJP Prime Minister and his principal secretary did in the past. Apparently during the tenure of Vajpayee, a certain touch-me-not member of a political family was detained in a US airport with cash beyond the legal limit of the US. Not only that the right strings were pulled to save the person from embarrassment, but also the report could manage to stay out of the public domain. Narendra Modi, judged by his speeches, seems to have no such civility in him, as the charge goes. Should Modi have followed the rules hitherto accepted as sacrosanct?

According to Richard King, author of *On Offence, The Politics of Indignation*, civility as preached is the civility of the Middle Ages. For common men, then it was a sin to speak against the nobility. 'To sin against nobility is to sin against God since it was He who set nobles above us.' On a practical note, it made sense for the common men to avoid criticizing the nobility. They had enormous power to hit back on the recalcitrant commoner. Thus was set the rule of civility. Introspection gives the impression that the Indian politicians' (and analysts, commentators and others) steadfast refusal to cross the Rubicon could be due to the concern of reprisal.[4]

Since India follows a semi-feudalistic approach towards democracy, there are good reasons to stay away from personal attacks by most leaders. The point one cannot miss is that those who will criticize today, say the family heirloom style of politics, will themselves indulge in the same style when in authority. The family-first policy of Congress is seen in regional parties like SP of Mulayam Yadav, RJD of Lalu Yadav, JMM of Shibu Soren, National Conference of Abdullahs, NCP of Sharad Power, SS of Thackeray, etc. Within Congress also, there are many who are in positions of authority due to family links; Shiela Dikshit, Sachin Pilot, Jyotiraditya Scindia and so on. People living in glass houses do not throw stones at each other. So the Rubicon has come to stay here.

But the principle of free speech is meaningless unless it includes the freedom to offend. In fact, the claim to find something hurtful or offensive should be the beginning of the debate not the end of it.

In an advanced democracy, the rules are similar to what the young India aspires to see now. More than a century and half ago, when a man of humble origin, born in a one-room log cabin, emerged as a political figure of the turbulent nineteenth century US, he was subjected to several personal innuendos. His rival Stephen A. Douglas, a democrat and member of the US Senate, repeatedly humiliated Lincoln for his humble background. Once he called Lincoln, 'a grocery-keeper' who sold cigars and whisky and was 'a good bartender'. Lincoln admitted that he sold whisky:

> I remember that in those days Mr Douglas was one of my best customers. Many a time have I stood on one side of the counter and sold whisky to Mr Douglas on the other side. But the difference between us now is this: I have left my side of the counter, but Mr Douglas still sticks to his as tenaciously as ever.[5]

Do we spot the voice of Mr Douglas in the barb of Manishankar Aiyar? But on personal attack, there was never a taboo in the US of 1850s and India of 2014. Now that in India a tea-boy emerged as arguably the most popular choice as leader and that there are many sly remarks hurled to denigrate him, there is no reason why some will hurl and enjoy the insults aimed at him from the safety of their ivory towers. Equality is the first principle of democracy. More important is Modi's invectives provided entertainment for those who came to listen to him or heard him on electronic media. Most TV channels had opted for showing his speeches live. The sharp oratory of Narendra Modi perhaps were unpalatable to the opponents and those who made it their 'dharma' to oppose Modi but as the election results have shown people at large loved those. Modi's humour—call it rustic, cheap, distasteful, offensive or repulsive—had been a primary factor for his receiving wide attention across the country and proved as the sure shot winner in the end. Modi could exploit to the hilt the weaknesses in all his opponents through his raw humour.

The other important element of a winning campaign, according to Quintas, was to offer hope. Even Narendra Modi in his speech acknowledging the support he received from his constituency Vadodara mentioned that people want to have a message of hope, of a bright future from their leaders. Negatives do not win their hearts. This is even more so when the majority of the electorates are young. Sixty-five per cent of voters in

India are in the age group of 35 years or less. They look for opportunity, opportunity to come up in life. For them religion, caste, freedom of expression and so on are vacuous meaningless terms if the alternative offers promise. They have little patience for criticism, of analysis of why things did not happen. But they are all attention when told how their future can turn brighter, if one delivers messages of hope. In all his speeches beginning from 15 September 2013 and ending on 10 May 2014, Narendra Modi kept harping on the story of hope—how India can prosper and deliver a happier time for the aspiring youth. In contrast, his detractors were busy either to deprecate what Modi failed to do in Gujarat or to emphasize on the religious divide that India has and why Modi is not suitable in such a diverse nation. Both had the opportunity to talk in detail and the nation voted thereafter, the election result of the largest democratic election in the history of mankind confirmed what Quintas had told his brother about 2,100 years ago. Provide the message of hope to the electorates. Modi did just that giving examples of Gujarat in the last 12 years. Indians believed and reposed faith in his leadership.

Ability to convey the message that the audience wants to hear is one aspect of a campaign. The other in case of Narendra Modi was his control over the audience. His body language had been bold. Even experts in communication, perhaps much more competent than us, were mesmerized by Modi's oratorical skills. When Modi started speaking to rallies, a report of India's intelligence authorities cited three factors that needed special attention. The attendance to Modi's rallies had been large and spontaneous. The allegations that BJP spent huge sum of money to hire the crowd was a fable for those who hated him. In fact in his first rally in Kolkata, the TMC which is the ruling party in the state used its bus unions to stop buses plying from Kolkata's suburbs to the venue so that people cannot go to attend the rally. The huge crowd apart, the officials sleuths observed that the majority of those attending Modi rallies were young people. Third and no less critical was their comment that the audience responses had always been spontaneous to Modi. To evoke such response, the orator also had to be equally adept in communication. For Narendra Modi, spontaneity has been natural not a laboured act. Thoughts should flow seamlessly, audience must respond to the pauses and punch lines, and in the end they should go enthralled. Just contrast Narendra Modi with the others who had declared war on him. Sonia Gandhi keeps reading from papers, so does Mayawati. Mamata at best is incoherent and more often than not abusive. Mulayam himself knows what he has been speaking. Nitish Kumar just keeps punching the opponent instead of outlining his own performance or unfurls the mantra of hope. Only Lalu Yadav is blessed with rustic humour, but that cannot be the only fodder to the restless young. No wonder that after Modi's victory Mulayam lamented that how he would face the oratory of Modi in the Lok Sabha, who in his party would match him!

Body language must be matched by style of delivery—voice modulation, for instance. Narendra Modi loved to act. He is also a poet of sorts in his native tongue Gujarati. As actor and poet, he knew how to deliver speeches, a style that was natural to another poet turned Prime Minister of BJP, Atal Bihari Vajpayee. Modi's speeches are a refreshing change from the plastic, monotonous speeches of most Indian politicians. Rahul tried to copy Modi's style that of heightening the drama through his loud proclamations, flourishing hand gestures to emphasize a point, punctuate with gentle pauses and evoking passion, all in order to hold the attention of the audience. During Modi's speeches, at least three times longer than those of Rahul's, audience waited with bated breath for the punchline, the full-throated sarcasm and the messages of hope they came to hear. In the end, people went home convinced of Modi's commitment to the cause. Unlike Modi, the Gandhi brother and sister duo made attempts to enthuse people with their personal losses, death of their father and grandmother. They forgot that not everybody is expected to shed tears over some incidents which happened as recently as 23 years back, when many young voters were not even born. The other person in the election drama, Arvind Kejriwal, who received media mileage disproportionate to the number of votes polled by his party had the faults of others, mostly Narendra Modi's, as his pet theme. He even went to the ludicrous extent of getting the water of Gujarat's Sabarmati river tested to show how much pollutants flow through the river. His skill for technicality and ability to repeat the same point over and over again even created media fatigue after some time. Communication is an art. Rudiments of communication skill must come naturally to the person. Barring Narendra Modi in the largest election in the history of democracy, Narendra Modi dwarfed all his adversaries. His oratorical skill will remain as one of the best in a democratic election campaign, overshadowing even those of Presidents Obama and Roosevelt, Americans accept it or not.

How could Modi excel in connecting with the mood of the people in such a huge country where people are different in culture, language and even practicing religious rituals despite all being of the same religion? The secret lies in the fact that Modi had travelled across the nation and spent nights in at least 400 districts as a pracharak of RSS and later as BJP worker. He developed the ability to understand India's angst and the frustrations of the Indian youth. This helped him to focus on just two thoughts, good governance and development. He judged the past performances on these two parameters and demanded to be evaluated on just these two. His track record in Gujarat helped. In one stroke, Modi turned debates on secularism and communalism as irrelevant despite the chatterati raising it ad infinitum.

Modi developed an inimitable way of hammering home the idea of lost time to the nation. His stock phrase that India wasted 60 years and now should consider giving him a mandate just for 60 months turned immensely acceptable. That Modi was being considered as the only alternative was evident. A casual encounter with a voter outside the election booth is a testimony here: A simple middle-aged person with apparent no political connect thus revealed that he would vote for Modi to try out the BJP alternative for the next five years. 'We will vote him out if he fails, what do you say sir', he persisted. This was not a stray case since the election result had shown that many others reacted the same way.[6]

This was not the only punchline Modi used. He took advantage of the *chaiwala* barb to proclaim the greatness of democracy—in his party BJP, in particular. It helped him to expose complete lack of democratic system in the family-run Congress party. So, when Modi said that the boy who used to vend tea in train compartments was standing before India, he developed an immediate affinity with the man on the street. His detractors, in politics or in media, had no answer to that. When Modi said his mother used to wash utensils in neighbouring houses to feed the family, it immediately touched the right chord in the hearts of common men. When he said that his mother still lived in a relative modest home of his brother, not in the residence of the Chief Minister, the contrast of lifestyle between Modi and his detractors was evident. Indians had seen images of Modi seeking his mother's blessings in December 2012 after the victory in the Gujarat assembly election. The images were available for those who did not see it then, thanks to YouTube. Indians living far away from the glares of TV channels and affluence of Delhi, Mumbai or Bangalore saw in him a saviour whom they were willing to repose faith at least for five years. So rich had been his background, so transparent was his ability to convey the message that despite visible hostility of Delhi-centric media, India opted for Modi.

Modi travelled across the country. He addressed 440 rallies, travelled more than 300,000 kilometres, touched 5,800 places for rally or other party work. There were 4,000 places where Modi's *Chai pe Charcha* (discussion over a cup of tea) were organized. Modi addressed 3D rallies—12 such rallies were beamed across 1,350 locations. He knew the mainstream media was hostile to him. He also knew that in direct connect with people, nobody could match him. His wide acceptance in public meetings aroused people's curiosity. TV channels could not ignore him since Modi's team had arranged for web casting of his rallies. These were uploaded on YouTube for viewers to watch later. In any case, Modi's speeches made news. And what is no less important was that the feed was available free from BJP organization. Most of these meetings took place during the lean hours of the day, say around noon when unless there is some earth shattering news TV channels somehow fill time. Modi's speeches came as a welcome filler for the channels. Thus, media too willy-nilly kept highlighting Modi campaign. Congress also attempted to emulate and provided free feed of Rahul Gandhi rallies. But Rahul's speeches were a dampener. Lack of crowd participation was stark. Congress campaign realized that such live coverage would hurt them more than help their prospect. In a clever use of technology, organization and the leader's ability to connect Modi campaign could position its leader as an iconic political brand.

The important point to note is that in a democracy, people elect people, not issues. In 1951 they elected Nehru, in 1971 his daughter, in 1984 her son—all for the high like quotient they brought in. Issues will remain but in an election, be it the Westminster-style or the US Presidential-type, people love to look at the leader in the eye and decide if they trust him. Unlikable people are those who jabber constantly about things meaningless to the audience. Rahul Gandhi's claim of introducing RTI would enthuse an activist in a city but not a villager from Hajipur. For him, the issue is daily survival with no intention to learn how much money the former President Partibha Patil spent on decorating her retirement home. Whatever be the medium of dissemination, likeability is the magic bullet.

Choice of medium is also critical. The leader must reach the target voters. Here also Rahul Gandhi faltered badly. He chose to speak to an English news channel for 1 hour 20 minutes. Most of the time, he avoided a direct answer. In fact, he gave the impression that he had no understanding of the issues but was thrust on the position of the lead campaigner of Indian Congress party. English channels in India have a minuscule 0.08 per cent of viewers—most of them hold strong opinions on issues as well as on likeability quotient. By giving the interview as early as in January when the election campaign just began, Rahul did not convert a single non-committed person to vote for Congress. Instead he became the butt of jokes on the social media.

Modi in contrast avoided TV channels till the elections began. In the nine phase election, he waited patiently despite many provocations till the campaign for the fourth phase reached the end. This was when 121 seats went for polls. Modi chose the TV news agency ANI so that all channels could air his interview. Thereafter, he generously spoke to all major channels one after another keeping the English news channel Times Now in the end. Modi knew which medium to use and when.

The other message that came out of Modi's TV interviews was his ease of handling tough questions. When needed, he snubbed the interviewer and never allowed the aggressive anchors to cower him down. This is the body language of a leader. The likeability quotient increased further. What is more, Modi's language of choice was Hindi, even to the English channels. Anchors from ANI and Times Now were distinctly uncomfortable in Hindi. Modi took advantage and used his double meaning sentences merrily, to the utter discomfort of anchors. He was however most courteous, friendly and warm when it came to the national channel of DD that has a wider reach than the English television channels. Clearly, he knew his audience, mostly in small towns and villages, will love this image than the image of a stern administrator. Even the choice of location was soothing, an early morning in the garden in Gandhinagar. It was a pleasant leader talking to people not an aggressive politician haranguing his detractors. The national channel had the most endearing interview of Narendra Modi.

During the gruelling election campaign what stood out was the indomitable spirit and capacity to work of Narendra Modi. Nobody could help asking him how he managed to put in that much work. Addressing five or more election rallies every day at far away places and then getting back to Ahmedabad at night, taking stock of the campaign progress and then on the road the next morning, Modi's schedule was inhuman. Chandrababu Naidu, the Chief Minister of the bifurcated state of Andhra Pradesh mentioned how Modi addressed five meetings one after another and took a cup of tea after completing the assignments. During the campaign was Navratra, a nine-day long auspicious time when devout Hindus fast during the day. Modi continued his rallies all over even during the Navratra fasting. At the end of the day, he was ready for TV interviews. Workaholic Modi scored on the likeability parameter that could not be touched by any other leader competing with him. Even TV interviewers known for their hostility towards Modi came back sobered by his punctuality, business like approach and simple living.

What was the edge of Modi campaign over its rivals? Was it the advantage of a tech-savvy professional team? Or could it be the money spent for the campaign? Or was it simple polarization of Hindu votes against others? The critics of Modi like it or not in the final analysis, it was the key message that Narendra Modi delivered. Both in the BJP's manifesto and through his speeches, he emphasized only one point that economic problems were the root cause of social evils and that development matters. Even *The Economist*, a left liberal magazine that announced haughtily that it did not endorse Modi as India's Prime Minister admitted that the victory he achieved 'is more the result of his talk of strong government and improvements to the material lives of voters than anything else'.

An electoral trend seen in Indian elections since 2007 assembly election in UP had been people opting against a hung assembly and choosing a single party majority. In UP, Mayawati-led BSP won absolute majority, five years later BSP lost to its arch-rival Mulayam Yadav's SP which won absolute majority. In West Bengal, Mamata Banerjee's Trinamool Congress ousted the Left coalition to win absolute majority. In the national election of 2009, Congress won more than 200 seats so that the second UPA government was not much dependent on the whims of its allies. Clearly, Indian voters had a preference for a stable government, and, therefore, they elected representatives from the party of their choice. Modi understood this feeling and exploited it fully.

The coalition that Modi formed was with only smaller regional parties barring its two longstanding allies SAD in Punjab and SS in Maharashtra. In all his campaign speeches, Modi's message was clear—vote him as the next Prime Minister. In terms of Game Theory, Modi opted for all or nothing strategy in the election. In contrast, the other political parties had been looking for post-election numbers and coalition arithmetic to stop Modi. They were banking on Modi succeeding in just about 200 seats and falling short of majority. Then it would have been their negotiation skills to keep Modi out of the national government. The electoral preference of the nation was just against such a scenario. Modi's strong campaign therefore found more takers than the feeble attempt of his adversaries to stop him. That emotions guide behaviour, including voting behaviour was a point missed by Modi's competing leaders.[7]

Emotion also turns violent. Often this results in riots. When emotions are strong, even a small spark can ignite a large fire. This is what happened in Muzaffarnagar of UP in August 2013. The district has substantial Muslim population (nearly 40 per cent) and also Hindu Jat community. With the increasing political clout of Muslims in UP after the 2012 election that saw Mulayam Singh Yadav's SP win a massive mandate , Hindus felt marginalized. There is hardly a unanimity regarding what caused this massive riot immediately before the 2014 national election. Two versions seem to have gained currency: on the one hand, it is believed that a mere traffic accident involving some youths triggered the Muzaffarnagar riot; the other version highlights, on the other hand, that an alleged harassment of a girl from the Hindu Jat community by a Muslim youth in Kawal village spiralled into communal skirmishes. Since eve-teasing has been a major issue in the state, the second version is usually referred to while tracing the roots of such a communal flagrance. Even Muzaffarnagar had its share of such incidents. Apparently on such issues, there were clashes between the youths of the two communities which flared into a full scale riot. The Jat community had turned into a warrior class during the rule of the lesser Mughals and are known for arising strongly as a community. In August 2013, Hindu Jats took the law in their hands since the administration, they felt, had been soft on Muslims. Once the riot broke out police could do little. Muslims had to leave their villages and live in relief camps. It was the worst riot in UP in 20 years. However, the situation was controlled in less than a month. But since the incident happened just about 100 kilometres away from the capital city of New Delhi and that too less than a year before the national election, the riot ruled the news space much after the same had stopped. The detractors of Modi alleged that if he became the PM candidate such riots would become the order of the day. The hardcore Hindutva supporters felt that they needed Modi to have an 'unbiased' administration. Both Congress and SP made tactical mistakes by blaming BJP for the riot. The Chief Minister of UP, Akhilesh Yadav in a TV interview even named Modi's aide Amit Shah as perpetrator for the incident. The opponents of BJP helped polarizing the people along communal lines even before the campaign for 2014 election started. The Modi campaign benefitted from such myopic strategies of its opponents in no small way. BJP did not take part in openly debating their favourite issue that of attack on Hindus but through small gestures made it amply clear where was its sympathy. In Modi rallies, the riot-accused leaders were facilitated. Sanjeev Balyan and Hukum Singh who took part in Jat mahapanchayat gathering before the riot got elected on BJP ticket. Balyan is now the Minister of State in Narendra Modi cabinet.

The question is whether BJP engineered the Muzaffarnagar riot as a part of its electoral strategy. No doubt BJP gained with the polarization of votes. In fact, Balyan won Muzaffarnagar with over 400,000 votes. But closer look at the events suggests that the responsibility lay more on the laid back administration that did not contain the incident in time than any political machination. The SP and Congress fomented the Jat disenchantment with the ruling parties in UP and New Delhi. Modi knew he was a Hindu leader. He did not need any riot to polarize Hindu votes in his favour. But since the riot took place, his campaign made intelligent use of the same in the pockets where it mattered. In 2014, state assembly election in the Jat-dominated neighbouring Haryana BJP formed its government for the first time as an after-effect that lasted for more than a year. Political campaign must be well planned and should not be impetuous based on some rigid ideas of yesteryear. Muzaffarnagar riot is a lesson to all non-BJP political parties.

As argued, opinions vary on what led to the Muzaffarnagar riot: for some, it was a manufactured design to endorse an ideology-driven campaign that Modi had launched.[8] An outcome of 'love jihad', the riot affected the election campaign by creating a solid Hindu vote bank in BJP's favour; the other argument, equally plausible, draws on the idea that the riot erupted due to communal hatred over the years which confirms that communal riot does not take place all of a sudden, but builds up in course of time. It may have been true that the Muzaffarnagar riot consolidated the Hindu votes in the 2014 election; but that, by itself, does not explain the landslide victory of the BJP in which the opposition parties were completely decimated. This was a rare achievement by all counts. While explaining the poll verdict, one thus has to factor in the prevalent politico-ideological conext in UP following the assumption of power by the SP in 2012. The appeal of the BJP and its leader, Modi seemed to have been far more effective in comparison with that of other contending parties. It was certainly an ideological failure on the part of non-BJP candidates to halt the BJP which hardly had any impact in the 2009 Lok Sabha poll. The context seemed to have been favourably disposed towards the BJP because of the failure of the incumbent government to defuse communal tensions that had its root in the Muzaffarnagar riot. The riot was a testimony to the declining law and order in the state which was manifest when it broke out. So, the argument that the riot was a manufactured design seems to be overstretched simply because it does not take into account the historical processes that finally contribute to a riot which is always a flash point. The criticality of the Muzaffarnagar riot in garnering votes for the BJP thus seems to be misplaced.

In the light of the previous discussion, it can fairly be argued that the 2013 communal did not seem to be as critical as is usually made out. How does one thus explain the remarkable BJP victory in UP? The available field research provides an answer to this query. It is evident that the success of Modi is attributed to the role that the RSS had played in mobilizing support for the BJP. Not only did the RSS monitor the campaign in the province, the acitivists also went to the remote villages to inculcate support for the party in the election. As per newspaper reports, nearly 100,000 RSS group leaders and 600,000 swayamsevaks from 42,000 units were reported to have participated in the election campaign. A control room was set up in Varanasi to supervise the activities of these swayamsevaks; Amit Shah, a top-ranking BJP leader who later became the party president after the 2014 election and Anil Bansal, another top-level RSS leader were in charge of the entire machinery for election campaign.

There were innovative designs that the BJP campaign team deployed:[9] one of the methods adopted by the RSS was to visit remote villages in a carriage called *Namo Rath*, for the purpose of spreading what Modi did in Gujarat for the development of the people at large. By promoting Modi with loud advertisement jingles, these carriages, nearly 400 of them, as per reports, were most effective in reaching out to the masses with a specific message. One of the reasons for its success was certainly the involvement of the RSS activists who, given their familiarity with the areas and acquaintance with the people, built, rather easily in comparison with other contending parties, a support base for Modi and his politics. The second device which also helped sustain the momentum of the campaign was 'the feedback mechanism'. The RSS activists were instructed to draw the feedback from those who listened to Modi speeches and what they received was sent to the Varanasi-based and Amit Shah-led team. These were very useful inputs to devise new strategies. Besides articulating issues which were locally relevant, these inputs were also critical in rearticulating newer issues which might not have received adequate attention earlier. It has, thus, been forcefully argued that through these inputs from shakhas:

> Narendra Modi's image is recreated and disseminated. Alongside, insights are gathered for Modi's future speeches and the mobilizational strategies of the BJP are then chalked out. In the context of the 2014 elections, Modi's speeches are considered most influential and effective mobilizational tool of BJP, which is why so much importance is being given to organizing his rallies and then gauging the impact of his speeches.[10]

By linking the local issues with the national agenda of the BJP, this strategy seemed to have paid massive dividends to the party in terms of parliamentary seats, as the election results show. The third effective method that the BJP had adopted happened to be booth management. By forming booth management committee with a minimum of 20 shakha members across villages and small towns, the RSS devised another effective strategy which also paid off in the election. These RSS-led booth committees supplemented the already-established BJP booth committee. What was unique in regard to the former was to select members for these committees preferably from within the communities in the areas; as a result, it was always the case that if an area was dominated by a specific community, the members should invariably be from that community in so far it was possible. To mobilize women voters, the RSS always selected women activists to persuade them. It was also the responsibility of the booth committee members to make sure that the voters in their area of operation vote in the respective boots on the election days. Although the tasks of the committee members were demarcated, their activities were always assessed by the centralized team, led by Shah and Bansal. Not only were they constantly monitored, they were stripped of their responsibility if they failed to deliver. As reports suggest, a team comprising highly skilled professionals was given the responsibility of assessing the activities of the local teams in districts, small towns and also villages. Known as Citizens for Accountable Governance (CAG), this team also engaged in political mobilization by participating in Chai pe Charcha (conversation over a cup of tea) wherever it was possible.[11] This also acted favourably for Modi by building an opinion in his favour.

The 2013 Muzaffarnagar riot may have created an atmosphere of uncertainty; but it cannot be said to have tilted the verdict in BJP's favour given the well-organized election machinery that formulated and also implemented an effective election strategy in support of Modi's development through governance agenda. The riot may thus appear to be incidental simply because the 2014 election took place after the Muzaffarnagar communal outbreak. Whether this was responsible for the BJP avalanche in UP cannot be said to be fact-based, as the preceding -discussion demonstrates. It would, therefore, not be misleading to suggest that the stupendous BJP success in the 2014 national election in India can, without qualms, be attributed to the hard work of 'the various arms of the Sangh Parivar, the RSS itself, the BJP cadre and a team of technically-equipped workers, the blue brigade'.[12] The 2014 poll verdict was, in other words, an outcome of long-drawn processes which were rooted in UP's socio-economic milieu and the BJP's election campaign team reaped the benefit by both projecting a relatively strong leader and employing effective poll strategies which were executed by committed activists.

10

The Role of Social Media in Political Mobilization

'Narendra Modi to be India's first social media prime minister' concluded the *Financial Times*. The newspaper cited tweet of Narendra Modi, 'India has won! Good days are coming' which became the most retweeted post in Indian history—'more than 70,000 and counting'—as a confirmation of victory of social media campaign over conventional election campaign in India. Euphoric indeed but rather blown out of proportion though this observation was, one cannot wink at the fact that Modi campaign had used technology carefully to overcome its handicap with the mainstream media. Although the BJP did not seem to have received a favourable media coverage, the amount of money that the party had spent on the media campaign was staggeringly high. A newspaper report thus claimed that the BJP's campaign cost might have been around 5,000 crore; it further stated that for its campaign, the BJP had booked 15,000 hoardings across India for three months; spent crores of money to get prominent ad-slots across national, regional and vernacular newspapers for 40 days, and bought about 2,000 spots a day in television channels.[1] The 2014 election campaign represented a paradigm shift because along with the traditional method of electioneering in which face-to-face contact was always preferred, the media campaign, especially through newspapers and television channels, had also played a critical role in political mobilization. In the formation of opinions, either in favour or against a party, what media presented had a direct bearing and it was evident that the major political parties fighting the election had spent a considerable amount in media campaign. A 2014 survey on the impact of media on election campaign thus argues that given the 'increasing live coverage of political rallies and presidential-style campaigning, the growing link between political interests and owners of media houses and agenda-setting political debates, Indian politics is likely to become more 'mediatized' and the electoral process more 'Americanized' in coming years'.[2] As the outcome of the 16th Lok Sabha poll confirms, the media campaign supported the BJP to a significant extent: by couching the campaign around issues of market-driven economic reforms, especially in the print and visual media, the BJP ideologues crafted perhaps the most effective mode of campaigning in the 2014 election. The Congress too resorted to vigorous media campaign; but, because of the all-pervasive anti-Congress wave, the media blitzkrieg did not seem to pay-off to the extent it was expected by the party activists. For the BJP ascendancy, it can now be argued, the media campaign yielded positive results presumably because of the prevalent sociopolitical context that was heavily tilted in its favour at the cost of its bête noire, the Congress and its alliance partners.

The constant barrage of criticism in the mainstream media of Narendra Modi holding him responsible for the 2002 Gujarat riot continued even after the convincing election victory. Much before the campaign had started, the team Modi knew well how every issue would be distorted and dished out to the people. They needed a safeguard since the mainstream print and visual media did not seem to be favourable, if not entirely opposed, to the BJP and the NDA partners. Social media came handy. But to assume that it was only social media that turned the tide against Modi will be wrong. The team used conventional wisdom, mostly lacking when someone comes from a secluded elitist background like the Congress family members did.

When Modi gave any interview, his team recorded the same in detail so that if the words are distorted to mean something not intended to, they could help correcting the mistake, deliberate in most of the cases. During the last phase of the election campaign, the national broadcaster DD interviewed Narendra Modi. The official media held on to the interview ostensibly to balance the same with an interview of Rahul Gandhi, the Congress Vice President. Under public pressure and when questioned by the chief of the holding body of DD, the Prashar Bharati, the same was telecast but it had two important points missing. One was Modi's comment on Ahmed Patel, a fellow politician from Gujarat who was the powerful political secretary of the Congress President Sonia Gandhi. Modi said that he had political rivalry but personal good rapport with Ahmed Patel—an innocuous feel good statement. The other was on Priyanka Gandhi who was aggressively calling names to Modi in the family boroughs of Amethi and Rae Bareilly in the state of UP. Here too, Modi refused to make any harsh comment and condoned Priyanka's hostility as that from a daughter and sister—another feel good statement. Since both these statements portrayed Modi as a warm human being but not a monster that was the theme in the mainstream media, the national channel perhaps in its own wisdom decided to delete those. But Modi's team uploaded the entire interview on YouTube, which received more publicity in urban India and especially among the young voters in India than the DD telecast. Another lie was nailed with the intelligent use of conventional and social media.

Modi had an advantage. He used the campaign tools quietly in the state assembly elections of Gujarat. Post-election results, Vinit Goenka who was national co-convenor of BJP's Information Technology (IT) cell shared this information. He said that contrary to popular belief, the IT cell had been functioning since April 2006 and gained momentum in 2008, when it was also used in Maharashtra. In election 2014, Narendra Modi put a lot of thrust to it. In his inimitable way, he said that BJP should focus on 'nine I's—issues, ideology, inter-personal communication, Internet, intensity, introspection, industry, integration with the party and ideating'. For the first time, IT was used widely in election campaign in India. In fact since Senator Obama used the social media in his debut campaign for 2008 and took it to another level in 2012 with thrust on Twitter, nobody did put social media to such an intense use as Modi campaign did. BJP's IT Cell used concepts like bloggers' meet, video conferencing with voters across cities and interactive call centres for voter registration. They also conducted two round-table sessions before the campaign started to expose the party leadership about the kind of challenges that were faced by the industry. Social media became both a listening and a broadcasting tool.

BJP's IT cell reached out to as many as 144 million people across India, most of them young, touching virtually every Internet user in the country. Success has many fathers. In Modi's successful use of social media saw the two prominent ones Twitter and Facebook exulting. Twitter started planning to replicate parts of its India election strategy across countries that go to polls in 2014. The company was happy that it emerged as a key tool for politicians and media companies during the world's largest democratic exercise. Facebook having more number of active users was quick to claim that 29 million people in India conducted 227 million interactions regarding the elections on Facebook. In addition, 13 million people engaged in 75 million interactions regarding Modi. Twitter claimed that it worked closely with politicians 'including the victor Narendra Modi who used the platform for election campaigning'. There were many late entrants to Twitter, a prominent one being Lalu Prasad Yadav, the Bihar politician. But his rival (who turned friend after Modi win in 2014) former Chief Minister of Bihar, Nitish Kumar opted to remain a dinosaur in the IT age. He stuck to his derisive comments on Modi's use of Twitter. Another surprising absentee from the social media platforms had been Rahul Gandhi. Perhaps their reticence and conceit for average Indians led them to believe that they were like Lord Brahma of Indian politics—beyond word and thought like the creator in Hinduism.

Social media is one tool for reaching out to people. It is wider than the mainstream media and effectively a check on the sponsored reports. Madhu Kishwar, a senior fellow at the Centre for the Study of Developing Societies (CSDS) and Director Indic Studies Project at CSDS who had researched on the Gujarat riot and the post-riot campaign had used YouTube to expose the machinations of the likes of Teesta Setalvad. Kishwar had videographed her interviews and posted certain selected parts on YouTube. Later during the election campaign, she had published her findings in a book *Modi, Muslims and Media*.[3] One English news channel had telecast a few parts of her video records. Kishwar is an independent researcher who did not accept any grant from BJP or Narendra Modi. She used both the traditional form of message dissemination articles and books with YouTube to back up her findings. Her aggressive exposure led to total silence of Modi baiters in Gujarat and outside.

Congress for some unknown reason did not use social media at all. One of its articulate ministers Shashi Tharoor was active on Twitter. But he was embarrassed on a tweet of his. It was when he said that he was travelling the cattle class referring to the economy class of India's domestic flights. Journalist Kanchan Gupta noticed it and the barrage of campaign embarrassed both Tharoor and his party. It coincided with the party's discussion on using Twitter actively and the party decided to junk the idea. It did not occur to Congress leaders that when the message is wrong, one cannot blame the tool. Tharoor was inadvertent in his comment and paid the price.

Modi campaign embraced the technology ahead of rivals, collaborating with thousands of volunteers to spread the leader's message and counter criticism on the Web. Not all of them were active party cadres. There were many who were critics of Congress leader Rahul Gandhi and turned Modi supporter since their ideas converged. On social media, both Twitter and Facebook, Rahul Gandhi emerged as a constant source of punching. His air of superiority made matters worse. The social media space was fertile for any Congress critic. Modi campaign reaped the dividend.

About two-thirds of India's population are under 35. The country has the world's third largest Internet user base of 239 million and more than 900 million mobile connections. Many access the Web on their phones. Mainstream media used Twitter enlarging its reach beyond the estimated 35 million India users. Nearly 400 multilingual news channels closely tracked politicians on the website and this reached 153 million households. Modi had the first-mover advantage in using these technology tools to reach out to India's huge youth demographic. Rival Congress had ceded the space completely to Modi campaign. Few Congress supporters and activists who were on the social media faced barrage of criticisms from Modi campaign volunteers and also independent Modi supporters.

Modi's early start on social media helped the campaign to gather a large fan following. When December 2013 assembly elections were concluded, he already had eight million fans on Facebook. On 6 March, when elections were announced, Modi had already crossed 11 million fans. By 12 May, he had 14 million fans—the second most 'liked' politician on Facebook after Obama. On Twitter, Modi's handle @narendramodi has 4.3 million followers, global rank a lowly 314—US President Barack Obama ranks third in the world with 43 million followers. But considering the fact that Indians find the microblogging site Twitter a tough one due to restriction of 140 characters and their inability to do so, Modi campaign must be rated as a highly successful one.

Twitter emerged as a combat zone for rival political parties. While Congress was mostly absent to take up the opposition space came a fledgling political party AAP of activist Arvind Kejriwal. Often their exchanges were entertaining. During the election campaign, Kejriwal developed the habit of getting thrashed or slapped by somebody or the other. These made good media visuals for AAP to remain in news. When a rickshaw driver slapped Kejriwal, within minutes he had tweeted to imply there was a conspiracy against him. On social media, there was—a hashtag, #SlappedAgain, and was used by users who made fun of Kejriwal. It was started by an ordinary non-political user from Andhra Pradesh to make fun of Kejriwal. AAP hit back with a hashtag #IStandWithArvind. There had been several such incidences, which turned the elections an entertainment on social media. Mainstream media found story ideas out of such Facebook or Twitter wars. In the process, the organized social media campaign of Modi received more and more attention. Twitter India reported that since 1 January, there had been around 58 million election-related tweets; of these, 11.85 million had been directly addressed to Narendra Modi's verified account. While it is not possible to estimate how much of the social media conversation got translated into vote for Modi, but the incontrovertible fact remains that the team could disseminate the key message of the election campaign theme effectively through social media. Thus, the Modi campaign overcame the perceived weakness of a hostile mainstream media.

How did the team Modi come into being? Narendra Modi picked up two of the country's sharpest minds to spearhead his election campaign on the Web, ahead of the national elections in 2014. Rajesh Jain, an entrepreneur who helped revolutionize the Internet use in India with his India World Web portal—a collection of India-centric websites, comprising news, sports, entertainment and education—ran Modi's political campaign alongside technology entrepreneur B.G. Mahesh. Mahesh was the founder of Greynium Information Technologies Pvt. Ltd., which owns OneIndia, one of India's first regional language news portals. They put together a team of 100 techies to drive the Modi campaign across social media platforms like Twitter and Facebook. This was formalized when BJP appointed Modi as its head of election campaign for 2014.

Jain was a supporter of Narendra Modi. In his blog Emergic, he wrote in 2011 how BJP should conduct the campaign.

> For the BJP to form a government at the Centre, it needs to focus on winning not just 175 but 275 seats (or 225 + 45 with the three current NDA allies). Winning 275 needs a dramatically different strategy from trying to win 175. To get to 275 seats out of 350-odd seats, the BJP needs to ensure a 'wave' election with a 75% hit rate.[4]

Jain predicted rightly that if BJP focused on forming coalition and contest based on its relative strength in various states, the party would have won around 175 seats. In that case, Congress with 150 seats would form the government. Jain, therefore, wrote in favour of creating what he called a 'wave' election. India had seen a major wave election in 1984 after the assassination of Indira Gandhi. In fact the election in 1971, too, was a wave election in favour of Mrs Gandhi and her slogan 'garibi hatao'. What was unique in 2014 was that both the ruling Congress and the opposition BJP had been suffering from negative feelings. For Congress, there were two strong negatives—the charges of a number of huge scams and complete failure of governance. For BJP, the party leaders' failure to play the role of constructive opposition was a critical weakness. This, we have noted earlier, allowed space to Arvind Kejriwal and his AAP to come to the fore. The other negative was the presence of Narendra Modi who had been at the receiving end of perhaps the shrillest campaign against a political personality in India for the longest period. Luckily for BJP, the disadvantages of having Modi as its leader was its biggest advantage as well since his very presence galvanized the supporters and nudged the non-committed voters to reassess him. Jain and his team sensed this latent strength of Modi and used the same in their social media campaign.

Realizing inacceptability of Narendra Modi among various regional political parties Jain wrote, 'Switch focus from maximizing allies to maximizing seats for 2014. All strategy needs to be focused on this.' And Jain thought of how to create a wave election in 2011 itself:

> I think various factors are coming together to create the foundation of a possible wave election in 2014. For one, look at the 90% hit rates that have happened in places in Bihar, West Bengal and Tamil Nadu. The same concerns and issues have resonated across a state. I believe that something similar can happen nationally in 2014.

The Modi campaign was lucky that it could have a bright mind like Jain's on its side. Jain too was equally lucky to have a perceptive political person like Narendra Modi to back up, what many would have thought an audacious suggestion.

Jain and Mahesh were said to be behind the Modi promotion sites Niti Central and India 272. Niti is an acronym for New Initiatives to Transform India. Niti brought journalist Kanchan Gupta from *Pioneer* to lead as editorial director. Kanchan was popular on Twitter. He was the tormentor of Shashi Tharoor was and cited as the reason why Congress stayed away from social media. Kanchan had prior experience of working in BJP party organs as well as in the office of Prime Minister Vajpayee. Niti Central broadcasted Modi's public appearances real time on its website. India 272 enlisted volunteers from the 150 million new voters in the 18–22 age group in the 'Vote for NaMo crusade'.

Apart from Jain and Mahesh, there was another non-political persona behind Modi's campaign. He was said to have ideated the 'Chai pe Charcha' campaign—Modi's encounters with people over a cup of tea. Prashant Kishor, reportedly shy and skinny man, headed a group called the CAG. It was a platform for youths to engage with the political and administrative establishment to usher in an era of greater accountability and better governance, euphemism for supporting Modi. Kishor in his mid-thirties had been associated with Modi for over two years. Many of Kishor's team members either left marquee jobs or are on a sabbatical who, it was reported, worked pro bono.

The other prominent face in the Modi social media campaign was Arvind Gupta. The head of BJP's IT cell was a product of IIT–Banaras Hindu University and the University of Illinois. Gupta sold his software firm in 2009 and started working for the BJP. His responsibilities included looking after the party websites, uploading videos of rallies and meetings, sending them to media houses, posting comments and releases and also rebutting BJP opponents on the Net.

Gupta, Jain, Mahesh and their colleagues brought in out-of-the box thought process. But only lateral thinking is not enough. What one requires is execution adapting the thoughts to suit the specific local conditions. In India, politics is different in character from one geography to another. Modi style of political campaign had its usual dose of detractors. One of them was K.N. Govindacharya, a former BJP leader who fell out with Atal Bihari Vajpayee. Govindacharya told media:

> Modi's campaign has not touched the lower social strata and the non-Hindi speaking states. It has only swayed people in the urban and semi-urban areas, including those from the upwardly mobile backward caste communities who have, over the years, aligned themselves with the upper castes and classes.

Govindacharya was not alone though others preferred to maintain silence. On hindsight, it seems even Narendra Modi knew that these outsiders were educated, committed and technically qualified but had little connect with the Bharat that was his target. To bridge the gap, there were at least two formidable political personalities—Amit Shah and on top of all Narendra Modi himself. Without these two brains, the Modi campaign would have remained a point for debate and discussion certainly not the focus for accolades for the stunning election result.

Before he was singled out to supervise BJP campaign in UP, Amit Shah was known more for the wrong reasons—as Modi's hatchet man. With this choice, Modi sent the message that Shah is the most important person for the campaign. Few knew that Shah was born in Chicago into a business family and is thus a US citizen by birth. He, like many other Gujaratis, worked as a stockbroker. He had served the RSS and was a member of the Akhil Bharatiya Vidyarthi Parishad (ABVP), in Ahmedabad. When RSS spotted Shah's talent for crafting political strategies and managing elections, the Sangh engaged him to work as BJP leader Advani's constituency manager in Gandhinagar. It was Shah who delivered victory after victory for Advani. It was a natural transition for Shah to assume a bigger role in the party when Narendra Modi assumed the charge of the Chief Minister of Gujarat. Modi drafted Shah as his principal political aide. He emerged as Modi's man for all issues, which saw him being sent to UP.

Amit Shah did justice to the faith reposed in him. The largest state of India delivered 73 members to the BJP-led NDA. Barring the family members of Mulayam Singh Yadav and the mother–son duo of Congress not a single candidate from outside NDA won in the state. For the first time in the history of independent India, the state did not elect a single MP from the minority Muslim community. The election result proved beyond any shade of doubt that the politics of appeasement did not work. If one looks for a single factor that swayed the election 2014, the campaign in UP must be singled out. The architect of this campaign had been Amit Shah.

Shah had his team in Lucknow, Varanasi and New Delhi. It was a dedicated team of youngsters who were on sabbatical to work for the Modi campaign, somewhat like the US presidential election style. Their task was to provide information on real time so that Modi could respond to whatever his opponents had been saying. Their tasks had been data mining, research, social media, polls and campaign management. Not that they had always been correct as Modi's faux pas on historical anecdotes—in Patna rally he was confused on the dynasty of the Maurya emperor Chandrgupta, location of Taxila and even mixing Syama Prasad Mukherjee with Syamji Krishna Varma in another speech. Given

Narendra Modi's superb memory and oratorical skill, it is reasonable to conclude that there had been some slip-ups in the brief provided. Also campaign inputs were not well researched for all geographies, West Bengal is a case in point. The socio-economic weaknesses of the state did not find much mention in the campaign speeches of Modi. The other weakness of the Modi campaign was that the general theme of campaign speeches for all candidates should have been circulated so as to have uniformity in campaign message. In the absence of such strict dos and don'ts, there had been controversies. For example, Giriraj Singh MP from Nawada in Bihar made communal insinuations when he asked Modi-baiters to move to Pakistan or questioned why all terrorists came from one particular community. Narendra Modi avoided any such issues even under intense provocations. The Modi campaign team failed to broad base its reach.

CAG had been the principal background force in the Modi campaign. On paper, CAG was not attached to or funded by BJP. In fact, members were not allowed to join the party while they were working at CAG though in effect, the nonprofit functioned as a full-fledged consulting and campaign solutions outfit for Modi. It was working out of a central office in Gandhinagar, with staff in eight other offices around the country. In Delhi, they were located away from the party office separated from the regular visitors. It is reported that CAG had between 200 and 400 full-time, paid members, apart from some 800 paid interns and more than 100,000 volunteers.

CAG remained elusive during the entire election campaign. Thus, Modi could avoid the usual problems of a political campaign—leaks, sabotage infighting, defections and so on. By getting a professional team to plan and execute big chunks of his campaign, Modi ring-fenced his campaign from detractors from within BJP and elsewhere. Professionals were entrusted with tasks and nothing was left to good faith. Not much information on CAG is available on public domain since the participants had been tight lipped, but it is rumoured that those who did not meet the high standards expected from a professional were even let go. In Delhi, the team reporting to Amit Shah had even hired a PR outfit to support in media outreach. The agency was expected to provide inputs for tweeting in the newly created account of Amit Shah. Unlike any other political campaign, here the engagement was clean with clear roles entrusted and payment made to the agency on time.

What were the activities undertaken by CAG. The group analyzed the past election data, produced detailed report on each of the 450-odd seats in which the BJP contested. They conducted regular opinion polls to gauge swings. During the Modi rallies, the members collected data and sent to their headquarters for further analysis. Probably, Modi's late attention to West Bengal and Amethi had been the result of certain positive swings seen in these surveys. CAG reports were used at grass-roots level to streamline the campaign. The organization was credited for certain unique and successful campaign strategies like 'Chai pe Charcha' and use of 3D rallies. These rallies were immensely popular in remote areas as were the Modi campaign vehicles touring the interiors. Particularly successful had been its campaign in UP, the *Modi Aane Wala Hai* (Modi's arrival is imminent) campaign. Some 400 video vans took Modi's speeches to thousands of villages that are deemed to be part of a so-called dark zone, where the mass-media penetration is poor.

BJP's advertisements were well planned, ensuring the delivery of the key message. The party used two of India's celebrated admen Piyush Pandey and Prasoon Joshi. Unlike CAG, this was supervised by BJP teasurer Piyush Goyal and Ajay Singh, a former advisor of late Pramod Mahajan. They brought in Soho Square to create the TV, print and radio campaign, roped in Prasoon Joshi to write the party's anthem and rolled it into a music video. They also appointed a Delhi-based advertising professional, Sushil Goswami, to create a second set of radio ads and hired three Pune-based graphic designers to create cricket ads around Twenty20 World Cup. Three campaign slogans stood out ; 'Abki Baar, Modi Sarkaar', 'Janata Maaf Nahi Karegi', and 'Achche din anewale hain'. While the first was taken from BJP's campaign to launch Vajpayee—'Ab ke bari, Atal Bihari', the other two were created to attack the stagnating political atmosphere placing the same against the achievements in Gujarat. A variation of the 'achche din' was 'Modiji Aa Rahein Hain'. The advertisements delivered the key messages clearly and touched on issues like corruption, inflation, unemployment and leadership. Since the solution to the ailments, according to the campaign, depended on the leadership and since this wanted to shun the failed collective leadership model of the Manmohan Singh government, there was no option of using anybody other than Modi in all campaigns. While Congress and other critics cried hoarse over such projection of an individual, the election result has proved beyond any shade of doubt that the people of the country had been longing to elect a strong leader. The Modi campaign had sensed it well. In fact the only advantage the campaign had was the personality of Narendra Modi, his strong leadership, oratorical skill, clean image, the humble background and the track record in Gujarat. The campaign took a huge chance by its complete focus on one person. In the end, the gamble paid off. Narendra Modi emerged successfully as the 'saugandh is mitti ki' (in the name of the motherland).

11

The Unique 2014 National Poll in India

The 2014 election campaign stands out because of two reasons: on the one hand, the poll campaign was drawn heavily, if not exclusively, on one individual, the Prime Minister designate, Narendra Modi who appeared to have cemented an intimate bond with the voters across the country; the poll verdict was, on the other hand, equally startling since after almost one and a half decade, it was possible for the BJP to secure an absolute majority in the parliament. The BJP fought the election, it is true, as a leading constituent of the NDA which largely became a label given the failure of other partners to win the Lok Sabha seats as per their expectations. In the light of the nature of poll campaign and also the outcome, the 2014 national election in India seems to have set a precedent; it was not an accident of history, but an offshoot of processes that were intimately linked with, among others, the failure of the government, led by the UPA to defuse crises in governance, if not misgovernance.

The nine-phase long 2014 parliamentary poll—from 7 April to 12 May—was the second longest in India's democratic history after the 1951–52 first Lok Sabha poll that continued for five months. This was an extraordinary election otherwise. With a vote share of 31 per cent—or nearly every third vote cast in the country—the BJP obtained an absolute majority by winning 282 of 543 seats in the lower house of Indian parliament. The Congress share had dwindled from 24 per cent in 2009 to 19.3 per cent in the 2014 Lok Sabha poll. Except the right wing BJP, none of the contending parties had succeeded in retaining its earlier tally. The loss of the Congress was most revealing: while in the 2009 Lok Sabha poll, it had won 206 seats which were reduced to only 44 in the 16th national election, the share of its popular votes had also declined; for the BJP, not only did the 2014 poll outcome register a massive increase of its tally in the lower house of Indian parliament, but the share of votes had also enhanced from 18.8 per cent in 2009 to almost 32 per cent of popular votes.

The 16th Lok Sabha poll, held in 2014, put the BJP onto the centre stage of Indian politics. The NDA won a sweeping victory with 336 seats in the parliament. Its leading constituent, the BJP, won 31 per cent of all votes and 282 (51.9 per cent) of all seats, while the NDA's combined vote share was 38.5 per cent. It is for the first time since 1984 general election that a party has secured enough parliamentary seats to form a government without the support of other parties. The Congress-led UPA won 58 seats, of which the Congress had 44 (8.1 per cent) Lok Sabha seats with a share of 19.3 per cent of total votes. It was the Congress party's worst defeat in a general election since India was introduced to Westminster-type parliamentary democracy; it was also for the first time that the BJP and its electoral/governmental partners had an opportunity to obtain an absolute majority in parliament. By focussing on the NDA poll victory, the chapter reiterates the argument that an effective election campaign, led by Modi along with the BJP's frontal organizations and also the Sangh Parivar, resulted in an unprecedented victory that the BJP did not witness since its arrival on the political scene in 1980.

Held in 2014, the 16th parliamentary poll in India is a watershed in her recent political history for at least three significant reasons: first, breaking the trend of the last few decades in which no party was able to muster a majority in parliament, the BJP with 282 of a total of 543 seats in the lower house shall no longer be dependent on the whims of her partners for survival. With the BJP winning a majority on its own, a remarkable shift is visible in the texture of India's parliamentary politics. The wave for the star campaigner, the erstwhile Chief Minister of Gujarat, Narendra Modi, that has caught the imagination of the large section of the voters has given the BJP-led NDA an unprecedented victory with 336 seats in the Lok Sabha. Not only has the principal partner of the NDA, the BJP increased its tally in the 16th Lok Sabha poll, but it has also significantly enhanced its vote share from that in the 2009 parliamentary poll. Second, the voter turnout was also unprecedented: in comparison with the all-time record of 64 per cent turnout in 1984 election that took place in the aftermath of the assassination of Indira Gandhi, the 2014 election witnessed an increase of more than 2 per cent in the total number of voters who exercised their franchise. This is indicative of voters' confidence in democracy as a powerful mechanism for change even in adverse political circumstances. The BJP's landslide victory was also illustrative of a mass desire for effective governance in the light of the failure of the erstwhile Congress-led coalition government to meaningfully address the policy paralysis and a series of financial scandals which not only exposed its weaknesses against vested interests, but also gave credibility to the allegation of the government complicity with those involved in corruption. Third and the last, the 2014 national poll stands out since the parliamentary Left registered an ignominious defeat even in both West Bengal and Kerala which remained the left citadels in recent past. The defeat of the left is attributed to the disenchantment of local voters with the left in these two Indian provinces where the parliamentary communists ruled for an extended period of time. In West Bengal, the left seems to have become irrelevant as it has succeeded in winning only two of a total of 42 Lok Sabha seats in comparison with its tally of 16 seats in the last Lok Sabha; by winning eight of a total of 20 seats in Kerala, the parliamentary left has not only enhanced its share of the Lok Sabha seats from four in 2009, but also sustained its vote share in the midst of a national wave for the BJP.

What is most striking is the fact that the rise of the right-wing BJP is proportionally linked with the decline of the left in India's parliamentary history. The writing on the wall is very clear: the left decline that had begun in 2009 Lok Sabha poll is confirmed. In Kerala, the CPI (M) of the Left Democratic Front had won in five constituencies with only 21.6 per cent of total votes; despite having 22.3 per cent of total votes, CPI (M) in West Bengal registered victory only in two constituencies. One of the factors for this debacle is certainly the shifting of the minority, especially the Muslim votes. Modi's anti-Muslim rhetoric pushed the minorities, especially the Muslims, to the Congress-led United Democratic Front in Kerala, while his virulent campaign against the Muslim infiltrators from Bangladesh in West Bengal drew them to the AITC. This is a significant change in the perception of the minorities who always found the left as their natural saviour in their day-to-day struggle for survival.

So, the parliamentary Left has become virtually irrelevant in the election to the 16th Lok Sabha, winning only nine seats in comparison with its tally of 24 in the last Lok Sabha. The total vote share of the constituents of the parliamentary left (CPI (M), CPI, Revolutionary Socialist Party (RSP), Forward Bloc) is drastically reduced from 7 per cent in the 2009 parliamentary poll to a mere 4.5 per cent in the 2014 election. The leading partner of the left, CPI (M) suffered the most: its national vote share declined from 5.3 per cent in 2009 to 3.2 per cent in the 2014 poll.[1] The immediate outcome of the poor show of the left resulted in CPI (M) losing its status as a national party, which left only the Congress and ruling BJP as national parties.[2] The left stands decimated and CPI (M), its mainstream face, recorded its worst electoral performance since its formation in 1964. In West Bengal, the state it ruled for more than three decades, it failed to increase its tally beyond two seats—the same number of seats that its counterpart in Tripura had won. The gradual decline of the parliamentary left, as it had happened elsewhere in the globe, confirms that 'the spectre of its political irrelevance is staring at in India as well'.[3] The poor result is the outcome of a combination of factors, including the failure of the leadership to address the genuine socio-economic grievances of the people at the grass-roots; there are indications that its so-called committed cadres have not only been disenchanted with the leadership, they are also reported to have worked for the AITC candidates perhaps exposing the failure of the party leadership to build a solid cadre-driven organization in the state. The left is thus not only faced with an existential crisis, but is also pitted against a new political rival in the state, namely the BJP, that has the potential to occupy the main opposition space because as against the CPI (M)'s vote share of 22.3 per cent, the BJP has 17 per cent of the total popular votes. The scene in Kerala is not very different: like its Bengal counterpart, it is worst hit by the indifference of the cadres who do not seem to be as enthusiastic as in the past. The impact was visible: Despite having won five Lok Sabha seats, the 2014 national poll is also a break from the past because the well-established political trend of alternating between the CPI (M)-led Left Democratic Front and the Congress-centric United Democratic Front was broken this time. The Congress-led front has walked away with lion's share of seats which is explained by reference to 'the minority consolidation in favour of the Congress in the face of the Modi factor'.[4] In view of the open and tacit internecine factional feuds among the leaders in Kerala and West Bengal, the party failed to address the rising resentments among the workers. Due to the constant tussle between the two top leaders of CPI (M), Pinarayi Vijayan and V.S. Achuthanandan, in Kerala, the organization could never put up a strong show against the opposition. Similarly, the continuity of the Stalinistic leadership in West Bengal cost the party heavily in West

Bengal. The leadership is 'captured by a Kolkata-centric clique' which is incapable of understanding 'the pulse of the people at the grassroots'.[5] So, the rivalry at the top and the disconnect between the cadres and the central leadership was responsible for the declining importance of the parliamentary left in those states of India which remained the left bastion not so long ago.

Except the BJP, all other contending parties stood almost decimated in the 2014 Lok Sabha poll. It was undoubtedly a Modi-centric election in which the BJP successfully persuaded voters to vote in its favour. The role of the BJP's subsidiary organizations, and above all, the Sangh Parivar, cannot be undermined; in fact, besides Modi's charismatic appeal to the voters, the organizational backing that Modi had in the election came from them, especially in areas where the Sangh Parivar is known to have a firm organization. It was evident in the poll outcome which is given in Table 11.1.

Table 11.1:
Share of Votes and Seats of Different Parties

Seat Share of Different Parties in the Election	*Vote Share of Different Parties in the Election*
BJP (51.9%)	BJP (31.0%)
INC (8.1%)	INC (19.3%)
BSP (0%)	BSP (4.1%)
AITC (6.2%)	AITC (3.8%)
SP (0.9%)	SP (3.4%)
AIADMK (6.8%)	AIADMK (3.3%)
CPI (M) (1.7%)	CPI (M) (3.3%)
BJD (3.6%)	BJD (1.7%)
Shiv Sena (3.3%)	Shiv Sena (1.9%)
TDP (2.9%)	TDP (1.9%)
TRS (1.9%)	TRS (1.8%)
Others (12.7%)	Others (24.5%)

Source: Prepared from the election data, available from the website of the EC of India (eci. nic.in), accessed on 17 June 2015.
Note: AITC: All India Trinamul Congress, AIADMK: All India Anna Dravida Munnetra Kazhagam, BJD: Biju Janata Dal; TDP: Telegu Desam Party, TRS: Telangana Rashtriya Samati.

The 2014 election has made the BJP a truly national party with significant presence in almost all parts of the country. The victory is also attributed to BJP's success in building a broad social coalition of upper castes with other segments of Indian society. This was a unique achievement for the party which was, so far, identified only with the business communities, located primarily in cities and towns. The 16th poll not only extended its geographic expanse, but also created and consolidated a social base cutting across various socio-economic strata. As the Table 11.2 shows.

Table 11.2:
Outcome of the Sixteenth National Poll

BJP's Performance in the Hindi Heartland	*Consolidation of Social Forces in the Hindi Heartland for the BJP*
Hindi-speaking area: 190 seats (43.7%)	
Rest of India: 92 seats (22.3%)	Upper caste: 65% (31%)
	OBC: 48% (24%)
	SC: 34% (16%)
Note: Figures in the parenthesis show the	ST: 55% (24%)
vote share in percentages.	Muslims: 11% (7%)
	Note: Figures in the parenthesis indicate BJP's vote share in percentages at the all-India level.

Source: Adapted from Pradeep Chhibber and Rahul Verma, 2014 (p. 55).[6]

The above figures confirm that the political party that gained most electorally in the 16th election happened to be the BJP which seemed to have swayed the voters in its favour by projecting itself as a better alternative than the incumbent Congress-led UPA government that ruled India for a decade since 2004. One cannot discount the popularity of Narendra Modi, the BJP's Prime Minister designate, cutting across the social and political cleavages. What was BJP's electoral gain was Congress' loss. While the BJP had consolidated its social base, the Congress Party had failed to even retain what it had in the past. The Congress defeat, thus, meant that voters cutting across social strata turned away from the party and, thus, weakened its base across all social sections. Despite having introduced several pro-people welfare schemes that potentially benefitted a large segment of India's populace, the Congress lost its social base largely because of 'the administrative failures of the Congress-led UPA in the years preceding the 2014 election [to contain] corruption and inefficiency'[7] which almost automatically created a constituency for the BJP-led NDA. The Congress was defeated conclusively: its decline was all-pervasive; the inability of the Congress to sustain its support base even in areas which were its strongholds in the immediate past also reveals the bankruptcy of the organization that never appeared to be adequately equipped to stop the Modi juggernaut in the 2014 election, as Table 11.3 shows.

Table 11.3:
Electoral Performance of the Congress in Different Regions

Regions	Parliamentary Seats	Share of Votes (in percentages)
East	06 (117)	12.3
North-east	08 (25)	29.8
North	06 (151)	17.2
Central	03 (40	35.9
West	02 (78)	23.7
South	19 (132)	18.6
Total	44 (543)	19.3

Source: Adapted from the table in Suhas Palshikar, 2014 (p. 58).[8]
Note: Figures in the parenthesis indicate the total number of parliamentary seats in the region.

The 2014 national election is a clear break with the past. Besides the misgovernance of the erstwhile UPA government in its second term, the BJP-led NDA seems to have swayed the voters in its favour on the basis of electoral pledge of inclusive governance. The BJP strategy of projecting Modi as its prime-ministerial candidate several months before the election provided the party a clear edge over its principal rival which appeared to be directionless and busy putting a brave face despite visible cracks in the organization. While the Congress was on the defensive, the BJP's projection of leadership as 'decisive, effective and experienced' put the party on a stronger platform. It has thus been persuasively argued that

> [w]hen what was ranged against the BJP was seen to be hopelessly want-
> ing in competence and capacity, the party appeared to score points not
> exclusively for what it and its leadership represented, but for what it was
> pitted against. The BJP victory had [thus] much to do with a well-planned
> leadership-driven campaign[9]

which worked miracle in the national poll when its bête noire, the Congress was busy putting the house in order.

The election campaign was undoubtedly leader centric and the poll outcome confirms that the strategy was most effective. The Prime Minister designate, Modi, turned the 2014 Lok Sabha poll into a referendum on himself. He thus emerged as the focal point of electoral campaign across the country. The election thus became, in other words, something of 'a plebiscite on the leader rather than a choice of candidates in constituencies or a new set of political elite'.[10] As a result, the issues, both national and local, did not seem to figure when the voters made up their mind. It was a rare thing to have happened since the 1971 5th Lok Sabha poll when the election was fought on the popularity of Indira Gandhi. The 2014 Lok Sabha poll was, thus, not a battle for ideological issues but for an appropriate leadership that voters were asked to choose on the basis of their appeal to them. Like the American presidential election, the 16th national poll in India can thus be said to have set in motion processes for personality-based election. In 2014, the strategy favoured the BJP-led NDA by infusing new life into the cadres who appeared to have lost the zeal to work for the right-wing conglomeration presumably because of infighting that remained unaddressed; what made the strategy far more effective was also the Congress failure to project a strong leader to counter Modi; the inexperienced Rahul Gandhi was no match for him despite having had the acceptability to the party and also supporters by being born in the Gandhi family. On the whole, as the poll outcome suggests, the 2014 election was primarily a leadership-driven exercise in which the voters appear to have decided, not on the basis of the election pledges of the contending parties, but on the appeal of the leaders that the BJP and Congress had projected.

Like other non-BJP parties, the poor performance of the parliamentary left is also illustrative of the gradual weakening of the organization that has consistently backed the left cause. The 2014 poll outcome also confirms that the left leadership did not seem to bother to address these weaknesses seriously even in the aftermath of the 2009 Lok Sabha poll when the left was trounced as well. Whether the 2014 poll debacle will wake them up cannot be answered now. It is clear, however, that the Indian voters cannot be taken for a ride, and it has again been established beyond doubt that mere ideological inclination of the voters shall not always get translated into votes unless there is an organizational back-up. So, the parliamentary left has become rendered virtually irrelevant in the election to the 16th Lok Sabha winning only nine seats in comparison with its tally of 24 in the last Lok Sabha. The total vote share of the constituents of the parliamentary left (CPI (M), CPI, RSP and Forward Bloc) is drastically reduced from 7 per cent in the 2009 parliamentary poll to a mere 4.5 per cent in the 2014 election. The leading partner of the left, CPI (M) suffered most: its national vote share declined from 5.3 per cent in 2009 to 3.2 per cent in the 2014 poll.[11] The immediate outcome of the poor show of the left resulted in CPI (M) losing its status as a national party which left only the Congress and the ruling BJP as national parties. The parliamentary left perhaps faced the most ignominious defeat ever in its journey as an alternative ideological discourse in democratic India. Despite not being participants in the democratic elections, the left-wing-extremists were reported to have explored the None of the Above (NOTA) option as an effective means to ventilate their grievances. This perhaps shows their willingness to engage with the Indian state that has opened a small window for further dialogues.

The convincing BJP victory in 2014 election was followed by its equally impressive electoral performance in Maharashtra and Haryana state assembly elections, held in 2014. In Jammu and Kashmir, the BJP had won in 25 assembly constituencies (out of a total of 87 seats in the state assembly) with a share of 23 per cent of the total popular votes. This was an impressive show of strength as well though it did not succeed in any of the constituencies in the valley of Kashmir. The success was, however, soon marred because in the Delhi assembly election that followed the assembly elections in Maharashtra, Haryana and Jammu and Kashmir, the nationally successful BJP cut a very sorry figure. Hence, no analysis of 2014 Modi campaign will be complete without looking at the drubbing his party suffered in the assembly election of the National Capital Territory of Delhi in February 2015. The electoral loss was humiliating with BJP managing to win a mere three out of the 70 assembly seats. In terms of vote share, BJP could barely retain its share of 33 per cent (a marginal loss of 0.9 per cent) that it won in the state poll in December 2013, that was before the Modi-wave hit the country. In contrast during the national election, BJP won majority in 60 assembly constituencies of Delhi, winning 46.5 per cent of votes polled. In 2015 assemble election, it was a loss of 14.3 per cent votes in just nine months. So conclusive had been the BJP loss that many concluded it was the end of the Modi magic in election campaign.

What many winked at is that no two elections are similar. Kejriwal and his fledgling political outfit AAP had a strong support base in the national capital Delhi. In December 2013, AAP vote share was 29.5 per cent which increased by 3.5 per cent in the Lok Sabha poll of 2014 despite the Modi wave. AAP had been emerging as an alternative to the two established national political parties, BJP and Congress. In the assembly election 2015, AAP could win almost the entire anti-BJP vote-share—leaving a mere 9.4 per cent to Congress. Modi in an election rally said, 'This election will decide how world perceives India. Delhi is the country's identity and every event that happens in Delhi impacts our image worldwide.'[12] No wonder that after the result, the New York Times wrote, 'Fresh from the diplomatic high of a successful summit meeting with President Obama, Prime Minister Narendra Modi has been brought down to earth by domestic politics.'[13]

Delhi's CSDS in its analysis, however, concluded that the AAP sweep was not exactly an expression of disenchantment with the Prime Minister Modi or his government. As per the CSDS, post poll data for the Delhi elections, two-thirds of the respondents said that they were satisfied with Narendra Modi as Prime Minister. Only 30 per cent of voters said they were dissatisfied with Modi's efforts in office. Even among the poorest voters, there was high level of support for the Prime Minister. Sixty-three per cent of the overall respondents said that they were satisfied with the performance of the central government.[14] Yet nearly 39 per cent who voted for BJP in the Lok Sabha election of 2014 shifted to AAP in the assembly election of 2015. Clearly, politically matured residents of Delhi had been looking for a strong pro-people leader with a clean image to manage Delhi. The factors that made them to vote for Modi in the Lok Sabha poll worked in favour of Kejriwal in 2015. People knew well enough that BJP did not have any strong leader to espouse the cause of Delhi residents and only Kejriwal could stand up to meet their aspirations. It was a mandate in favour of Kejriwal with nobody coming remotely close to challenge him. Modi as Prime Minister could not have competed with Kejriwal. Clearly, BJP agenda of 2014 laid the ground work for Kejriwal's stunning election win.

While people used the same logic and voted in favour of AAP, Kejriwal, too, learnt from his misadventure of 2014 and reorganized his campaign learning from the Modi campaign. Kejriwal knew that media would mock him for his abrupt resignation in 2014 as Chief Minister of Delhi and also for cutting a sorry figure in challenging the Modi campaign in the Lok Sabha election. His campaign, therefore, concentrated on addressing people in their localities through nukkad sabhas (street-corner meetings). What is more, he started when BJP was euphoric from its Lok Sabha victory, Congress was still sulking and media was using AAP as a joke.

Kejriwal started in September. First, he began introspecting what went wrong. He realized people in Delhi who expected him to be different did not like his ambition of quickly attempting a national position betraying their faith in him. It was time for Kejriwal to pick up pieces. He realized that people still had hope in the alternative politics he propounded. At the same time, they had hope in Modi. This is when BJP national leaders were busy planning their electioneering in the larger states like Maharashtra, Haryana, Jharkhand and J&K. The local leaders in Delhi were relaxed and busy infighting. They were hoping that the Modi magic would see them through. For Kejriwal, it was a battle for survival. If he had failed, it would have been the end of Kejriwal as a politician. The stakes were too high for him like it was for Modi in the general election 2014.

Kejriwal reached out to the voters direct, keeping his media exposure to minimum. Pratap Bhanu Mehta wrote in the *Indian Express*:

> Sociologist Daniel Bell once said that the challenge of the modern state was that it was too big for the small problems in life and too small for the big problems in life. It has to articulate an idiom that addresses ordinary problems or ordinary people: petty corruption, electricity, water. The AAP hammered home these themes in a homely way.[15]

What is more, Kejriwal did what most politicians do not do. He admitted his mistakes—the mistake of resigning just after 49 days as the Chief Minister of Delhi in 2014. His candid admission of guilt and promise never to repeat it blunted all criticisms on that count. The second important decision of Kejriwal was never to criticize Modi knowing well that many of his potential supporters still admired Prime Minister Modi. In contrast, politician Modi made the mistake of criticizing Kejriwal for leaving Delhi abruptly and also for his *dharna* (sit in demonstration) in front of central government office in Delhi when he was in power. What Modi winked at was the fact that people had already accepted Kejriwal's apology.

Election campaign is not merely unfurling of cold statistics nor is it mere creation of grand events and winning over people. If Modi campaign drew people out, it was because he touched the heart of ordinary Indians. When in power, he could not have whipped up that passion since Modi is the establishment now. Columnist Swapan Dasgupta assessed it rightly, 'To my mind, the most significant change that has happened in the past 10 months has been the transformation of the Modi image from that of a crusader against a decrepit and venal establishment to the leading light of a new but aloof establishment.'[16]

When AAP volunteers were busy doing what BJP did before the Lok Sabha election 2014, BJP Delhi unit was acting the way its predecessor Congress had been acting. They were complacent thinking that a few Modi rallies would prove decisive in their favour. There was no effort by the party to reach to people, find out their issues and bringing the same before the central government to resolve the same. Of the seven members to Lok Sabha, one Dr Harshavardhan became health minister to lose his portfolio in the first reshuffle of the Union Cabinet. The remaining six members were never seen working in their respective constituencies. BJP, thus, conceded its position to AAP even before the assembly election was announced. Point missed by BJP was that in Delhi, the party was the ruling one since Delhi was under the President's rule. In addition BJP had been managing the civic bodies for last few terms. The performance of these bodies is full of corruption and harassment to people. It was, therefore, easy for AAP to resume its role as the populist crusader. Closer to the election, Modi committed a critical mistake. He wore a pinstriped suit with his name monogrammed all over. In one suit, he surrendered his carefully cultivated 'tea boy' (chaiwala) image. In contrast, Kejriwal carried on with his muffler wrapped on his head, a style reminiscent of the poorer sections of the society.

Kejriwal's volunteers spread to every corner of Delhi. It created intense publicity but not of so high decibel ones like BJP. AAP booked time slots in radio, a cheaper option against BJP's full page advertisements. In Delhi, half of the 13 million voters belong to the poorer sections of the society. AAP had its foothold in the capital with their support in 2013. Majority of them were willing to move back when Kejriwal and his team came back to them for support after the Lok Sabha election debacle. AAP's down to earth approach in campaign won over many from the middle class who saw arrogance in BJP's high cost election campaign. In addition, a large section of central government officers were unhappy with the new Modi dispensation. The party initiated timely attendance, change of work culture and elimination of delay in file movements. This not only affected their cosy lifestyle but also in more cases than not dried up their extra source of money from the speed money collected. The voting pattern revealed that in constituencies where the government quarters are located, BJP vote share came down sharply compared to the same in 2014 Lok Sabha election. BJP's loss was AAP's gain.

If the success of the Modi campaign 2014 was in its ability to occupy the mindspace of the people, Kejriwal's success in Delhi, too, lay in the same narrative. Loss of Modi's BJP in Delhi is, thus, a failure of the party to stick to its narrative and communication of the same. In contrast, Kejriwal successfully adapted it with stunning victory.

The message is clear. In Indian elections, be it for Lok Sabha or state assemblies, a leader must touch the sentiment of its voters, tell them a narrative on how to attain a better future. Like the candidate, Bill Mc Kay in the Hollywood movie *The Candidate*,[17] the leader must say:

> There has to be a better way ... time has passed when you can turn your back on the fundamental needs of the people ... Don't think you can distract them any more ... All a man can say is here I am ... I am willing to give in all I got.

This was Modi's message to India in 2014, this was what Kejriwal told Delhi in 2015. That is what a campaign is about.

Examples can be multiplied to substantiate the point that for the Indian voters, democratic election is a powerful mechanism to articulate their voice that the contenders for political power can afford to ignore only at their peril. The 2014 poll outcome has unambiguously established the point. Empowered by the constitutional guarantee to the citizens, the Indian voters chose the candidates in accordance with their priorities which cannot be fathomed so easily. Challenging the conventional wisdom on democracy, as articulated by S.M. Lipset in his *Political Man: The Social Bases of Politics* or J.S. Mill in his *Considerations on Representative Government*, the Indian voters have proved beyond doubt that neither the Lipset's notion of nation's financial health[18] nor Mill's concern for social homogeneity[19] is enough to consolidate democracy. So, in the ultimate analysis, the 2014 poll may have sealed the fate of some of the contending parties, including the parliamentary left; nonetheless, it has confirmed once again that democracy in India is organic in character and spirit and in that sense, the 2014 epoch-making election celebrated Indian democracy in no uncertain terms.

12

Reinventing Political Communication—The Modi Interlude(?)

According to experts on political campaign communication, the necessary condition a candidate for office must satisfy is demonstrating fitness for office.

> During the campaign especially the earliest portions when public images of potential candidates are beginning to be formed, the electorate draws inferences from campaign actions about how a particular candidate would behave as mayor, or governor, or even president.[1]

Electorate does not want those who are viewed as dishonest, dull or incompetent. The higher the post, the more stringent the checks. Normally people gather the impression from media. Hence, the political leaders are ever obliging to media persons. In the initial days of the Indian democracy, media did not have the reach. Television was not there, and only All India Radio was the mass media. Indians could see their leader Jawaharlal Nehru on the news features that movie halls used to show before the movie and during the intermission. In any case, Indians knew Nehru was the leader who fought for freedom along with Mahatma Gandhi. There was no second choice as long as Nehru was around. For him, the challenge was to set up a democratic system. For Nehru, it was not one of getting elected.

The rub off effect of Nehru's unchallenged position worked in favour of his daughter Indira Gandhi in 1967 and again in 1971. There was no doubt among the electorates in most parts of the country, of the capability of Nehru or his daughter to rule the country. As long as Indira was the vote puller, she had the control of the party. Even when in 1971 the 'syndicate'—consisting of the senior leaders of Congress—broke away, Indira emerged as the choice of the electorates. The liberation of Bangladesh and Indira's role in the Indo–Pak war positioned her as the undisputed leader of the nation. Unfortunately, she squandered that advantage and in 1977, she failed over the issue of being just and democratic. Her failure to manage people's aspirations in the early 1970s and also visible dictatorial tendency saw the first defeat of Congress in national election in 1977. The important point to note is that in 1977, people voted against Indira and not in favour of any alternate leader. Clearly, neither Morarji Desai nor Charan Singh the two Prime Ministers between 1977–80 were the people's choice. Their tenure was destined to collapse, which happened. Their inability to offer charismatic leadership, as alternative to Nehru and his daughter, brought back Indira in 1980.

Rajiv Gandhi inherited not merely the good look of Nehru and Indira, but also the sympathy Indians had for the family, especially due to the brutal killing of their Prime Minister Indira by her security guards. Rajiv's election campaign was perhaps the smoothest in the history of any democratic election. There was no challenge to Rajiv's choice as Prime Minister anywhere in the country. But what Rajiv failed to realise was that time had been changing. India in late 1980s was not the same as in late 1950s. The changed circumstances—of the economy, society and tools of communication—created a challenge that Rajiv Gandhi could not manage in 1989. The 9th general election was arguably the first one in 40 years' history of Indian democracy that saw the emergence of an alternative leader to the incumbent Rajiv Gandhi, a member of the Nehru–Gandhi family. This was the first 'surfacing' of an alternate prime-ministerial candidate that of Rajiv's former Finance Minister V.P. Singh. In 1977 when Congress lost power for the first time, nobody was projected as the prime-ministerial candidate. The anti-Indira campaign was headed by an old and ailing leader JP who had assembled the anti-Congress forces. In terms of political campaigning that was not surfacing of any alternative leader but a collective opposition by the political leaders who were against Indira Gandhi. Since they had no other reason to work together, their association started weakening the moment their objective of defeat of Indira was achieved. In contrast, the emergence of V.P. Singh as an alternate option to Rajiv Gandhi in 1989 reflected the maturing of anti-Congress forces in Indian politics. The 9th General Election led to a structural change in Indian election scene, and therefore campaign tactics.

The change in the campaign trend seen since 1989 was the result of the change in technology as well. In the early 1980s, the Central Government under Indira Gandhi spread the signals of DD through setting up of relay transmitters at different parts of the country. This brought political

leadership closer to the people. In addition, India witnessed a video par-
lour boom during this period. Video news release brought independent
views closer to the people. Political parties like BJP used the technology in
spreading their messages. Political campaign in India took a new decisive
turn from this period. The move turned into a tidal wave with the launch
of private channels in 1991 when the government relaxed rules. It changed
further with the rise of social media. Like the Obama campaign in the
US, the Modi campaign in 2014 had shown how the same could be used
even to neutralize the influence of well-established mainstream media.

Elections are important because they allow the citizens the freedom to
actively participate in selecting the leaders. For the leaders, elections give
them the legitimacy with which to govern. Like in the US, Indians elect
the Panchayat Pradhan to the Prime Minister, to govern various tiers of
administration, be it from a village unit or the whole nation. Elections give
the citizens of all hues an opportunity to participate in the decision-taking
process. When Nehru launched campaign for the first general election,
his worry was to encourage people to participate in the electoral process.
If he had to travel across the nation, it was to create this awareness.
Not only could he draw Indians out to vote, his efforts turned elections
as carnivals of sorts for the average citizens.[2] 'On this one day', wrote
Mukulika Banerjee, 'the inequality of wealth and status that dominated
normal life... was briefly set aside ... elections in India are carnivalesque,
in their noise and colour...'

In any carnival, there must be novelty along with localization to attract attention of the target participants. A politician must therefore plan
the campaign carefully. For Nehru, his daughter Indira and grandson
Rajiv, the task was easy. The family acquired a star value unmatched by
even the most popular superhero of India's immensely popular Hindi
movie world from Mumbai. This star value helped Rajiv's widow Sonia
Gandhi to hold the oldest party, the INC together and remain its longest
serving party president. Sonia Gandhi had the added advantage of being a foreigner yet adopting the country as her own. Ordinary villagers
from far-flung areas had sympathy for her. The same star value worked
in favour of her son Rahul Gandhi to emerge as the Prime Minister-in-
waiting in 2014. Sonia's clever use of her children—daughter Priyanka
and son Rahul—in her election campaign since 1998 when she joined
the electoral politics—too helped nurturing the family's star value. The

Congress strategy was an adaptation of what in the US is known as the use of surrogates. In 1972, Richard Nixon in his re-election campaign used surrogates to tour the country, while he spent longer hours at the White House.[3] In 2004, twin daughters of President George Bush, Jenna and Barbara, travelled around the US focussing on young voters. His parents, former president George H.W. Bush and mother Barbara also campaigned for their son. Sonia Gandhi had her son Rahul to share the burden of campaigning with her, while daughter Priyanka could keep busy in the two pocket boroughs of Amethi and Rae Bareilly for her brother and mother respectively. Narendra Modi did not have the luxury to use any surrogate, no illustrious family member coming in as he hailed from a rather humble background, neither could there be any political friends or officials from his party BJP or coalition partners, busy as most of them had been in having their own share of the pie.

The robustness of Indian democracy, despite the long line of leadership of Nehru family, was first tested in 1977. Indira Gandhi's Emergency was India's Watergate moment. Like democracy emerged stronger post-Watergate, so did the Indian electoral system post-emergency. The result of 1977 illustrated that despite poverty, lack of education, varied culture, language and religion, the electorates knew well enough how to behave on the election day. Role of money, mob, mafia or muscle power got reduced with every passing election and improvement in communication technology. Instant reporting through 24-hour TV channels empowered the electorate, heightening the carnival spirit. India does not have televized debates as the US has since 1960, but appearances before TV anchors for interview by the top claimants are watched with more than ordinary care. The more the world turned into a global village, the faster has been the spread of new technology. While TV started playing an increasingly important role in the US election campaigns since the days of Eisenhower in 1952 and again in 1956, TV was introduced in India only in 1965 on a regular basis. It took another 15 long years before TV transmission could spread to larger towns across the country. Only in 1991 came the private TV channels which finally led to TV boom in the country.

TV had clinched Rajiv Gandhi for a historic victory in 1985. The country had seen how Indira Gandhi was shot dead by her own security guards and felt offended. They saw the grief-stricken Rajiv and his family, the young kids Rahul, Priyanka and even Varun, son of Indira's deceased son Sanjay, at the funeral. India decided to vote for Rajiv in sympathy. The event and its visuals that reached every nook of the nation were so powerful that nobody cared to think even once before casting the ballot in favour of Rajiv Gandhi. It was a tsunami in favour of Congress created in no small measure by television. If one cares to draw parallel with the US, 1985 was India's 1960 when Kennedy defeated Nixon largely due to his success in the first televized debate of the US.

Electioneering turned to the visual media since 1991—after Rajiv Gandhi's assassination. The effect of the brutal killing of the former Prime Minister on his campaign trail stopped BJP's pro-Hindutva campaign using video vans. Rajiv's assassination turned the scale in favour of Congress. Since 211 constituencies had gone to polls before the incident, the effect was on the remaining 323 seats. Congress thus missed absolute majority yet got enough seats to govern for five years.

The polarization factor, division between Hindu and Muslim voters, got exacerbated due to demolition of the Babri Masjid. This helped BJP during this period. In addition, what helped was the absence of any charismatic personality in the national political scene other than BJP's Atal Bihari Vajpayee. But the appeal of BJP was confined largely in the Hindi heartland. BJP, therefore, needed alliance partners. In 1996, the party failed to have sufficient number of allies. In 1998, it did barely manage to have majority that did not last beyond a year. In 1999, BJP had its coalition government. In Vajpayee, BJP had all the necessary ingredients of successful electioneering. He had been in the national politics since the beginning of the democratic process. He was an excellent orator. His record as a parliamentarian was non-controversial and nationalistic. What is more, his image was soft, not that of a rabid anti-Muslim, Hindu fanatic. Thus, despite all hard work, his long-term colleague L.K. Advani had to remain content as the second in command to Vajpayee.

With the spread of technology, no political entity, in power or not, could any longer control information. The election for India's 14th Lok Sabha in 2004 was held at this juncture. The only charismatic face of BJP, the incumbent Prime Minister Vajpayee, was unwell. It was clear that if BJP-led coalition won, Vajpayee would make way for Advani. But the hardcore Hindutva image of Advani unified the anti-BJP votes. Evidently, the electorate opted for any available political face over the certainty of Advani after Vajpayee. The charisma factor, thus, did not work. Nor did its high voltage 'India Shining' campaign. Congress led by Rajiv's widow Sonia Gandhi emerged as the choice of the multiple political parties. In 2004, it was not any rub-off effect of Nehru–Gandhi family charisma that helped Sonia Gandhi. This was a factor for her remaining as Congress president and holding the party together. But nationally, the result was the effect of people's reluctance to opt for a pro-Hindutva government. Incidents in Gujarat were too vivid in the mind of Indians. The year 2004 was India's post-Watergate moment. Even if Abraham Lincoln had contested as the Republican candidate in 1976, perhaps he would have lost the US presidential contest. Defeat of Vajpayee was on the cards despite a spirited campaign.

Like Ronald Reagan's 'Morning in America' in 1984, for India's Dr Manmohan Singh, 2009 was a no contest though many in Indian media predicted a win for BJP. The factors that worked in his favour were many. The economy was booming. People viewed governance as fair and honest. The terrorist attack in Mumbai made people think in terms of a stable government. The incident made people cautious against BJP's candidate Advani. After rejecting him in 2004, Indians had no reason to vote in his favour. What is more important is that the no confidence motion against the Singh government on the Indo–US nuclear deal rallied the vocal middle class in favour of Congress. Effort of Advani to copy some elements of Obama campaign in 2008—like writing a memoir—did not help his cause. The social media campaign of BJP was half hearted at best.

Narendra Modi came amidst all these turmoils. He knew the winning formula. James Carville wrote in the Foreign Affairs[4] on campaign tips given by Quintus some 2000 years ago. 'Quintus starts with what we campaign advisers call "confidence building", assuring the candidate that he has what it takes to win.' Narendra Modi demonstrated the same by winning Gujarat elections despite a concerted campaign against him by the central government and forces outside. A leader, according to Napoleon, has to be 'a dealer in hope'. Modi became one—the front-runner among all the chief ministers espousing development as his mantra. What is more, he used modern technology for 'micro-targeting, crafting specific appeals to the narrowest of segments of the voting public'. According to Carville, Quintus in effect recommended what was used by several American presidents:

George H. W. Bush's courtesy, Bill Clinton's total recall of names and faces, and Barack Obama's focus on getting out the youth vote. He argues for campaigning constantly and incessantly, and cautions against taking vacations during the campaign, since your absence will suggest that you are taking voters for granted.[5]

Narendra Modi did use all these mentioned by Carville. Election 2014 was Indian election campaign turning matured, at par with the US, the oldest running democracy in the world.

When Nehru was campaigning in the first general election of the newly independent India in 1952, the US had its presidential election which the US war hero Dwight D. Eisenhower won. While Nehru had to traverse the country to reach his audience with back up from Radio and maybe news reels in movie theatres, 1952 saw introduction of TV in the US election campaign. Both Eisenhower and his rival Adlai Stevenson used TV for advertising. TV debate came later in 1960. In India, TV played a role much later, in 1984. In 1992, the US saw the use of the Internet in election campaign. Bill Clinton used the emerging medium to spread his message, but those were the days of one-way campaign through the Internet. Social media came only in 2008 when President Barack Obama used it extensively for his campaign and repeated the same in 2012. Indians are fast learners, at least in terms of political campaign methods. Post 1991 election video campaign picked up, TV played an increasingly important role and even social media found its users. But nobody used all these mediums like Modi did in 2014. The campaign simply overtook the US Presidential campaign in terms of the use of social media which was so intense that even mainstream media, including TV, had to follow the social media lead. The 2014 Modi campaign positioned India as an innovator of sorts in political campaign technique. The largest democracy on earth overtook the oldest and the richest democracy in campaign technique.

The other record was that Narendra Modi is the first outsider in New Delhi to contest and win a decisive mandate in India. His brief stay in Delhi as one of the General Secretaries of BJP in the 1990s was uneventful. He was certainly not a prominent face in the party that lost amidst the crowd comprising more prominent faces like Pramod Mahajan, Arun Jaitley, Rajnath Singh, Venkaiah Naidu, Sushma Swaraj and others. Never could anybody in the more than 60-year history of Indian electoral democracy become a Prime Minister without being present in Delhi politics. The only exception perhaps was H.D. Deve Gowda who was appointed as the Prime Minister in 1996 for just one year. Point to note is that he was chosen by the leaders active in Delhi politics who could not agree on anybody from among themselves. Hence, they opted for the 'humble farmer' from Karnataka. Modi had one of the most negative start as a political leader. With no administrative or legislative experience, few expected him to succeed. The riot was his 'agni-pariksha'. For novice Modi, the Chief Minister, Gujarat riot was his baptism by fire. It gave him the opportunity to prove both his political skill and administrative ability. Once firmly on the saddle, Modi did not let the opportunity slip by and built on a reputation as a leader committed to the development of his state.

While his position in the state was unchallenged, the critical question for Modi was to reach the people outside Gujarat. He knew well enough that he enjoyed the name recognition as well as reputation of sorts as a Chief Minister who delivered growth. It was also clear that the mainstream media would be reluctant to carry Modi's message the way he would like it to be disseminated. Clay Shirkey wrote in the Foreign Affairs:

> Political freedom has to be accompanied by a civil society literate enough and densely connected enough to discuss the issues presented to the public. In a famous study of political opinion after the 1948 U.S. presidential election, the sociologists Elihu Katz and Paul Lazarsfeld discovered that mass media alone do not change people's minds; instead, there is a two-step process. Opinions are first transmitted by the media, and then they get echoed by friends, family members, and colleagues. It is in this second, social step that political opinions are formed.[6]

Here, Modi campaign had a gap which was bridged effectively through social media. Social media created a debate, mostly against the mainstream media, which was slow to catch up with the public mood. By the time India's mainstream media woke up to the fact as to how it had lost its ability to influence the public opinion, it was too late. The speed and precision of execution with the social media tools caught everybody unaware as was the final mandate. Modi campaign 2014 in totality was an improvement over any other campaign in the history of democratic electioneering. It was a mixture of stump oratory, clever use of visual media, intense use of social media technique to catch the fancy of an electorate where a large section did not even have regular supply of electricity, forget about the use of the Internet. In such corners, BJP used its video vans loaded with Modi message. The campaign cleverly used the phased polling schedule to keep alive its core message. Had the election been held in one single day, Modi campaign would not have enjoyed this advantage. Viewed from a purely PR point of view, the Modi campaign 2014 was an optimum one. It had used in right doses the advantages it had—Modi's oratory, his tenacity to campaign every day at far corners of the nation, his ability to create theatrics to arouse interest of the audience and no less important the weaknesses of his opponents. The campaigners knew well enough the carnivalesque nature of Indian election. Wherever Modi went for rallies, the campaign created the pre-carnival atmosphere. With such presale, Modi campaign ensured large turnout on the polling day.

Every country has its own peculiar characteristics. PR tools, therefore, need to be adapted suiting the specific character of the electorates. Modi campaign in 2014 did it successfully by creating an effective case study for students of election campaign. The important point is that:

> ...everything was not that new in Modi's campaign. He focused on tried and tested tactics and themes, including anti-corruption, caste politics, and some Hindu nationalist overtones where and when they were relevant. The RSS network, a traditional asset of the BJP, also played a very important role.[7]

Positioning a person as a political brand, in addition to the political party and that too in a parliamentary democracy, does not come cheap. In case of Nehru or Indira, both were synonymous with the Congress brand which was deeply rooted in the country. They did not need much extra effort to position themselves as undisputed leaders. For Modi, the task was difficult. He was a regional leader, one among several other chief ministers in BJP-ruled states. Therefore, he had to embark on a more than a year-long campaign. He started in February 2013 with the students of Delhi University's SRCC. The campaign turned intensive due to four state assembly elections in December 2013. Then, he moved over to the general election campaign till May 2014. Evidently, the cost for such a campaign was huge—₹712.48 crore. This was the expenditure incurred during the official 75-day campaign period—money spent after the election was officially notified. In contrast, Congress spent ₹486.21 crore during this period. Total amount spent by all national parties in 2014 Lok Sabha poll was ₹1308.75 crore—BJP spent 54.4 per cent of that.[8]

On publicity which includes expenses on advertisement, campaign material and for public meetings, BJP spent ₹463.17 crore against ₹346.41 crore of Congress. Expenditure on travel including that of star campaigners for BJP was a high ₹159.15 crore against ₹129.50 crore of Congress. BJP expenditure on candidates was also more than that of Congress—₹159.81 crore against ₹96.70 crore. Important points are that while BJP had only one star campaigner, Narendra Modi, Congress had at least three, the party president Sonia Gandhi, Vice President Rahul Gandhi and Prime Minister Manmohan Singh. Then, no less important is that Congress had put up more candidates than that of BJP—464 against 428. Clearly, Congress campaign could not keep pace with that of BJP's. Expenses on public meetings reveal the aggressive campaign style of Modi. BJP spent ₹89.46 crore on meetings compared to just ₹33.08 crore spent by Congress.[9] Modi campaign's attention to details was more expensive and in the end proved more effective.

According to Suhas Palshikar, in 2014 election India's state-level leaders like the Chief Minister of West Bengal, Mamata Banerjee, Chief Minister of Bihar, Nitish Kumar, Chief Minister of Odisha, Navin Patnaik and others were caught unaware. They never could imagine 'the rise of popular leadership immersed in narcissism and catching people's imagination across states—something the Mamatas and Lalus could never do'.[10] Curiously, no analyst ever pointed out narcissism in the campaigns of Nehru, Indira or Rajiv. Even the great grandson of the Nehru–Gandhi lineage, Congress Vice President Rahul Gandhi, qualifies to be painted in the same brush. But the Indian mindset accustomed to genuflect before a 'feudal' family member found narcissism in Modi campaign. After all Modi was not fortunate enough to be born as Nehru's grandson. The other point missed is that in their own jurisdiction, the Mamatas and the Lalus follow no less the style of narcissism. What Modi did in his spirited campaign was to point out to people everywhere what they received from their political feudal rulers and what he gave to his people in Gujarat. He was not apologetic but contrasted his delivery against the delivery of others and the final take away for the common men.

According to Christophe Jaffrelot, the kind of exaggerated self-promotion, what Palshikar called narcissism is not unusual during an election campaign.

What was new was the way Modi toured India to contrast the 'Gujarat model' with the situation of the other states in India, making the Nehru-Gandhi family and non-BJP Chief Ministers responsible for socio-economic backwardness. Never before had a Chief Minister showcased his achievements in this manner in order to rule at the Centre.[11]

In Rahul Gandhi's Amethi constituency, while campaigning for his nominee Smriti Irani Modi said, 'Your dreams are my dreams. For 40 years, one family has destroyed the dreams of three generations. I will ensure your dreams are fulfilled.'[12]

Expressing deep concern for the abject lives of the people of Amethi, Modi spoke of how the region lagged behind its counterparts across the country. Be it agriculture or trade, the region lagged far behind its neighbouring districts, not just the nation. From the severe lack of basic amenities like water and sanitation to erratic power supply and insufficient educational institutions, Modi pointed out that Amethi was just a vote bank for the Nehru–Gandhi family. Addressing the issue of lack of toilets in schools, which had led to the alarmingly low figures of girl child education, Modi showcased the initiative taken in Gujarat, where 76,000 toilets were constructed in schools so as to enable girl students to pursue their education.[13]

Rival leaders started making fun of Modi's Gujarat model questioning what was that model. Modi responded in Gorakhpur mocking at Mulayam Singh Yadav, known as Netaji to his followers, 'Netaji, do you know the meaning of converting to Gujarat? It means 24 hour electricity in every village and street. You can't do it. It requires 56 inch chest...'[14] In his speech at Domariyaganj in UP, Modi mentioned that he was born in a low caste. In his first speech, after he was declared by BJP as the prime-ministerial candidate, he shared personal anecdotes of his desire to serve in the army but could not sit in the exam due to financial constraints and how he volunteered to give tea and snacks to soldiers during the 1965 India–Pakistan war. He added that years later in 1995, the BJP gave him the responsibility of North Indian states like Haryana, Punjab, Himachal Pradesh and Jammu and Kashmir, which is when he got to visit cantonments and meet officers. He opined that it is some divine indication that out of all this, ex-serviceman rally became his first public meeting after the PM announcement, even though the public meeting was planned long before that. 'I want to tell those who divide the nation in the name of secularism—to see real secularism see the army. We can learn the true essence of secularism from our armed forces.'[15]

From the outset, Modi trapped his opposition to attack him and his performance in Gujarat as the Chief Minister. He mentioned Gujarat only to rub in the failure of the other states to meet the needs and aspirations of the people. This attracted the young voters. An examination of age-wise voting and preferences in the 2014 elections reveals that the BJP benefited from youth and first-time voters showing a high preference for the party relative to other age groups.[16]

The empirical analysis presented by Basu and Misra 'shows that BJP's electoral success in 2014—measured as the change in vote share between 2009 and 2014 was crucially dependent on the support of younger, especially first-time, voters'.

The reason was simple since in the entire campaign, Modi presented a picture of a leader who has delivered and if elected in the national scene would deliver more than what others could do. 'The image that was projected was that of a "doer" which echoed the skills of a CEO'.[17] What added further spice to the broth was how Modi mixed a dose of his poverty and low-caste birth in the would-be CEO. If a poor boy who used to sell tea in his father's stall in the small town's railway station could deliver so much happiness to the state of Gujarat, he certainly deserved a chance.

Conclusion: Marketizing an Ideology-driven Dream

India's election results belied many expectations—it surpassed the best estimates of the BJP supporters; for the Modi baiters, it brought in their worst nightmares; for the knowledgeable, it showed the limit of their intellect; and for the common men, mostly swing voters, it came with the hope that *Achhe Din Aane Wale Hain* (good days are coming). Whatever be the point of view, nobody can deny that the spectacular victory of Narendra Modi rewrote the rules of election campaign in an underdeveloped, diverse nation adopting the Westminster-style democracy.

What was unique in Modi campaign? Did he adopt any strikingly patented method that nobody ever did? Or did he adopt and adapt the winning campaigns in India and abroad?

The overwhelming view was that Modi ran a completely presidential-type campaign for votes. Modi in his election meetings openly asked people to vote for *Kamal* (lotus, BJP's election symbol) and strengthen his hands. Very rarely did he mention why the candidate in the constituency deserved support. It was Modi all the way. But so had been the campaign of Nehru and later his daughter in 1971. Even in 1998 and 1999, BJP used their leader Atal Bihari Vajpayee for support and nominated him as their prime-ministerial candidate. It was a mixture of the British style of electioneering where the leaders of respective parties contest for the prime-ministerial position. Modi simply followed this practice and should be credited with an innovative presidential-style campaign as in the US.

Apart from the fact that the electioneering was centred on Modi, the stark reality was that it was spearheaded by Modi alone. But, this too was not unique. Nehru was his lone warrior, so was his daughter Indira. Whenever a medley of leaders campaigned for votes, the results had been fragmented. Many might cite the election of 1977 as an aberration. But if one looks carefully it was actually a victory of the assortment of leaders who gathered together with the single point agenda of defeating Indira Gandhi. The moment that objective was achieved, the leaders lost the reason to be together. Finally, the internal dissension saw the ouster of the Janata government and even disintegration of the party. India's election campaigns had always been personality driven and fronted by the star campaigner. There was nothing unique in the Modi campaign.

Should we say that the extraordinary ability of Narendra Modi to traverse the subcontinent amidst the summer heat, sometimes going without food due to the Navratra fast, was an exceptional characteristic of Modi campaign? In terms of sheer enormity of the large rallies addressed by Narendra Modi, it indeed is record breaking. While Nehru, too, had campaigned in every corner of the nation during the first election in 1951–52 in particular, he did not speak to so many persons in so many different destinations. But, this is a question of mere number. This shows the tenacity and the physical capacity that Narendra Modi has, but by itself it cannot merit citation as a unique feature of the campaign. Nor can one attribute the spectacular election result to this factor alone.

In the age of communication, when election campaigns in nearly all democracies have shifted to TV, Narendra Modi exhibited his preference for stump oratory. He proved himself to be a dinosaur in the age of communication. But this, too, is not exclusive. In India, rallies are an essential feature of campaign. Despite TV reaching out to a large part of the country, Indian electorates love their leader to travel and speak in their midst. Even the audience travels for hours to attend the rallies.

But Modi was not alone, all political leaders like Rahul Gandhi, Sonia Gandhi and others addressed rallies in different parts. There were two striking features in Modi campaign that were not seen in rallies of anybody else. First was the sheer tenacity of Narendra Modi of crisscrossing the country. Second was the spontaneous response of people to come and listen to him.

As far as technique of campaign is concerned, what stood out was the use of social media by Modi campaign. This blunted the mainstream media, which had been anti-Modi. After the campaign was over on 12 May, Narendra Modi acknowledged the power of social media in his campaign. He tweeted, 'Due to social media, lies & false promises of several leaders could not go beyond the podiums of their rallies! More power to social media.' Even here, the Modi campaign did not reinvent the wheel, but merely used what President Barack Obama did in his presidential bids. If earlier no other Indian leaders could use the tool effectively, the reason lies in the fact that it is a new medium coming into prominence only in the last few years. For Congress, the tool was irrelevant since the ruling politicians had unstinted support from the mainstream media. In social media all publications and channels have their overwhelming presence. Their editors and anchors have huge following. So, why would Congress bother to make a separate effort to manage social media? The Congress' reluctance also perhaps was due to the aggressive comments from individual participants in social media dialogue against its heir apparent Rahul Gandhi. From the very beginning, the perfect textbook style effort to build the image of the younger Gandhi was marred by stringent attacks on Facebook and Twitter, the two most popular social media platforms. In addition, there had been several posts on the YouTube where the Congress star fared poorly. Spoofs were also galore. Another factor, the reticence of the Gandhis, perhaps was behind the party's reluctance to reach out direct to people through social media. Social media is a two-way dialogue between the initiator and the respondent. The approach of the Gandhis had been one way, distant and condescending to the citizens. The signals emanating from them and through their courtiers had been as if they had been doing a favour to the people by acquiescing to be at the helm of Indian politics. Nobody can access social media under such circumstances. Modi campaign, thus, had an unchallenged field in social media. What is more important, disgusted with the governance and the pliant mainstream media a large number of social media participants kept on taking the cudgels on behalf of Narendra Modi. It was impossible for the mainstream media to outshout the spontaneous participants in the debate. This indeed was a unique feature of India's political campaign 2014.

Still, the question remains what was so special in Narendra Modi that a large number of Indians supported him so spontaneously! The secret lies in the message that Modi propagated. It was a message of hope, that of future, a message of a change from the rot the country was sinking in. If his Patna rally in October 2013 delivered the 'daisy and the little girl' moment, the winning stroke was in his assertion that a poor irrespective of his religion must fight poverty. In his entire eight-month long campaign, Narendra Modi stuck steadfastly to this single theme. This single theme helped the campaign to overcome caste, social and regional bias of the electorates. The net result was seen in India's largest and arguably the most complex state of UP. It elected 73 MPs for BJP, leaving just seven to family members of regional strongman Mulayam Singh Yadav and two Gandhi family members Sonia Gandhi and her son Rahul Gandhi.

A comparison to this election theme could be found in Indira Gandhi's campaign in 1971 when she adopted the slogan *'Garibi Hatao'* (remove poverty). Indira Gandhi could win two-thirds of majority in the Lok Sabha, so overwhelming was the support for her. Clearly, in a poor country, the majority of the voters get attracted to any strong leader promising to eradicate poverty. Here, too, the key message of the Modi campaign was nothing unique but a variation of Indira's messaging in 1971.

Any election campaign must remember the characteristics of voters. They are changeable perhaps fickle in their opinion. Voters do not have permanent friends or enemies. They are selfish, act for their own interest with hardly any concern for the nation. They do not mind subsidy on their electricity bill or fuel and food even if this means that such subsidies hurt the long-term growth prospect of the economy. Voters are highly emotional, prejudiced and irrational as far as the big picture is concerned. The electoral gain of Arvind Kejriwal in the Delhi state assembly election in December 2013 and again in 2015 is a case in point. This also had demonstrated how voters focus only on short-term benefits. Clearly, voters are incapable of making a rational choice, they lack the necessary experience, knowledge and even the capacity to make appropriate judgements. Naturally, they rely on media. This made media persons feel more important than they actually are. Election 2014 is an example. Media picked up issues which were non-issues for the voters. Take the example of Modi's marital status. The more dirt the media tried to hurl at Modi, the higher went the support graph of Modi. The concerted effort to drag Narendra Modi and his political assistant Amit Shah into a controversy over alleged snooping on a lady from Gujarat similarly did not cut much ice with the large number of voters. By playing such cards, which were liberally used by the leaders of Congress, ended up a majority of common men equating media with the corrupt people they wanted to throw out. Instead of influencing public opinion, media ended up as a villain of sorts. This was a unique feature of election 2014 not seen before.

The campaign style of Narendra Modi helped paint mainstream media as one of the villains waiting to be uprooted. Narendra Modi was not available for any media interaction till the last phase of the election. His absence forced the Indian media to rely on Modi rallies and the feed that came from BJP campaign sources. People saw the spontaneous crowd, their animated participation in the rallies and the festive scene everywhere.

Even those who were not overtly Modi supporter thought it prudent to try him out. One masterstroke was Modi campaign decision to hold an impromptu rally when Narendra Modi went to file his nomination papers in Varanasi. There was no religious ceremony. He simply went and filed his papers with a huge crowd in tow. In contrast, Arvind Kejriwal, his main opponent, who had been hoisted by the Modi baiters from Gujarat and elsewhere, went for religious symbolisms shunned by the so-called icon of Hindutva Narendra Modi. Media by showcasing Kejriwal drew attention to the contrast. Kejriwal's dip in the Ganges in Varanasi, a photograph widely splashed in the Indian media, presented the picture of a desperate politician trying to outdo the Hindutva image of Modi. In contrast, Modi did not even walk along the ghats of Varanasi. At every stage, the Modi campaign outwitted the adversaries which received support from the mainstream media.

When the long-drawn elections went into the fourth stage, Narendra Modi consented to his first major interview on television. His choice was the TV news agency ANI. The interviewer was a relatively lightweight lady journalist who was evidently not very conversant with the intricacies of politics in India. It was not that she was uninformed, but against Narendra Modi, she was lighter than a butterfly. As the interviewer herself wrote in her blog later, she was so overwhelmed by the distinctive style of Modi and the Spartan office of the Chief Minister of Gujarat that she could not afford to be belligerent.[1] The ANI team entered the residence of one of India's Chief Minister who faced acute security threat without much of a show. There was no aide waiting to take or to give brief to Modi. What is more, the furniture of the Chief Minister's residence was simple. Not even a carpet was available for the team to absorb the glare of the floor. Unlike most VIPs, Modi came on time, exchanged just few pleasantries as a host and went straight for the interview. The interviewer was shocked that never did Modi ask her after recording was over how was the interview or when would it be telecast. He simply finished his appointment and flew out for his rallies. This nonchalance had been an inimitable trait in the character of Narendra Modi. Even more well-prepared and hostile interviewers who got the opportunity to grill Modi thereafter faced this business-like approach in the BJP leader. Hostile questions met with equally stringent but subtle responses. These interviews came when a large number of constituencies were going in for polls and, therefore, were out of bound for Modi campaign due to polling rules. But the televized campaigns through carefully planned interviews ensured that the key messages of the campaign reached all. This careful planning was a masterstroke of the Modi campaign, never used in India before. Nor could it be used elsewhere in the world since only in India elections are held in phases spread over few days and not on a single day in the entire country.

According to a former Danish Prime Minister Anders Fogh Rasmussen (later Secretary General of NATO), the answers to the problems facing the society in the twenty-first century are different from those in the twentieth century. Thus, despite certain similarities between the Modi campaign and those of Nehru and his daughter Indira, Narendra Modi had to address the issues differently. One glaring difference between then and now is the way a family is revered and accepted. While to most of the cronies in Congress and stakeholders who benefitted from out of the relationship with Nehru family linkages, this was not apparent but Narendra Modi sensed the mood correctly. In the twenty-first century, people, particularly the younger generation, are much less reverential even to their own family elders. To expect them to continue voting a certain family to power is impractical. More so, since Rahul Gandhi failed to enthuse people with either his wit, oratory or thoughts. Narendra Modi scored on this count. Tony Blair, the former British Prime Minister explained in his party conference speech in 2004 as to how the system has changed. 'The relationship between state and citizen has changed. People have grown up. They want to make their own life choices. In an opportunity society, as opposed to the old welfare state, government does not dictate; it empowers.'[2] This was the key message of Narendra Modi. He had been the first twenty-first century politician of India. This had been the reason for the success of the Modi campaign.

Politicians address the electorates as their consumers. They do not intend to meet their demand but look at the voters to supply what the politicians want. This needs a special art of communication so as to convince the consuming voters as to why the leader would be the right choice to meet their aspirations. Narendra Modi scored on this point. His humble background, first-hand experience of how a large sections of Indians live that he gathered during his travels through at least 400 districts of the vast nation, his sharp wit and equally sharp but well-controlled emotional touch and finally the excellent oratorical skill had been tailor-made to reach out to people face to face. He used these qualities to the hilt in his election rallies and also through the 3D rallies. Mere television interviews would not have given him this exposure. Narendra Modi, to the TV-savvy American poll pundits could be a dinosaur of the modern age, but in effect, he proved himself as a dinosaur that harbingered new style of political campaign in the twenty-first century India.

The more important question, however, is as to whether the Modi campaign will change the campaign style in India. In other words, should Modi's detractors learn their lessons and adapt the elements of the campaign so as to meet the challenge called Narendra Modi? Such reaction would require equal or even stronger oratorical skill than Modi's, deeper connect with the people cutting across geographies, and ability to showcase some groundwork. Narendra Modi, the Chief Minister, had been responsible for bringing in development as a political agenda. Now, states try to compete with one another on the parameter of growth. The success—even if one concedes the points of Modi-critics—though a limited one, was in such a stark contrast with the non-governance of the UPA government for nearly 10 years that no opposition to Modi could hold its ground in 2014 elections. To meet the challenge of Narendra Modi, the political parties must therefore showcase the fact that they could also govern and meet the expectations of the people. This is a huge task since now their efforts will be benchmarked against those of the Modi government in New Delhi. The bar is rising; if the opposition wants to face the challenge, they need to reinvent their politics.

One option for the opposition would be to oppose the Modi government at every stage and project it as incompetent. It will be possible provided the government takes steps, which seem preposterous to the people of India. If not and the government attends to the critical issues staring at the nation, undue opposition would find more detractors than supporters for the opposition parties. This applies to Indian media as well. Both need a course correction if they want to pose a serious challenge for Mr Modi after five years.

Successful political campaign need not be confrontational only. One must be judicious as well. The bifurcation of the southern state of Andhra Pradesh is an example. BJP supported the ruling Congress resolution of bifurcation of the state. But, in the elections, BJP fared better than Congress, which was held responsible for the division of the state. The opposition parties to the Modi government must tread carefully.

According to Narendra Modi, India's Prime Minister, the 2014 elections has seen the demise of the caste-based political parties. The three caste-based parties from UP SP, BSP and RLD and RJD in Bihar did not fare well. When development is the expectation and hope is the theme, caste takes a back seat. But more important question for India is if it saw a restructuring of politics on the religious lines? The left and liberals who are staunch Modi-critic feel that the elections saw the majority community voting out the minorities. They cite the fact that from India's largest state UP with sizeable Muslim population not a single Muslim MP could be elected. Also, despite winning absolute majority, BJP failed to get a single Muslim leader elected to the Lok Sabha. Viewed from their perspective, the single most important feature of election 2014 had been the majority community voting to power a strong leader of their choice. In other words, Modi got elected for representing Hindutva.[3]

The point one may not like to explore is the role of emotion in voting behaviour. Every appeal to a voter is ultimately an emotional appeal to voters' interests—what is good for them and their families.[4] The question that decides an election is how strong is the appeal. Clearly, no voter is moved by a leader whose appeal does not touch the heart. Westen had an interesting anecdote on Adlai Stevenson who was running against Dwight Eisenhower. A woman impressed by Stevenson told him that every thinking person would certainly vote for him. Stevenson responded, 'Madam, that is not enough. I need a majority.' The candidate was right, he lost to Eisenhower.

In early years of elections, Indians voted for those who took part in the freedom struggle. The emotion encouraged Indians to vote for Nehru since the first election. Wasn't he responsible for India's freedom? Was he not the chosen one by Mahatma Gandhi? The emotion was so strong that even the partition of the country was forgotten. This went on till 1967 when Nehru's daughter Indira was leading the country as the Prime Minister. The allegiance shifted to Nehru's heir. It had a temporary break in 1977 when the emotional chord with Nehru was weakening. Even though weak, occasions like assassinations of, first, Indira in 1984 and, then, her son Rajiv in 1991 made it strong enough for people to vote for Congress. The sentiment helped Congress-led UPA to come back to power in 2009 election as well.

But with the changing times, the voters were feeling restless. They were keen to hear different views. Modi sensed it correctly.

In this context, Modi could learn from the experience of his 'Barack'. When Barack Obama threw his hat in the presidential contest for 2008, he was just the first-term senator with little experience to back up. Against him contesting for the democrat ticket was the formidable Mrs Hilary Clinton. Initially, the Obama campaign was listless with the candidate trying to explain his position on issues. After a couple of losses in primaries, Obama broke free with his narrative on how he, an outsider, would clean up Washington. There was no looking back for Obama thereafter. The outsider always has a romantic appeal.

Modi, too, played merrily his USP—a successful leader with a good track record keen to cleanse the dirty system of governance in New Delhi. Indians had been waiting to hear such a voice. None of his adversaries, in BJP and outside, had the credentials he offered. None was as good an orator as Modi. Most importantly, nobody could tell a story the way people were keen to hear. Modi used all the tricks available in a campaign. He made fun of his opponents, criticized the past policies sharply, was unsparing on every other leader even in their home turf. The governance failure since 2009 helped Modi to sharpen his attack. Media, particularly the electronics media, though hostile in general could not afford to miss Modi's highly successful rallies. They could not afford to miss all the drama. For them, it was a question of TRP. Modi, thus, turned the table on everybody else. In the end, the individual candidates became irrelevant. In most constituencies, it finally ended up as a fight between Modi and a rather insignificant non-BJP candidate.

To assess Modi's victory merely from a communal angle will be unfair for the masterly tailored campaign. During his gruelling campaign trail, never ever did he mention anything against any religion. He stuck steadfastly to the theme of growth, aspiration of the people and future prosperity. Even under most trying circumstances, like in Patna, Modi was not provoked. Whether there were signs of rethinking among the Muslim or not the fact remains that even in the state of J&K PDP, a regional party from the Muslim-dominated Kashmir valley formed a coalition government with Modi's BJP. Clearly, Modi could touch the emotional chord of a majority of voters.

Modi's style of political campaign is based on people's aspirations. He understood that people look forward to future and like to shake out from the problems faced in the past. The saddest thoughts might be the sweetest songs in media but not when one is deciding on whom to vote. The sooner the opponents of Modi realize the trick, the better it is for their political future.

The Final Word

It is conceptually wrong to be judgemental and theoretically myopic to make conclusive statements on political processes which are never static; its flexible nature is obvious since it draws on the constantly transforming socio-economic context. Nonetheless, one is encouraged to make certain specific comments on the basis of this extensive study that has already been undertaken. The massive Modi-led BJP victory is an offshoot of long-drawn processes that seem to have had its roots in the misgovernance or the visible administrative lapses that the erstwhile UPA government failed to meaningfully address. It is strange that despite having introduced effective pro-people rights-based social schemes, the UPA and especially its leading partner, the Congress almost completely failed to consolidate its support base. Contrarily, the BJP gradually became a serious contender for power although its electoral performance in the 2009 Lok Sabha poll was dismal. This means that while the Congress had an advantage of being the ruling party for a decade, its election campaign never became as effective as that of the BJP in garnering votes for a variety of complex reasons. The BJP campaign was unique: despite the fact that it was the NDA which fought the poll, the 2014 election virtually became a Modi affair in which Narendra Modi remained most critical in the entire campaign; as the campaign gained momentum, the other important BJP leaders seem to have lost their appeal, to a significant extent, and they also needed Modi to address the voters in those areas in which they were contesting. Reflective of the American presidential-type election campaign, the 2014 election, thus, set in motion processes whereby an excessively popular leader appears to have prevailed over the ideological appeal of the party to which he belongs.

The other distinction of the 2014 election relates to the exploration of different modes of political communication besides the traditional means of election campaign (television, print and radio). Political parties resorted to several newer e-techniques, such as Facebook, Twitter, Google Plus, YouTube, among others to reach out to the voters; not only did they redesign their websites to make them more user-friendly, they also opened accounts on various social-networking platforms to fulfil their electoral ambition. These techniques might not have had a national appeal given the fact that they remained confined to the urban areas; nonetheless, they appeared to have been effective in persuading the young voters who are believed to be technology-friendly. Despite their obvious limited role in mobilizing voters in India, the importance of these e-instruments cannot be undermined given their growing importance in the daily walks of life. The fundamental point that deserves careful attention is about the modes of political communication involving both the traditional media and modern e-means. What is significant is the content of communication or the ideological goal that the parties seek to attain, if elected to power. As the election outcome confirms, neither the Congress nor its alliance partners were able to halt the BJP and the other major NDA constituents because of their failure to persuade the voters given their disappointing track record while in administration. In the light of such a well-entrenched mass disappointment, Modi's slogan—minimum government and maximum governance—did work miracle in the campaign. By stressing the goal of inclusive development and underplaying the typical right-wing sociopolitical aims (which are linked with Hindutva), the BJP created a hope for the mass of voters who felt cheated by the erstwhile UPA government. And, appropriate modes of political communication translated this into votes for the BJP in the 2014 national poll.

There is one fundamental point that should not escape our attention. Election is generally fought on contextual issues, and an effective political campaign is an aid to success in the electoral battle. As is evident in elections in India since 1952, specific ideologies, articulated in specific designs of governance, gain precedence. There is however a pattern: the issue of misgovernance and corruption seems to sway the voters to a significant extent. Whether it is the defeat of the Congress in the wake of the Bofors scam in 1989 or the 2G scam in 2014, or whether the losing of power of the Janata government in 1970s or of NDA government in 2004—the critical issues happened to be the misuse of authority and public trust. Campaign strategies are designed highlighting the mass disenchantment with the political party holding power for its involvement in activities which are believed to have hurt the mass sentiments. This is a basic formula which appears to be universally true. It is, thus, possible for the BJP to win over the majority of the voters in the 2014 Lok Sabha poll since the Congress, despite having adopted widely acclaimed rights-based socio-economic programmes benefitting the majority, failed to convince them presumably because of the public disillusionment with the government that it had run for a decade. Now, the same BJP was trounced in the 2015 Delhi Assembly poll by a new political entity, AAP, presumably because of its success in building trust with the majority of Delhi voters through the transformational goals that it had projected. That the BJP that won a thumping majority in May 2014 failed to sustain its momentum in less than a year confirms the argument that the campaign strategies and also the machinery to implement them do not seem to be adequate by themselves. The key to the success of a party in winning the mandate lies in appropriately comprehending the contextual issues and their meaningful articulation in election campaigns. Despite being unique in some respects, India's 2014 national poll, thus, confirms once again the pattern, namely the contextual issues, as articulated through strategies in election campaign, remain critical in fashioning the decisions that the voters make once they reach the polling booth to cast their votes.

Postscript

The Bihar Assembly Election, 2015—Revival of Coalition Dharma

The evolution of India's parliamentary democracy is full of surprises. Voters' behaviour remains unpredictable; the outcome often tends to defy the well-argued and theoretically sound assumptions. The past is replete with examples perhaps showing how mature the Indian voters are. It is not, therefore, odd to find that pollsters are generally wrong in their predictions in exit polls. There is, however, one fundamental assumption which comes out of the unpredictable nature of election in India, namely, the poll outcome is heavily dependent on the contextual pulls and pressures which usually vary from one region to another. This means that Indian election cannot be conceptualized in derivative wisdom and for a meaningful analysis, one has to take into account the contingent factors and how they shape the voting patterns. The 2015 Bihar assembly election is illustrative here. Unlike the 2014 Lok Sabha polls and elections in Haryana, Maharashtra, and Jammu and Kashmir that followed where the BJP triumphed, the Bihar election sealed its fate in favour of a new conglomeration of parties which is being christened as Mahagathbandhan, or Grand Alliance comprising the Janata Dal (United), RJD and Congress. Historically speaking and also as the trend shows, the result is not an exception since the BJP-led NDA lost its ground presumably because of its failure to comprehend Bihar's complex socio-economic and political reality which can never be grasped in a straightforward matrix of conceptualization. The idea is to take into account the unique contextual compulsions of Bihar to devise effective electoral strategies. As the results demonstrate, the BJP and its alliance partners have failed while its bête noire, the Mahagathbandhan of JD(U), RJD and Congress reaped the benefit by way of creating a strong support base involving specific caste and religious groups.

The aim of this postscript is to understand the dynamics of elections specifically with reference to the 2015 Bihar assembly election. The argument that is being made here relates to the nature of election which provides a battlefield for the political parties in fray. Election is as much an ideological competition as a strategic battle to win over voters. On both counts, the Grand Alliance seems to have been well placed in comparison with its opponent, the NDA, as the poll results show. The claim that the BJP is invincible needs to be reviewed because what was evident in the 2015 Delhi election was not an exception but illustrative of a trend that was well articulated in the 2015 Bihar election.

Setting the Scene

The lure of the ancient city of Pataliputra, now Patna, had seen many a mighty, starting from the Alexander the Great and now Narendra Modi, attempt to conquer the rich Gangetic land of Magadha. The richness of the land, Bihar, is long gone. It is now among the laggard states of India, known for its workforce migrating to other parts of India seeking livelihood. The poor of Bihar are badly fragmented along caste lines. Its 17 per cent Muslim population suffers no less amidst poverty and lack of opportunities as much as do their Hindu neighbours. Poverty and suffering instead of bonding have divided them all—lower caste Hindus, Muslims and even upper caste poor. What Bihar lacks in development it compensates in terms of its political sensitivity. It was the state which saw Mahatma Gandhi assuming the charge of Indian freedom movement. It was here Mohammed Ali Jinnah revived Muslim League, Subhas Chandra Bose launched his Forward Block after separating from Congress, JP started his movement that saw eventually the first defeat of Congress in national election in 1977. No less important, it was here at Gandhi Maidan in Patna in October 2013 Narendra Modi had his 'Daisy and the Little Girl' moment when bombs went off during his rally. Bihar and its capital Patna is a historic city not merely because of its ancient lineage but also for figuring in prominently at different points in time in the national political events. Bihar state assembly election of 2015 was one such momentous event—mother of all electoral battles in the largest democracy of the world.

For onlookers, battle for Bihar proved to be a real-life drama. It had several firsts in the history of political rivalry. Here was a popular Chief

Minister Nitish Kumar aligning with his bête noire Lalu Prasad Yadav, a caste leader and former Chief Minister of the state. Both tied up with Congress, a fading power having some committed pockets of support in Bihar. The objective was to stop Narendra Modi, India's Prime Minister and leader of right-wing Hindu nationalist party BJP. The former foes turned friends since Modi had outwitted all of them during the national election 2014. In coalition with a few regional caste-based politicians, Modi won 29 of the 40 seats from Bihar. Nitish Kumar, Lalu Yadav and Congress lost largely due to splitting of votes. Had they formed an alliance, the electoral arithmetic indicated that Modi would not have won so many Lok Sabha seats in 2014. Subsequent by-elections when these three parties contested together proved this conclusively. It thus made immense sense for the three adversaries to come together and stop Modi's march.

Not that Modi did not lose any election since winning the mandate to govern India in 2014. His party BJP lost badly to Arvind Kejriwal's AAP in Delhi assembly election in early 2015. But Delhi is just a city with the government having little more authority than a corporation but much less than a state. Despite the massive loss of BJP, Delhi election was not an indicator of Modi's loss of charm with electorates in the country. Bihar was a proper testing ground for judging relative political muscle of BJP and its rivals. One point to note is that it was seen since the national election of 1977 that whenever the opposition political parties could combine so as not to let votes getting split the national party—then Congress—lost. The exception was 1985 when India voted Rajiv Gandhi with a massive sympathy mandate. BJP vote share in the successful 2014 national election too was not enough to defeat a combined opposition defence. In other words in Bihar, BJP started on a weaker note than the alliance christened Mahagathbandhan of JD(U), RJD and Congress.

For Nitish Kumar, Bihar was not merely a prestige battle but also an opportunity to emerge as the face against Narendra Modi. Nitish Kumar had been an ally till BJP chose Modi as its PM candidate for 2014 election. The separation came essentially due to two factors. First, Nitish Kumar feared that by siding with Modi, he would lose his Muslim support base. Indian politics particularly caste-based regional parties depend on combined support from the backward castes, Dalits and Muslims. JD(U), the party Nitish Kumar leads, works on that premise. Second, Nitish Kumar harboured the same ambition as Modi's—to become the Prime Minister of

India. He knew his JD(U) was essentially a regional party but felt that in case of a hung Lok Sabha if he had some numbers, other parties including Congress would nominate him as PM. In 2014, the hope did not fructify due to a blitzkrieg of election campaign of Narendra Modi. But if Nitish could get his third term in Bihar and given the inability of Congress leadership to recover from the blow in 2014 election, he would certainly emerge as the principal opponent to Modi in 2019 national election. For the same reason, Modi needed to cut Nitish Kumar down to size. If the Bihar chief minister can be mauled on his home turf, Modi would remain an unchallenged leader for 2019, unless somewhere an Arvind Kejriwal surfaces.

Campaign Unfolds

As far as election campaign is concerned, one cannot doubt that Nitish Kumar had been very much in awe of Modi campaign 2014. The Nitish campaign 2015 in Bihar smelled like a carbon copy of Modi 2014 campaign. So, he hired Prashant Kishore who as the head of CAG, devised certain key facets of the spectacular Modi campaign. It is said that he was behind Modi's virtual presence via hologram before distant audiences and also the vastly popular 'Chai pe Charcha'. Kolkata newspaper, *The Telegraph* spoke to one Professor Nawal Kishore Chaudhary, who taught economics at Patna University. He said, 'Nitish has got hold of Modi's *brahmastra* (critical weapon) of the 2014 campaign and is trying to use it against Modi himself.'[1]

Nitish campaign not only used Modi's techniques but also with it adopted after some modifications certain successful campaign initiatives of Modi. JD(U)'s 'Parcha pe Charcha' (discussion on the pamphlets), though sounded deceptively similar to Modi's 'Chai pe Charcha' was an initiative informing people about the work done by the Nitish government. Using a four page pamphlet:

> ...it explained in detail on the work done by the JD(U) government in the fields of law and order, governance, women empowerment, roads, power, etc. More importantly, it sought feedback on issues affecting the everyday lives of the citizens of Bihar from across the state, thus connecting the party and government to its people at a more substantial level.[2]

The other tool used by the Nitish campaign was 'Har Ghar Dastak' (visiting every house). This was a volunteer-driven campaign of the JD(U). The aim was to take the message of Nitish government to the people. To encourage the volunteer workers, *karyakartas,* (workers) who visited more than 500 homes, were promised the star karyakarta title. How much this helped to keep the tempo of the campaign high was reflected in the result. Incidentally, Nitish Kumar had to tie up with his arch-rival Lalu Yadav not only to stop division of votes but also to have cadres working on ground for his party. Unlike BJP or Lalu's RJD, Nitish's JD(U) did not have cadre base which is crucial for any election campaign. Kishor could create ideas but in election you need foot soldiers to execute the same. Evidently, the Har Ghar Dastak programme helped bringing together cadres from two different poles and deliver an electoral magic.

Nitish-campaign initiative, 'Ask Nitish' on Twitter was an attempt to a two-way communication campaigns unlike PM Modi's 'Mann ki Baat' (straight talk), which Nitish campaign felt was a monologue. In contrast, 'Ask Nitish' attempted to provide answers to the questions raised in detail and with humility unlike Modi's campaign what the CM's campaign felt was haughty.

> Just like the CM's famous janata durbar, #AskNitish has led to the resolution of concerns raised by many citizens. Not just that, the campaign has also focused on real time interviews with the media on Twitter—thus setting the agenda and narrative for the elections.[3]

Clearly, there was emphasis on media in Nitish campaign while Modi and his campaign head BJP President Amit Shah knew well that the national media had adopted an adversarial position to them.

A well-publicized campaign by team Nitish was the Swabhimaan (self-dignity) campaign also called the 'Bihari DNA' campaign by the Kishor led I-PAC team. This was in response to Modi's DNA dig at Nitish and had little to do with the Gujarati *asmita* (dignity) narrative, though seemed similar by many. While rolling out NDA's campaign for assembly polls in Bihar, Modi singled out Nitish Kumar and said there was something wrong with his DNA. In a rally in Muzaffarpur Modi said there was something wrong with Kumar's 'political DNA' that led the JD(U) leader to ditch friends who worked with him. 'I was hurt when he withdrew his support. But when he did the same thing to a Mahadalit such as Jitan Manjhi, then I figured out there is something wrong in his political DNA,' Modi said, referring to the JD(U)'s split with the BJP in 2013.[4] 'What happened to those who worked with (Kumar)? To George Fernandes? To our (BJP's) Sushil Modi who once worked shoulder to shoulder with him?' he asked. Modi said Kumar broke up with the BJP for personal gain. 'If you hated me so much you could have come into my room and slapped me or strangled me. But you throttled the development of Bihar because of your problems with one man,' he said. The mutual animosity between Prime Minister Modi and Bihar Chief Minister Nitish Kumar came out in the open. From this point onwards, Bihar election campaign turned personal. The Prime Minister had also lashed out at Kumar's ally Lalu Prasad, saying his RJD stood for 'rozana jungle raj ka dar' (fear of jungle raj everyday). Modi had asked Bihar's voters to pick a 'single-engine train' to drive growth, a reference to the combination of the RJD, JD(U) and the Congress for the polls to be held later this year. In a later campaign speech, Modi called it derisively as combination of three idiots, taking the term from a popular Hindi movie.

The Nitish-campaign saw the vulnerability of their leader in Modi's DNA barb. They were quick to launch a battle on the issue. First came a riposte in which Nitish Kumar sent a tweet alleging that PM Modi had insulted all Biharis. 'The Prime Minister said there is a problem in my DNA. I'm a son of Bihar, so it is the same DNA as the people of Bihar... I leave it to the people of Bihar how they judge a person who maligns their DNA,' his response on twitter. The Nitish campaign tried to turn the PM's barb as an attack against a democratically elected representative of the state and to that effect the entire state. According to Payal Kamat, their counter campaign was also an assertion of Bihari selfhood.

> The campaign has generated great enthusiasm with already more than 20 lac samples of hair and nails being submitted by people across the state, thus making the point that attacking the DNA of Bihar, is attacking its self-respect. These samples are being sent to PM Modi in batches.—Kamat wrote in an article to a website.[5]

The national media played in favour of the 'Bihari selfhood' claim of the Nitish-campaign. The Bihar election campaign from then onwards turned into a battle between two personalities Narendra Modi and Nitish Kumar. It could never get out the personality clash issue with Nitish campaign winning successfully a large section of national media to its side. Instead of taking a relook at the impact of his personal attack, Modi went on with his barbs.

Nitish Kumar on the other hand was once beaten twice shy. During the national election, Nitish dismissed Modi as a leader of no consequence. But in the assembly election, where his personal stake was very high, he took time off to follow Modi's speeches carefully and reacted well prepared. The cautious move and the ability to judge correctly the strength of his adversary helped Nitish campaign to turn a factual statement of Modi on past record of Nitish in deserting his allies into a campaign of attack on self-respect of all Biharis. The later campaign of Bihari vs. Bahari (outsider) by team Nitish was another clever twist that caught Modi-campaign in a trap.

In contrast, the Modi campaign was elated at the size of the crowd the Prime Minister was attracting in his rallies mistaking the same as spontaneous support as was the case in 2014. Nitish Kumar and his allies were better prepared now not any more oblivious to the popularity Modi enjoys. Nitish campaign also had the worry of how the coalition with his arch enemy Lalu Prasad Yadav was working on ground. This led the Nitish campaign to argue that the Prime Minister merely talked big without any record of success in the last 18 months. Constant negative campaign against the Modi government made people easily accept the argument. Political analyst Sanjay Singh concluded:

> ...so his (Nitish's) best chance lies in convincing people that Modi and the BJP aren't offering any solution to the problems of the state. Nitish is hoping to argue that the Prime Minister is only insulting wisdom of the people and make the elections an emotive one about Bihari pride.[6]

This strategy worked while Modi went on abusing his rivals.

People at large did not take kindly to Prime Minister Modi's '*chunawi jumla*'—*attack during election* mode. As the results showed clearly that Modi should have left for some other party functionary to call JD(U) as *Janata Ka Daman aur Utpidan* (party of suppressing people and torture) and RJD as *Rojana Jungle Raj Ka Dar* (party that would bring in jungle raj every day). Evidently, Modi, the master orator, was carried away by his success and also the massive crowd his rallies attracted. Unfortunately, unlike the 2014 campaign, there was no team of professional gauging the mood of the audience and resorting to course correction for BJP campaign in Bihar. Nitish Kumar had the advantage with the professional support from Prashant Kishore and his team.

An interesting analysis of election rallies by the star campaigners Modi, Nitish and Rahul Gandhi showed the different style and response to their campaign. They were as different as chalk and cheese reported Aman Sharma in the *Economic Times*.[7] 'Three rallies in a radius of 30 kilometres and within three hours of each other turned out to be as different as chalk and cheese when PM Modi, CM Nitish Kumar and Congress scion Rahul Gandhi landed in Seemanchal on November 2nd.' Modi rallies had a sea of crowd, 'a two–three km walk required to reach the venue and a shoulder-to-shoulder jostle to get out'. This led to the trademark Modi statement, 'This ground has also fallen short. What to do? There is no bigger ground in Purnea. Many can't see me also.' Since the crowd was not swayed to vote for BJP coalition, why did they go to his rallies? Aman Sharma quoted an aged member of the crowd, 'Only his oratory is good, *tabhi zamaana diwana hai inka* (that is why people are mad for him).' In fact, one BJP MP confided that there had been huge crowd in all Modi rallies, but there was no enthusiastic response from them as was seen during campaign 2014.

Nitish Kumar knew that he was no match for Narendra Modi in oratory, but unlike Rahul Gandhi he did not attempt to change his own style. Knowing well that Nitish Kumar's rallies are more like open-house sessions, more orderly and sedate, with a mediocre attendance that tends to fill smaller grounds. In his rallies, women were offered chairs to sit in a separate enclosure. He spoke like an elder brother or senior school teacher without going much into technicalities and certainly avoided history which was incidentally the main plank of NDA campaign. Nitish knew well that ten years have elapsed and his tenure managed to wipe out the wounds of the Lalu Prasad rule. More important for two long years, Nitish ruled with RJD support without denting his record of governance. Perhaps consciously, Nitish Kumar projected an image of a local wise man unperturbed over the Modi onslaught but asked his people to continue having their faith in him. With the caste equation firmly in his favour, Nitish knew his strengths and weaknesses. Modi on the other hand winked at his weakness—the fact that the changes brought by his government were yet to percolate to the people in a big way. Given the experience of ten years, Nitish was viewed as a man of development in

Bihar while they judged Modi on the basis of constant media report as 'all sound but little substance'.

Rahul Gandhi's party Congress received a big boost with Bihar assembly result—from a measly four seats in 2010, the party reached 27 seats—a strike rate of close to 70 per cent though less than those of JD(U)—73 per cent and RJD—80 per cent. But the credit goes entirely for the accommo-dation by the two regional strong men perhaps as an appreciation for its helping hand in forming the Mahagathbandhan in the first place. Rahul's rallies had been sparsely attended with nothing much to hear from him though he received media attention disproportionate to the content and quality of rallies. Clearly, Congress had been the collateral beneficiary of the successful coalition forged in Bihar.

For BJP, Bihar was an uphill struggle from the very beginning. Immediately after the national election, BJP lost by-elections in the state when the three parties JD(U), RJD and Congress tied up. The state is known for its caste divide. The caste question overshadowed the question of development. Sevanti Ninan who runs the media analysis website The Hoot pointed out how caste issue dominated the Bihar poll discourse.

Are you a forward or a backward? An EFC (extreme forward caste) or an EBC (extreme backward caste)? And how extreme is that? From seat distribu-tion to media reporting and analysis, it has been caste all the way in these elections. So in the current context, a voter on camera will proudly declare himself to be an 'atipichra' (extreme backward) as a badge of eligibility for benefits, Ninan wrote.[8]

She observed that not only media but even star campaigners includ-ing Prime Minister Modi focused unrelentingly on caste. BJP had no option since the NDA coalition knew that the caste equation of the Mahagathbandhan was perfect combination to win an election in Bihar. In addition, there was an unforeseen statement on reservation by BJP's parent body RSS chief. To turn a complex caste situation even more daunting for BJP coalition, Mohan Bhagwat, Chief of RSS suggested in an interview to the two mouthpieces Organiser and Panchjanya that reservation policy should be reviewed in the country. 'We believe, form a committee of people genuinely concerned for the interest of the whole nation and committed for social equality, including some representa-tives from the society, they should decide which categories require reservation and for how long', Bhagwat had said. 'The non-political committee like autonomous commissions should be the implementation authority; political authorities should supervise them for honesty and integrity', he also added.[9] Coming close on the heels of the beginning of the five-phase Bihar assembly election, BJP coalition could not have a more formidable foot in the mouth situation. RSS is widely seen as the organization setting up policy guidelines for its political arm BJP. Coming from its Sarsanghachalak (supreme chief) Nitish campaign used it to their delight. For a caste-based coalition that hoped to forge an alliance of lower caste, backward caste and Muslims the statement from Dr Bhagwat was manna from heaven. The first die of NDA loss was cast. Muzamil Jaleel of *Indian Express* wrote after visiting students of Magadh University, 'It's hard to escape caste in Indian politics, but more so in Bihar, where politicians, with their enviable grip over caste arithmetic, play the game like no one else can.' Filed just a week after the statement of Mohan Bhagwat on reservation, Jaleel wrote:

> ...the RSS chief's remarks were just bad timing. Bihar's voter, especially the young voter who has grown up on a diet of Mandal politics and politicians, is all too politically astute to have missed the significance of the remark. Lalu only sharpened the lines further with his call for Mandal II.[10]

Jaleel noticed that there had been occasions in the past when students rose beyond the caste arithmetic. For instance, the assembly election in Bihar in 2005 was about Lalu Yadav's 'misrule', 2010 was a test of Nitish-led JD(U)–BJP government's 'vikas' and the 2014 Lok Sabha polls were only about Narendra Modi. But Bihar-2015 saw complex caste calculations ruling again. Clearly, BJP poll strategy failed to change the discourse. Mere presence of Narendra Modi and his oratory could not bring in any new factor to sway the voters away from the near invincible caste equation forged by Nitish Kumar and Lalu Yadav which ensured support from Muslims as well with Congress in the fold. Predictably, media sensed how caste would be the decider in the assembly election. Even reputed TV channels went on to ask respondents what were their castes. One well-known reporter, wrote Ninan, went on to mention that one-third of BJP's candidates were from upper castes while they constituted only 16 per cent of the state's population. How sensitive were Biharis on caste could be gathered from reports of Muzamil Jaleel. Jaleel too recorded the caste sensitivity of the students when they discuss 'vikas' (development) and on how to 'free the state from the clutches of caste' which they felt was the single biggest divisive factor, they ended up being deeply entangled in it.[11]

Caste loyalty clouds their final judgement. One student told Jaleel:

> The truth is, to us students, the reality of caste hits hard on two occasions— at the time of marriage and during elections. For four and a half years, we pretend as if caste doesn't matter. Then the elections happen and we are made aware of our caste differences.

Caste is so deep rooted in parts of Bihar that 'if a person needs to go to a doctor, he checks the doctor's caste first'.[12]

For Muslim students, the biggest concern is the rise of communal politics, which will turn the Muslim community 'into a common enemy to be kicked around'. 'Anyone but the BJP,' one student said of his voting preference.[13]

If the fact that caste and development issues are interlinked matters less for the younger generation, the older voters particularly those who are less educated and exposed to the world, like women, will blindly follow their caste loyalties. In such a state, BJP, viewed as an upper-caste party, was not expected to match the winning combination of Lalu and Nitish. Brand Modi was not what Bihar had been looking for. BJP's campaign strategist Amit Shah read the Bihar election pitch wrongly.

The Bihar campaign of BJP clearly had put its entire emphasis on the popularity of Prime Minister Modi. Despite losing Delhi election in February, the party did not learn its lesson. By overusing its valuable brand in a wrong market, the BJP campaign not only diluted the Modi brand but also put its government in New Delhi at a great disadvantage. The high-pitched campaign of BJP against the low-key Nitish campaign with the soft-spoken Nitish Kumar as the leader of the coalition did the trick. Member of Rajya Sabha and editor of *The Pioneer*, Chandan Mitra wrote:

> But ultimately Bihar demonstrated that it is far from rejecting caste as its main political currency... when voting for a government in the state, caste reared its ubiquitous head... .It is an established fact that when casteism determines voting intentions in North Indian States, the BJP ends up as the main loser. And in the attempt to match caste with caste, BJP strategists erred in their calculations.[14]

The other weakness of the campaign had been the failure to project a local leader to head its campaign. According to Mitra, the 'Bihari sub-national pride did not reconcile itself to the party not projecting local leaders—the Bahari versus Bihari slogan, craftily coined by the Lalu–Nitish duo, seemed to receive traction as the campaign progressed.'

Mitra also pointed out a unique character of Indian elections. 'As in real-life dramas, elections in India are contested in a hero-villain syndrome. Whichever party is able to portray its opponent as a villain, has a natural advantage.'[15] In 2014, national election Narendra Modi had a villain in Congress party in general and the Gandhi family in particular. But the Bihar poll was fought without a villain in the picture.

> For the BJP, its regular villain, the Nehru–Gandhi dynasty, was only a bit player, almost without a speaking role in the long-running drama. By opt-ing for a back seat, Lalu ensured he did not fit that role either. And Nitish, with the fully deserved epithet 'Susashan Babu' (good governance leader) could not have been acceptable to the people as the villain. So it ended up as a contest between two heroes—Narendra Modi and Nitish Kumar. The campaign was devoid of any rhetoric against the incumbent Chief Minister, a rarity in Indian elections.[16]

What Mitra called sub-national pride is present in all states in different doses. In none of the eastern states barring Jharkhand in 2014, BJP had ever formed a government of its own. In Bihar, the alliance with Nitish Kumar succeeded in 2005. But alone and in coalition with some caste leaders who did have very local influence, BJP was not in a position to sway a caste-based population with socialist bias to its way. Brand Modi was squandered in a wrong market. Surajit Dasgupta in an analysis for *Swarajya Magazine* wrote:

> Modi's Lok Sabha election campaign was so refreshingly full of hope for a new India that large sections of Yadavs had dumped Mulayam Singh and Lalu Prasad while Dalits dumped Mayawati and went for 'sab ka saath, sab ka vikas'. That vision, that hope was conspicuous by its absence at the Bihar hustings.[17]

BJP failed to demonstrate clearly to the voters that it has a different vision for the country.

That differentiator, Bihar has proven, cannot be the cow. Not in eastern India (remember, it is Bengal next). It has to be pro-market reforms coupled with a social education programme for the masses that must kick in much before an election starts; that education must impress upon the electorate that the seven decade-long government-driven economy can do them no good; it is time for a new paradigm.[18]

Brand Modi had its problem due to an assortment of his colleagues in the party and the government.

You cannot have a leader talk 'development' while an assortment of his colleagues is constantly working on distracting, communal issues, and yet expect to pull off stunning victories in polls. …That the party ruling at the Centre is 'intolerant', going by uncontrollable incidents like Dadri[19] happening across the country, however, was a message the opposition-friendly media was directing to the Bihari voter for months, which aggravated the crisis for the BJP that could come up with no convincing riposte to the charge.

What is more the arrogance of BJP was visible at every stage of the campaign. Its President Amit Shah was particularly responsible for giving such an impression. He said on October 29th while addressing a rally in Raxaul, 'If by any mistake BJP loses, victory and defeat may be in Bihar but fire crackers will go off in Pakistan. Do you want crackers being burst in Pakistan?' A party fighting an election should never talk of the possibility of defeat. In whatever manner you complete the sentence, even trying to petrify Hindus by invoking Pakistan, the message that is conveyed is that you are bracing for defeat. That may well have been the message voters of the fourth and fifth rounds got from the BJP chief.[20]

The copybook style spectacular election campaign of Narendra Modi in 2014 lost its shine in two massive electoral losses in NCT Delhi and Bihar. In both the states, BJP faced a two-way contest. Brand Modi was pitted against a popular but maverick activist turned politician Arvind Kejriwal in Delhi and a veteran and successful Chief Minister Nitish Kumar in Bihar. Kejriwal had his dedicated set of cadres who understood nuances of modern communication. Nitish Kumar hired the professional services of Prashant Kishore who played an important role in Modi 2014 campaign. Both in Delhi and in Bihar, BJP campaign was left to the party machinery headed by its President Amit Shah. In both the states, BJP failed to encash the Modi magic. Clearly, elections in India depend on the time and place of the contest. Even in the highly successful Modi-2014 campaign, BJP failed to make a dent in at least four states—West Bengal, Odisha, Tamil Nadu and Kerala. The electoral success of Modi 2014 campaign should be seen in this context.

The other critical factor in a country like India is whether the leader is an incumbent or not. In 2014, Narendra Modi was an outsider with some success report from the state of Gujarat where he was the Chief Minister. In 2015 for Bihar, he was an incumbent Prime Minister. The anti-incumbency factor of Nitish Kumar got cancelled out with Prime Minister Modi's record in office. Other things remaining similar, people of Bihar opted for its local and tested leader instead of an unspecified leader to be appointed by BJP if the party came to power. The brand loyalty for Modi in Bihar was strong as could be seen from the massive crowd attending his rallies. But the same was not strong enough to defeat two formidable factors in favour of Nitish Kumar—the perfect caste equation in a state where caste matters and the past record of Nitish Kumar as Chief Minister. The Bihar package announced with much drama by the Prime Minister did not influence much since voters knew well enough that even if Nitish Kumar won, the package would be implemented. It was not linked to electing BJP-led government. Analyst Suraji Bhalla who predicted a landslide in favour of the Mahagathbandhan summed up as to why Nitish enjoyed better brand equity in Bihar than that of Modi:

> Nitish Kumar has followed a four-dimensional development model. First was to decrease lawlessness, second to build roads, third was electrification and fourth was to enhance and encourage girls' education. That's a very nice spectrum to fight an election on. I think people saw the work he did.[21]

Most analysts agreed generally that caste equation overtook brand Modi. But a Lokniti–CSDS survey for the *Indian Express* revealed that the emphasis of the BJP campaign to equate Bihar with a backward state did not go well with the aspirations that the Modi-2014 campaign infused. Between mid-day meal and computer education, the survey observed, more than two-thirds of the respondents opted for the latter. 'This aspirational preference was spread robustly across age-groups and was irrespective of the respondent's education.'[22] Bhalla too questioned the disproportionate importance given to the caste factor:

> There is zero evidence, and I emphasise, ZERO evidence to prove that people vote based on caste.... Is it the caste of the politician that the people are voting for? Did Jitan Manjhi then get all the Mahadalit votes? Or is it the caste of the voters that matter? Then why did the same people vote for Modi during the Lok Sabha elections?

He felt that it was the coalition of competing political forces that sealed the fate of BJP in Bihar, 'The two-party versus three-party contest played out and that's why I say the alliance really worked. It is obviously not caste.'[23]

Brand Modi shone in 2014 since it was pitted against the UPA government that was a miserable failure. Indians everywhere were angry not only at the Manmohan Singh government but also with the Congress President Sonia Gandhi and her son Rahul Gandhi. Having a much highlighted villain was easy for Modi to spread his message of development. But in 2015 Bihar, the message of growth was rusty. Instead of development what came to the fore was eating of beef, relook at reservation, and anti-minority utterances of BJP associates. Value of brand Modi was diluted by its internal public more than any outsider. Inability to forge a working relation with opposition so that parliament functions also went against Modi's leadership quality further weakening the brand. Not all faults lay with Modi or BJP but as a former Bangladesh politician, Maulana Abdul Hamid Khan Bhashani had said, 'In an underdeveloped country you start losing popularity the moment you are in power,' Narendra Modi, too, lost his popularity rating somewhat. By pitching him in an election that was completely loaded against BJP-led coalition, Amit Shah dealt a severe blow to brand Modi. It is for the brand manager to use a brand effectively. The same formula fits all types of campaign attitude of BJP led to its ignominious defeat both in Delhi and Bihar state assembly elections.

Political campaign is complex. It is even more complex in India, a country which boasts of the costliest residential house on one side and thousands having no roof on top of their heads, people who speak different languages, eat completely different food and what is more practised varied in religious rituals even when they espouse the same Hinduism. The sum total of sub-nations leads to people casting votes differently in national and state elections. Brand Modi is a national brand but was not enough to vanquish brand Nitish, a brand for Bihar. A coalition that could be stitched together for a compulsion in Bihar might not even be formed when national election comes. State elections merely illustrate the limitation of Modi under certain conditions, anything beyond that is speculation.

Distinct Flavour of the Election Campaign

Elections are not peculiar to democracy; it takes place at regular intervals to enable the voters to elect their rulers. So, the 2015 Bihar election is just a routine matter though in four unique ways, it stands out in the annals of India's recent political history.

First, the Grand Alliance of JD(U) and RJD reconfirms the idea that in politics, there is hardly a permanent foe or a friend. It was simply inconceivable just before the preparation for the assembly had begun that the incumbent Chief Minister, Nitish Kumar would fight his former ally, the BJP in alliance with his erstwhile political foe, Lalu Prasad Yadav. Despite being characterized as an opportunistic coalition, the coming together of Nitish Kumar and the RJD supremo was undoubtedly governed by a grand strategy drawing on caste considerations. Both these leaders are assumed to be effective in building a solid vote back for the grand alliance. So, two former arch-rivals agreed to forget the past primarily for electoral dividends which they badly need to trounce electorally their bitter enemy, the BJP.

Second, for the BJP that is in saddles of power at the centre, the Bihar election was a life-and-death question. If it could win, the ruling BJP would have proved its unquestionable popularity as a party of governance with the incumbent Prime Minister Modi as the mascot of victory. If it lost, as it did, its claim as a party with solid mass base would further be weakened and perhaps strengthen the detractors within the party who are opposed to Modi and his Man Friday, Amit Shah to raise their heads against them. Moreover, camping in Patna to monitor the campaign, the BJP boss, Shah, had left no stone unturned to reach out to the voters even in remote villages with the help of RSS cadres. Besides providing organizational support, Shah had also created an enviable record of election rallies to be addressed by the Prime Minister; it is a record since no other Prime Minister in the past addressed so many election rallies in an assembly election.

Third, even from the point of view of the nature of the election campaigns, the Bihar election is a class apart. One notices visible metamorphosis in the nature of the issues that figure prominently in the campaign as it progresses. In the first two phases, the campaign was generally confined to the issues of development: the BJP promised 'a golden Bihar' while its rivals chart out a course of action to continue with the developmental plans and programmes that the incumbent JD(U) government had initiated since it came to power in 2010. There was suddenly a change of gear: drawing on the Jungle Raj that Bihar encountered when the RJD was in power before 2010, the BJP highlighted the inevitable adverse consequences in case the grand alliance was allowed to form government. Given the exclusionary policy designs of the erstwhile RJD government, both the Dalits and upper castes, the BJP candidates warned, are likely to bear the brunt of such partisan measures. In view of the Dadri brutal murder merely on the suspicion of having eaten beef, the grand alliance held the BJP responsible for growing communalization in India and also sharpened their attack by highlighting the possible adverse effect of communalism in India. Furthermore, the statement of RSS Chief Mohan Bhagwat on the need for reviewing the reservation scheme was utilized by the alliance to suggest that reservation for the OBCs was likely to be withdrawn; this had been continuously mentioned in the election campaign to garner support of the sections of society which might have felt threatened with this utterance of Bhagwat. For the BJP's super campaigner Modi, Nitish Kumar's characterization of Modi being 'bahari (outsider)' gave a fillip because he switched over to refer to Sonia Gandhi's foreign origin to support his contention of Sonia being a bahari and not a Bihari; Modi attacked Sonia Gandhi because she happened to be a part of the grand alliance. So one saw the relative decline of socio-economic issues in the election campaign that seemed to have hovered around even personal attack! Furthermore, the BJP Secretary Amit Shah's contention that 'if NDA loses, there will be celebration in Pakistan' appears to have disturbed the Bihari voters to a significant extent who dubbed this as a threat to their personal integrity. Whether this statement was directed to create a nationalist fervour is difficult to say though it certainly had adverse impact on the voters, especially those in the fringe who instantly became adversaries to the BJP.

Finally, the campaign in the 2015 election also draws on memories of brutality, being perpetrated by both the upper caste supported Ranveer

Sena and the reign of terror that Shahbuddin, Munna Shukla and Sadhu Yadav unleashed during the RJD's long rule. Although Ranveer Sena seems to have lost its sheen because of lack of leadership, voters were being reminded by the grand alliance partners of the 1997 Laxmanpur Bathe incident where more than 50 Dalits were mercilessly killed by the upper caste had supported Sena. This is a past incident; nonetheless, it was being highlighted to alienate the Dalits and OBCs from the BJP which, if elected to power, was likely to establish the upper caste hegemony. Similarly, the BJP had been constantly harping on the Jungle Raj that was established with the support of the ruling RJD when the history sheeters had a free hand! The definite poll outcome in Bihar reveals how the voters decided on the basis of what they deemed appropriate, as the following discussion confirms.

Analyzing the Poll Results

Bihar is perhaps one of those few Indian provinces where the identity issues always remain a critical variable in election. The 2014 Lok Sabha poll seem to be an aberration since the identity consideration did not appear to be an effective vote-catcher tool; the BJP's plank of development and Modi's charisma and the backing of the Sangh Parivar were important factors in winning a landslide victory, of course, in the context of the failure of the Congress-led UPA to effectively combat corruption. The alternative that the BJP stood for appeared to be real, to the Bihari voters who seem to have supported the NDA candidates clearly for a corruption-free and development-driven government. Bihar was no exception since this was the trend in the entire north India where the opposition parties, including the ruling Congress were almost completely trounced.

In the 2014 Lok Sabha poll, the BJP and its allies in the NDA reaped the advantage of the so-called Modi wave. The entire north India seemed to have been swayed by the wave which sealed the fate of most of the contesting candidates belonging to the incumbent ruling conglomeration. With its promise to provide 'good governance as against misgovernance', the BJP managed to build a solid vote bank comprising people from different socio-economic strata. The claim seemed to have persuaded the voters presumably because of its projected candidate, the sitting Chief Minister of Gujarat, Narendra Modi, who was credited with the impressive development that the state had during his tenure as Chief Minister. It was, therefore, the track record of Modi which acted favourably in the 2014 national poll. The main losers in the election happen to be two dominant regional parties, the RJD and JD(U) that managed to win only in five parliamentary seats. The 2014 Lok Sabha poll is thus a story of BJP's ascendancy and decline of the state-based parties as Table P.1 shows.

Table P.1:
The 2014 Lok Sabha Poll in Bihar

Party	Seats, Won	Percentage of Votes, Polled by Each Party*
Bharatiya Janata Party	22	29.9%
Janata Dal (United)	02	14.5%
Indian National Congress	02	8.6%
Nationalist Congress Party	01	1.2%
Lok Janshakti Party	06	6.5%
Rashtriya Janata Dal	04	20.5%
Rashtriya Lok Samata Party	03	3.7%
Total	**40**	

Source: Adapted from the figures provided in the website of the EC of India, 2015, accessed on 9 November 2015.
Note: * These inputs are taken from *The Economic Times*, New Delhi, 9 November 2015.

As Table P.1 shows, the BJP had a very impressive vote share which allowed them to trounce the divided opposition presumably because of the first-past-the-poll system of voting. If the RJD and JD(U) fought together, as they did in the context of the 2015 assembly election, it would have been difficult for the BJP to get more than half of the total Lok Sabha seats from Bihar, as the total of votes that they had polled was more than the BJP's share. So, one can safely argue that the impressive BJP victory was largely due to the split of votes which was avoided in the recent assembly election when the Mahagathbandhan convincingly defeated the BJP and its coalition partners in more than two-thirds of the assembly constituencies. The strategy that Ram Manohar Lohia had devised to avoid the division of opposition votes in the context of 1967 state assembly election continues to remain effective and needless to say, it also worked in the Bihar assembly election.

As argued previously, by avoiding vote splits, the conglomeration of RJD, JD(U) and Congress became invincible. This is one part of the story; the other equally important segment of this narrative is liked with how a right kind of caste combination allowed the BJP's opponents to reap electoral dividends in the 2015 election. Undoubtedly, caste considerations remained paramount since the contesting political parties had begun choosing candidates for each constituencies. Whatever might have been the election pledges, the political leadership took ample care to select the candidates essentially in terms of their caste appeal. Despite the fact that the BJP kept highlighting the development agenda, it also chose candidates on the same considerations. This was evident in the list of candidates that the party had fielded; since Yadavs are estimated to constitute almost 14 per cent of the Bihar population, the BJP had chosen at least one Yadav candidate in every large district. The fact that a Yadav was made party's general secretary in Bihar is also a testimony to the fact that the identity issue was given precedence over development which seemed to have received less attention. As the list shows, the NDA continues to bank heavily on upper caste as the alliance had fielded not less than 85 upper caste candidates; there were 28 Yadavs, 40 SCs, nine Muslims, 29 belonged to the Extremely Backward Classes and Kurmi-Koeri-Vaishya had 58 candidates. For the Mahagathbandhan, the scene was clearer: as many as one hundred and 34 candidates were from OBCs and Maha Backward Classes (extremely backward classes), 40 SC/Scheduled Tribes, 33 Muslims and 35 upper castes. These figures direct our attention to the fact that the candidates were selected by the parties in fray on the basis of their caste affiliations since it would help them win the election. It also shows that the party ideologues seem to have been swayed by the consideration that caste remained a vote-catcher device. So, the context was ready: the election did not seem to be an ideological battle, but an occasion to establish caste hegemony of specific caste groups. The RJD of Mahagathbandhan chose candidates to consolidate its Muslim–Yadav vote banks while its alliance partner, JD(U) sought to strengthen the Maha Backward Classes–Mahadalit coalition by being favourably disposed towards the candidates from this combination. On the basis of above inputs, one can thus safely argue that though the BJP and Mahagathbandhan had emphasized the clamour for development, in the end, they resorted to caste calculation to tilt the outcome in their favour which is manifested in the proportion of votes they polled, as the following table shows.

Table P.2:
Performance of Selective Political Parties in Bihar Assembly Election 2015

Political Parties	Seats, Won	Percentage of Votes Polled
Janata Dal (United)	71 (115)	16.8% (22.6%)
Rashtriya Janata Dal	80 (22)	18.4% (18.8%)
Indian National Congress	27 (04)	6.7% (8.4%)
Bharatiya Janata Party	53 (91)	24.4% (16.4%)
Lok Janshakti Party	02 (03)	4.8% (6.8%)
Rashtriya Lok Samata Party	02*	2.6%
Hindustani Aam Morcha (Secular)	01*	2.3%
Communist Party of India (Marxist-Leninist) Liberation	03**	1.5%

Source: Adapted from the figures, provided in the website of the EC of India, 2015, accessed on 9 November 2015.

Notes: (a) Figures in the parenthesis show the number of seats, won by the contesting parties and the percentages of votes, polled by them in the 2010 Assembly election.

(b) While Janata Dal (United), Rashtriya Janata Dal and Indian National Congress formed the Mahagatbandhan (Grand Alliance), its bête noire, the National Democratic Alliance was constituted by the Bharatiya Janata Party, Lok Janshakti Party, Rashtriya Lok Samata Party and Hindustani Aam Morcha (Secular).
*These parties were not even formed in 2010;
**this party did not open its account in the earlier assembly election.

Table P.2 confirms, the Mahagathbandhan is well ahead of its opponent, the NDA coalition not only in terms of seats, but also in the proportion of voters that supported the alliance. The Modi effect did not seem to have worked favourably for the BJP while an effective electoral strategy and an appropriate caste-combination made the Mahagathbandhan seemingly unassailable. This is evident in the vote share for the respective conglomeration, as Table P.3 shows.

Table P.3:
Share of Votes of Contesting Political Parties in 2014 and 2015

Party	Vote Share in the Lok Sabha Poll, 2014	Vote Share in the 2015 Assembly Election	Change
BJP	29.4%	24.4%	−5.0%
Lok Janshakti Party	6.4%	4.8%	−1.6
Rashtriya Lok Samata Party	3.0%	2.6%	−0.4%
Hindustani Aam Morcha (Secular)	—	2.3%	+2/3%
NDA	38.8%	34.1%	−4.7%
Rashtriya Janata Dal	20.1%	18.4%	−1.7%
Janata Dal (United)	15.8%	16.8%	+1.0%
Indian National Congress	8.4%	6.7%	−1.7%
Mahagathbandhan	44.3%	41.9%	−2.4%

Source: The Times of India, New Delhi, 11 November 2015, p. 10.

Table P.3 is self-explanatory. Not only has the NDA's vote share considerably eclipsed, the constituents of Mahagathbandhan did not do well in this respect because their vote share has also declined, but not to the extent it has for the NDA. Nonetheless, the results show the convincing victory for the Mahagathbandhan candidates presumably because of the first-past-the-poll system of election. The winning candidates may not have had support of the majority, but of the candidates in the fray, they had won maximum number of votes which made them winner. So, the Grand Alliance of three major Bihar-based political parties reaps the benefit of coalition by avoiding vote splits. It is admitted by the BJP when one of its senior ministers of the incumbent NDA government, Arun Jaitley, commented while seeking to explain the electoral debacle by saying that

> ...in the 2014 general election, the three partners in the Grand Alliance had fought separately. In the Lok Sabha polls, we found that polling percentage was 38.8% while various constituents of the Grand Alliance had got 45.3% but separately. We felt that may be, when coalitions happen, partners cannot transfer their votes totally to each other. So we thought that combined with the Prime Minister's appeal, the three of them would not be able to beat us. We were proved wrong.[24]

Why did it happen? The reason has to be located in an effective social engineering that Mahagathbandhan's ideologues and also strategists
affected to sway the majority of the voters in their favour. So, with the
alliance, it was possible for Mahagathbandhan to develop a formidable
bloc to oppose the NDA conglomeration. By avoiding the division of votes
among their supporters, the constituents of the Grand Alliance reinforce
the coalition dharma which gave them electoral benefits beyond expectations. This is one part of the story; the other equally important part is
linked with the image of the incumbent Chief Minister, Nitish Kumar,
as an icon of development. His track record as an administrator reveals
that by concentrating on *sadak* (road), *bijli* (electricity), *pani* (water) and
shiksha (education), he created his own constituency of supporters across
the length and breadth of the state which always remains at the bottom of
the development chart in the past. Hence, it has been rightly argued that:

> Nitish may have scored on election arithmetic because he was able to har-
> ness Lalu's formidable caste bloc. But the scale of this triumph shows that
> this is not just a vote for caste combinations but also a reward from Biharis
> for his consistent efforts in trying to make their lives better.[25]

The argument is supported by a field report which suggests that 'not
only did the Grand Alliance get its arithmetic right through Lalu [Prasad
Yadav's] formidable social coalition, Nitish [Kumar's] track record as the
man who brought development to one of India's most backward regions
added winning chemistry.[26] The favourable poll outcome is thus a creative
blending of arithmetic and chemistry: while by preventing split of votes,
the Mahagathbandhan fixed the dice in its favour by building a solid
supportive social blocs among the OBCs and also Extremely Backward
Classes, its constituents, JD(U) and RJD, in particular, eclipsed the chances
of the BJP-led NDA of repeating the 2014 story.

A study of the Bihar poll outcome also underlines the point that the
RJD supremo, Lalu Prasad Yadav and the JD(U) mascot, Nitish Kumar
are complementary to each other; it was their joint effort that pushed the
NDA to the periphery and put the Grand Alliance in the saddles of power.
While the former retained the support base by reiterating the demand
for social justice, Nitish Kumar sustained his popularity by dint of hard
work for Bihar's socio-economic progress. There are detractors of Lalu
Prasad Yadav because of his attacking style of politics, his partner in the

Grand Alliance seems to have swayed the voters by his charisma which 'comes not from an impressive appearance or ringing voice, but from a sincere earnestness, and the subliminal aura of Mr Nice Guy [who was hailed for being] an achha aadmi (good guy) who accomplished what he had promised.'[27] Furthermore, Modi's exhortation for development seems to have convinced the voters since they were not persuaded by mere promises; whereas, what the incumbent Chief Minister did to translate his promises into reality was visible: villages are connected by metal roads; school buildings have been built in villages; power cuts are no longer a recurring phenomenon; and law and order situation has considerably been improved. Nitish Kumar's development plank is thus a reality while Modi's has little to showcase for the hinterland and small town voters. The huge financial package that the Prime Minister announced at the beginning of the campaign did not seem to tempt the voters to vote for the NDA. It is not, therefore, surprising that Nitish Kumar suffered virtually no anti-incumbency backlash even after nine years in power as Chief Minister which perhaps explains why Nitish Kumar struck a chord of familiarity with local Biharis which paid off in the 2015 assembly election.

One of the weaknesses of the NDA's campaign strategy, which helped the opponent, stems from an exclusive dependence on Modi–Shah's capacity to garner adequate number of votes. As a result, the local leadership was neither allowed to intervene nor had a chance to guide the campaign in accordance with what they deemed appropriate. The BJP went into campaign with only two of its popular faces, Modi and his party president, Amit Shah. The local leadership was completely ignored even in the campaign posters and hoardings which was a source of irritation for the local party units; not only did this strategy weaken the organization in Bihar, it also gave a fillip to the opponents who now used this to lead the Bihar versus Bahari campaign. Till the third phase of the election, the pattern continued which, however, changed in the last two phases when the top BJP leadership seemed to have understood how damaging the strategy was. It is surprising that the BJP ideologues failed to comprehend the adverse effect of such a strategy despite its drubbing in the 2015 Delhi assembly election when the local leadership was simply bypassed to accommodate an outsider, Kiran Bedi, who was imposed from above which displeased the BJP workers who built the organization in Delhi brick-by-brick. This was a wrong strategy which drew on the overconfidence of the BJP's national leadership of Modi–Shah's ability to sway the voters for the BJP as they did in 2014 Lok Sabha and selective assembly polls that followed. For local voters, this also created a negative vibe for the BJP which was charged with disrespecting Bihari asmita (dignity). Even the committed BJP voters, it was reported, found it very humiliating since it was based on a misconception that the Modi–Shah combination had a capacity to sway the voters irrespective of socio-economic circumstances.

It was not merely electoral arithmetic or social justice plank that sealed the fate of the BJP-led NDA, the Hindutva strategy did not seem to work as was expected. The Dadri incident, Amit Shah's statement that if NDA lost there would be celebration in Pakistan and the prevalent atmosphere, being charged with the allegation that the NDA government was intolerant of diversity had an impact on the voters who did not appear to be convinced of electoral pledges that the star campaigners often made in the grand election rallies. Furthermore, Modi's strong arguments for development were also dismissed as vacuous in view of the failure of the government in 18 months of being in power in Delhi to deliver on the promise of development which was meant to translate into jobs and raise the standards of living for the people. Nobody was willing to take what Modi announced during the campaign seriously because of growing importance of those issues which had, according to the common Bihar voters, had hardly any relevance whatsoever in their daily existence. For instance, the party advertisement portraying a woman hugging a cow and state leaders calling the election a choice between those who eat beef and those who want to stop cow slaughter boomeranged because instead of creating a support base for the BJP, it resulted in alienation of a large contingent of even committed BJP voters from the alliance. None of the BJP stalwarts involved in the campaign realized the adverse outcome of an endeavour that reflected a clearly partisan ideological stance. In consequence, the election campaign that had begun with promises for good governance and development gradually diverted to cultural wars and personality clashes which went on unheeded. In such a context, the clamour for Hindutva was always interpreted as a design to divert people's attention away from livelihood concerns. As the election results show, none of their grand strategies allowed the BJP to reap political dividends in a situation when the anti-BJP forces came together regardless of their ideological differences and personal enmities to fight a common foe. So, the BJP's failure to comprehend Bihar's peculiar socio-economic context and Mahagathbandhan's ability to successfully read the pulse of the people seem to have been critical in understanding the 2015 poll outcome which is likely to set in motion processes of change in India's political texture.

Concluding Observations

India is not only the largest democracy in the world, it is perhaps the most creative laboratory of democracy as well. Elections are generally the occasions when voters elect their representatives to form a government of their choice. There are however elections which are also trendsetters: the 2015 Bihar assembly election is one of them for a number of reasons which have been explored further.

First, the 2015 Bihar assembly election reinforces the importance of coalition dharma in bringing together even political foes under one platform. This was tried in the past both at the national and regional levels. By forging an alliance of the anti-Congress parties in the context of 1967 state assembly elections, Ram Manohar Lohia initiated a trend that continues to survive even today. Notwithstanding winning a majority in the 2014 Lok Sabha poll, the BJP is part of the NDA coalition; so, technically speaking, the BJP is running a coalition government in India in alliance with its coalition partners. Experiments were made at the state level: the Left Front government in West Bengal that was trounced by the Trinamul Congress-led *Mahajot* (Grand Alliance) in 2010 was another example of a successful coalition government that lasted for more than three decades since 1977. The Mahagathbandhan in Bihar is a testimony to the trend that is illustrative of the fact that coalition is perhaps the only politically viable means in government formation. There is however a major change in the texture of coalition in Bihar. As is evident in the past, the coalition partners flock together around a dominant political party: in case of national coalition, the two pan-Indian parties, the BJP and Congress, remained the focal points and smaller parties are drawn to them to remain politically viable and meaningful. This was also true of the Left Front government in West Bengal and Trinamul Congress followed the pattern when it formed government following the defeat of the CPI (M)-led coalition. Bihar is an exception in two major ways: on the one hand, despite being a pan-Indian party, the Congress is not a dominant partner in Mahagathbandhan leaving space to the regional/state-based parties, the JD(U) and RJD. Even the assembly seats were allotted to the parties, the Congress agreed to accept its secondary role allowing the dominant partners to keep a major share of candidates. The election results also show, on the other hand, that there is hardly a dominant partner though the RJD wins in 80 constituencies while its partner JD(U) registers victory in 71 seats in an assembly of 243 seats. So, none of them is actually a dominant partner and also the pre-election declaration of Nitish Kumar being the Chief Minister resolves the issue rather amicably.

Coalition is thus a great leveller in the sense that the partners are taken as equals when it is forged either to combat a political foe or to form a government. This is a paradigmatic shift in Indian politics when neither the contribution to the freedom struggle nor communally divisive agenda became critical in building consensus. With the articulation of the traditionally peripheral voices in politics, what have become significant are the issues of governance and development and not false assurances for socio-economic transformation in distant future. Unlike the European states, which are more or less uniform ethnolinguistically and thus culturally, the Indian version of coalition is thus a noteworthy contribution to democracy by locating the experiment in an essentially multicultural social context. And, in that respect, coalition is complementary to democratic processes, articulated not only in the ritualistic participation of the people in elections, but also in their day-to-day involvement in governance. In this fundamental sense, coalitions are unavoidable and cannot be wished away as a mere ripple.

Secondly, although it was a state assembly election, the Bihar election had ramifications at the national level. A script was written and the BJP's mascot that rallied voters in the 2014 general election no longer remained as effective as in the past. The convincing victory of Mahagathbandhan halted the juggernaut by devising strategies which the BJP failed to match. This has two serious implications: on the one hand, it exposes the claim that BJP cannot be defeated presumably because of its success in polarizing voters along with religious axis; the Bihar election also confirms, on the other hand, that any attempt in this regard hardly creates a vote bank for the party indulged in such a practice. The BJP needs to reinvent itself if it wants to remain a viable competitor in the forthcoming assembly elections and also the 2019 grand finale of the Lok Sabha poll. While election results firmly indicate the weakening of the BJP, they also substantiate the idea that Mahagathbandhan is a precursor of a grand alliance of anti-BJP political parties in the days to come. The Bihar poll has shown, in other words, that a combined opposition with a credible leader can defeat the BJP-led conglomeration, sparking speculation about the revival of a Third Front in a new garb. The results are, therefore, indicative of possibilities for future.

The Bihar poll outcome is also a powerful comment on the idea of India; that diversity is the core of the nation that can never be diluted, and efforts towards building a homogeneous nation in the Western sense seem to be suicidal. Drawing on the bogey of Pakistan, the BJP ideologues endeavoured hard to sway the mass of voters in their favour which harmed its campaign to a significant extent, as the results show. By asking the voters whether they prefer those who eat beef, the BJP campaign managers seem to have made a blunder which gave enough fodder to its opponents to attack the NDA for being divisive in its appeal. Instead of helping the BJP to garner votes, the fiddling with the inherent character of India as a nation-state appears to have consolidated the supporters for Mahagathbandhan. To this was added the BJP failure to project a local leader to take on the Grand Alliance. The distinction that the Mahagathbandhan campaigners made between a Bihari and a Bahari (outsider) helped the Alliance to play the subnationalist card that was strategically characterized as an insult to the Biharis when Modi accused Nitish Kumar of having wrong DNA. To put across the message, the incumbent Chief Minister asked the voters at the end of his address to the election rallies whether they wanted a Bihari or a Bahari Chief Minister. The response was always in favour of a Bihari Chief Minister. It is this subnationalist emotion that helped the Grand Alliance to knit a bond among the Biharis in favour of the Grand Alliance of caste and religious groups despite being placed differently in the social hierarchy. Although the Bihari-versus-Bahari distinction may have given political dividends to Mahagathbandhan, it is likely to foment trouble for the Biharis, settled elsewhere, as was evident when the Shiv Sena attacked them in Mumbai claiming that Maharashtra was for *Maratha Manus* (sons of the soil) only. Moreover, the insistence on communal harmony as a necessary precondition for development seem to have made

Mahagathbandhan an acceptable conglomeration in contrast with the BJP-led NDA that was alleged to have instigated communal disharmony by defending specific Hindu cultural practices. The appeal of the duo of Nitish Kumar and Lalu Prasad Yadav was most effective also because they insisted on inclusive growth involving different strata of society and also diverse religious groups. In contrast with the strategy of capital-intensive growth which Gujarat had pursued at the behest of Modi being its Chief Minister, the BJP opponents succeeded in creating a favourable vote bank by devising a socialistic developmental package insisting on social justice, communal harmony and freedom of choice. The new rhetoric that the NDA championed did not appear to have many takers while the old socialistic design of growth became an effective vote catcher tool.

Thirdly, in the context of a high-octane election campaign, it is the Indian voters who had the final laugh. It is being proved again and again that there is hardly a theoretical format to conclusively conceptualize the voting behaviour in India. Most mature in their preferences, the voters have shown that they cannot be taken for a ride although they get their chance generally once in five years. The usual charges that Indian voters do not seem to be politically alert appears to be overstretched in the light of the pattern of voting that voters have evinced in independent India. This pattern is evident both at the national and regional levels: for instance, while Indira Gandhi was ousted from power in 1977 as voters expressed their resentment over the imposition of 1975–77 Emergency, she was again brought back because of the misgovernance of the Janata Dal, a conglomeration of parties which came together against Indira Gandhi-led INC. The 2015 Bihar election further confirms how astute the Bihari voters are; instead of being swayed by the Modi rhetoric, they retained their independence while deciding a distinct course of action which was contrary to what was believed to be voters' choice in view of the convincing victory of the BJP in 2014 Lok Sabha poll. So, the Bihari voting behaviour was not unique, but governed by what the voters deem appropriate at a particular juncture of Bihar's history.

Finally, the election victory of the Mahagathbandhan confirms that democracy in India has developed firm organic roots and can never be diluted. The fact that democratic elections create an environment in which voters express their preferences without fear and hurdles, in the presence of an alert and vigilant Election Commission of India, is a further proof to those who doubt the depth of Indian democracy. Defying the conventional wisdom, democracy in India has evolved as a system of politico-ideological mechanism with a clear Indian flavour. The supremacy of the participants can never be ignored; it is they who shape the path which democracy follows. The 2015 Bihar election may have worrying moments of divisive rhetoric though at the end, voters made a prudent choice to scuttle the divisive design that appeared to have gained momentum temporarily. This seems to have reinforced processes which, besides challenging the hegemony of a single party, appear to have contributed to the rise of strong political forces highlighting socio-economic and political issues relevant to the respective areas. Democracy thus always creates conditions for the growth alternative centres of power, which provide useful political forums for articulating peripheral voices. It is constantly being reinvented which makes an analyst to argue that 'it is the peculiar dignity of Indian democracy that it so often provides a new dawn'.[28] The idea reverberates throughout India's political history since independence in 1947 when democracy was considered as a mere window-dressing. History is replete with examples showing its peculiar unfolding which caught the commentators by surprise. Implicit here is the idea that there is hardly a settled format for democracy to follow; it is clearly contextual in character. This is being proved time and again. Being organic in nature, democracy in India provides newer challenges which cannot be grasped, let alone conceptualized, in derivative wisdom. The 2015 Bihar election is just another persuasive illustration corroborating the idea that democracy in India is not merely a structural edifice, but also comprises certain fundamental socio-economic and political values to meaningfully articulate the participatory character of governance in which citizens are not merely passive recipients, but instigators of change.

Notes and References

Introduction

1. Rajdeep Sardesai, *The Election that Changed India* (New Delhi: Viking, 2014), Chapter 10.
2. Harish Khare, *How Modi Won it: Notes from the 2014 Election* (New Delhi: Hachette, 2014), 133.
3. Khare, *How Modi Won it*, 202.
4. Khare, *How Modi Won it*, 128.
5. *The Times of India*, 30 April 2014, report by Surajit Gupta.
6. Neerja Singh (compiled), *Gandhi Patel Letters and Speeches: Differences within Consensus* (New Delhi: National Book Trust, 2009), 172.
7. M.N. Roy, *Men I Met*, reprint (New Delhi: Ajanta Publications, 1981), 19.
8. Neerja Singh, ed., *Nehru–Patel: Agreement within Differences* (New Delhi: National Book Trust, 2010), 33.
9. Neerja Singh, *Nehru–Patel*, 33.
10. Roy, *Men I Met*, 19
11. Roy, *Men I Met*, 12.
12. Roy, *Men I Met*, 12.
13. Pranab Mukherjee, *The Dramatic Decade: The Indira Gandhi Years* (New Delhi: Rupa Publications, 2015).
14. Election Commission General Election 2014 data, available at http://eci.nic.in/eci_main1/ElectionStatistics.aspx
15. Election Commission website: Results of state assembly election. Available at http://eci.nic.in/eci_main1/ElectionStatistics.aspx

Chapter 1

1. Report on the First General Elections in India, 1951–52, Volume 1, Election Commission India, 9.
2. Available at http://eci.nic.in/eci_main/eci_publications/books/genr/FirstGenElection-51-52.pdf
3. Rajni Kothari, *Politics in India* (New Delhi: Orient Blackswan, 2005), 103.
4. Nehru Report Wikipedia, available at http://en.wikipedia.org/wiki/Nehru_Report
5. Bipan Chandra, Mridula Mukherjee and Aditya Mukherjee, *India after Independence*, 1947–2000 (New Delhi: Penguin, 2000), 238.
6. When Indira Gandhi split Congress in 1969 in the wake of the Presidential election her part of Congress came to be known as Congress (I)—I for Indira and the leaders who formed the other part were known as Congress (O)—O for old or organization. Morarji was a leader of the second group.
7. Ajit Balakrishnan's blog, available at http://blogs.rediff.com/ajitb/2009/12/08/the-congress-part-ad-campaign-for-the-1984-lok-sabha-elections/

Chapter 2

1. Judgement by F.E.A Chamier, District Judge of Faizabad on 18th March 1886 as recorded in BJP White Paper on Ayodhya and quoted by T.P. Jindal in his book *Ayodhya Imbroglio* (Delhi: APH Publishing, 1995), 160.
2. Several books, notes and reports on the dispute are available. Available at http://en.wikipedia.org/wiki/Babri_Masjid
3. A summary is available at http://en.wikipedia.org/wiki/Mohd._Ahmed_Khan_v._Shah_Bano_Begum
4. For Supreme Court judgement, http://en.wikipedia.org/wiki/Babri_Masjid
5. Shilyanas is laying the foundation stone. In case of a temple through an elaborate ritual the land is purified so as to ward off any evil influence. Normally an auspicious part of the construction site is selected where this "puja" is held.

Chapter 3

1. Ineresting anecdote in http://www.rediff.com/money/2004/apr/02shining.htm
2. Advani's speech to CII, available at http://www.echarcha.com/forum/showthread.php?t=20124
3. L.K. Advani, *My Country My Life* (New Delhi: Rupa, 2008), captures the political developments till 2004.

Chapter 4

1. Madhu Kiswar, *Modi, Muslims and Media* (New Delhi: Manushi Publications, 2014), has detailed investigation of the developments, generally supportive of Modi.
2. See www.youtube.com/watch?v=DleuqZUwHk8

Chapter 5

1. *Indian Express*, 'Rahul: If I'd not Come from Gandhi Family, I wouldn't be Here', 21 November 2008. Available at http://expressindia.indianexpress.com/karnatakapoll08/story_page.php?id=375820
2. Exclusive interview of Rahul Gandhi with Arnab Goswami on 29 January 2014, available at http://youtu.be/UVOBQ8NVxeo
3. Rahul Gandhi's team carefully revealed all his political exploits suitably in all sections of the national media. Some critics wrote blogs which got featured prominently only in a section of media.

Chapter 6

1. Arvind Kejriwal managed his media exposures carefully. His unconventional style attracted media. Despite his electoral loss in 2014, he continued to attract media attention even in the Delhi assembly election in February 2015.

Chapter 7

1. Akshaya Mukul, 'Editors of Two RSS Weeklies Lose Jobs over Pro-Modi Stand', *The Times of India*, 6 April 2013.

2. In a private conversation with Sugato Hazra, co-author, Prakash Javadekar, the senior most BJP spokesperson in Delhi, discussed the point and explained the need for silence within the party till the Karnataka result was over.

3. Aditya Menon, 'It's all Go in Goa: Modi looks to BJP National meet to get PM Nomination in the Bag', *Daily* Mail, 6 June 2013 http://www.dailymail.co.uk/indiahome/indianews/article-2337097/Its-Goa-Modi-looks-BJP-National-meet-PM-nomination-bag.html#ixzz3cOSWdcec

4. Laurence Rees, *Selling Politics* (London: Random House, 1992).

5. Rees, *Selling Politics.*

Chapter 8

1. *The Times of India*, 5 December 2007, New Delhi.

2. *The Times of India*, 2 December 2007, New Delhi.

3. *The Hindu*, 3 and 4 December 2007, New Delhi

4. *The Indian Express*, 7 July 2011, New Delhi.

Chapter 9

1. Quintus Tullius Cicero, *How to Win an Election* (Princeton: Princeton University Press, 2012).

2. Quintus Tullius Cicero, *How to Win an Election* (Princeton: Princeton University Press, 2012), Amazon Kindle Edition.

3. Report, released by the Press Trust of India, 12 July 2013.

4. Richard King, *On Offence: The Politics of Indignation* (London: Scribe Publications, 2013).

5. Ray B. Browne, ed., *Lincoln in the Popular Mind* (Chicago: Brown and Howell, 2013), 55.

6. Personal experience of one of the authors at East Delhi Parliamentary constituency's Trilokpuri assembly segment which earlier had elected debutant Arvind Kejriwal's AAP representative to the state assembly.

7. Drew Western, *The Political Brain: The Role of Emotion in Deciding the Fate of the Nation,* (New York: Public Affairs, 2007).

8. For instance, Harsh Mander believes that it was a manufactured riot. See, his, 'Yet Another Doctored Riot', *Hindustan Times*, 27 September 2013.

9. The entire discussion is drawn on Badri Narayan, 'Modi's Modus Operandi in the 2014 Elections', *Economic and Political Weekly*, 17 May 2014, unless otherwise stated.

10. Narayan, 'Modi's Modus Operandi in the 2014 Elections', 13.

11. Narayan, 'Modi's Modus Operandi in the 2014 Elections', 14.

12. Narayan, 'Modi's Modus Operandi in the 2014 Elections', 14.

Chapter 10

1. Himani Chandra Gurtoo, 'BJP's Advertisement Plan may Cost a Whopping ₹5,000 crore', *Hindustan Times*, New Delhi, 13 April 2014—cited in Rahul Verma and Shreyas Sardesai, 'Does Media Exposure Affect Voting Behaviours and Political Preferences in India?' *Economic and Political Weekly* (27 September 2014), 83.

2. Rahul Verma and Shreyas Sardesai, 'Does Media Exposure Affect Voting Behaviours and Political Preferences in India?' *Economic and Political Weekly* (27 September 2014), 87.

3. Madhu Purnima Kishwar, *Modi, Muslims and Media: Voices from Narendra Modi's Gujarat* (New Delhi: Manushi Publications, 2014).

4. 'BJP's Project 275 for 2014'. Available at http://emergic.org/2012/06/17/blog-past-bjps-project-275-for-2014/

Chapter 11

1. The total vote share of CPI is 1.4%, while RSP obtained 0.3% and Forward Bloc got only 0.2%. *The Indian Express*, 17 May 2014.

2. As per the criteria set by the Election Commission of India, a party is eligible to be declared as a national party provided (a) it secures at least 6% of total votes, polled in four states and wins four seats in the Lok Sabha or (b) it wins at least 2% of total seats of 543 from no less than three provinces of federal India.

3. Akshya Mukul, 'Red Star Fades out, CPM Faces Total Eclipse', *The Times of India*, New Delhi, 17 May 2014.

4. *The Hindu*, New Delhi, 17 May, 2014.

5. Quoting a member of the central committee of CPI (M), *The Times of India*, New Delhi, 19 May 2014, thus reports.

6. Pradeep Chhibber and Rahul Verma, 'The BJP's 2014 Modi Wave: An Ideological Consolidation of the Right', *Economic and Political Weekly* 49, no. 39 (27 September 2014): 55.

7. Chhibber and Verma, 'The BJP's 2014 Modi Wave', 50.

8. Suhas Palshikar, 'The Defeat of the Congress', *Economic and Political Weekly*, 49, no. 39 (27 September 2014).

9. Sandeep Shastri and Reetika Syal, 'Leadership in Context: Impact of Leadership in the 2014 Election', *Economic and Political Weekly* 49, no. 42 (27 September 2014): 81.

10. Suhas Palshikar and K.C. Suri, 'India's 2014 Lok Sabha Election: Critical Shifts in the Long Term and Caution in the Short Term', *Economic and Political Weekly* 49, no. 39 (27 September 2014): 39.

11. The total vote share of CPI is 1.4% while RSP obtained 0.3% and Forward Bloc got 0.2% only. *The Indian Express*, 17 May 2014.

12. *Economic Times* (Delhi), 11 February 2015, quoted from a Modi rally on 1 February 2015.

13. *The New York Times*, 'A Defeat for Prime Minister Modi'—Editorial, 10 February 2015.

14. *Indian Express*, 'Decision 2015–How Delhi Voted', 12 February 2015.

15. Pratap Bhanu Mehta, 'A Victory of Possibilities', *Indian Express*, 11 February 2015.

16. Swapan Dasgupta, 'Modi must Retain his Anti-establishment Image for BJP to Recover', *Hindustan Times*, 12 February 2015.

17. The 1972 movie, *The Candidate*.

18. According to the SM Lipset, 'The more well-to-do a nation, the greater the chances that it will sustain democracy'. S.M. Lipset, 'Some Social Requisites of Democracy: Economic Development and Political Legitimacy', *American Political Science Review* 53, no. 1 (1959): 102.

19. According to J.S. Mill, 'Free institutions are next to impossible in a country made up of different nationalities.... It is in general a necessary condition that the boundaries

of government should coincide in the main with those of nationalities'. J.S. Mill, *Considerations on Representative Government*, reprint (New York: Oxford University Press, 2008), 223.

Chapter 12

1. Judith S. Trent, Robert V. Friedenberg and Robert E. Denton, Jr., *Political Campaign Communication Principles & Practices*, Seventh Edition, (Plymouth UK: Rowaman & Littlefield Publishers, 2011), Kindle Edition.
2. Mukulika Banerjee, *Why India Votes?* (London: Routledge, 2014).
3. Trent, Friedenberg and Denton Jr., *Political Campaign Communication Principles & Practices*.
4. Quintus Tullius Cicero and James Carville, 'Campaign Tips from Cicero: The Art of Politics From the Tiber to the Potomac', *Foreign Affairs* May/June (2012) issue.
5. Cicero and Carville, 'Campaign Tips from Cicero'.
6. Clay Shirkey, 'The Political Power of Social Media: Technology, the Public Sphere, and Political Change', *Foreign Affairs* January/February (2011).
7. Christophe Jaffrelot, 'The Modi-centric BJP 2014 Election Campaign: New Techniques and Old Tactics', *Contemporary South Asia* 23, no. 2 (2015): 151–66.
8. Analysis of funds collected and expenditure incurred by National Political Parties—Lok Sabha 2004, 2009 and 2014: Association for Democratic Watch (ADR), 2 March 2015.
9. Analysis of funds collected and expenditure incurred, 2 March 2015.
10. Suhas Palshikar, 'Lalu, Nitish aur Woh', *Indian Express*, 10 June 2015.
11. Jaffrelot, 'The Modi-centric BJP 2014 Election Campaign', 151–66.
12. 'Top 10 Quotes from Modi's Amethi Speech', 5 May 2014. Available at http://www.rediff.com/news/slide-show/slide-show-1-ls-election-top-10-quotes-from-modis-amethi-speech/20140505.htm
13. 'I Have Come Here to Share your Sadness and Make your Problems Mine' Narendra Modi campaign in Amethi from www.narendramodi.in
14. Jaffrelot, 'The Modi-centric BJP 2014 Election Campaign', 151–66.
15. Ten memorable speeches of Shri Narendra Modi from 2014 Lok Sabha election campaign www.narendramodi.in
16. Dipankar Basu and Kartik Misra, 'BJP's Youth Vote Dividend', *Economic Political Weekly*, 17 January 2015.
17. Jaffrelot, 'The Modi-centric BJP 2014 Election Campaign', 151–66.

Conclusion

1. Available at http://www.rediff.com/news/special/ls-election-smita-prakash-meeting-modi-spartan-surroundings-no-fuss-all-business/20140421.htm
2. Available at http://news.bbc.co.uk/2/hi/uk_news/politics/3697434.stm
3. Harish Khare, *How Modi Won it*, p. 213: 'At every milestone in his political journey that began in 2002, he has craftily experimented with polarization as a strategy. The 2014 campaign was no different. It was built around themes and tactics of polarization.'
4. Drew Westen, *The Political Brian—The Role of Emotion in Deciding the Fate of the Nation* (New York: Public Affairs, 2007).

Postscript: The Bihar Assembly Election, 2015

1. Report by Shankarshan Thakur in *The Telegraph*, Kolkata, India http://www.telegraphindia.com/1150723/jsp/frontpage/story_33229.jsp#.VjxemrcrIgs (accessed on 9 November 2015).

2. Payal Kamat a political communication professional and a member of CM Nitish Kumar's campaign team I-PAC.
   http://www.thenewsminute.com/article/bihar-polls-cm-nitish-kumar-champions-people-centric-campaigns-34733#sthash.lnCDVHbm.dpuf (accessed on 9 November 2015)

3. Payal Kamat, a political communication professional and a member of CM Nitish Kumar's campaign team I-PAC.
   http://www.thenewsminute.com/article/bihar-polls-cm-nitish-kumar-champions-people-centric-campaigns-34733#sthash.lnCDVHbm.dpuf (accessed on 9 November 2015).

4. Available at http://www.hindustantimes.com/india/something-wrong-in-nitish-s-political-dna-modi-at-muzaffarpur-rally/story-ENXfYCxX4bggcONJMkoqIL.html (accessed on 9 November 2015).

5. Payal Kamat, available at http://www.thenewsminute.com/article/bihar-polls-cm-nitish-kumar-champions-people-centric-campaigns-34733#sthash.lnCDVHbm.dpuf (accessed on 9 November 2015).

6. Sanjay Singh in the First Post http://www.firstpost.com/politics/collateral-damage-modi-also-hurt-bjp-going-nitish-gaya-2385232.html (accessed on 9 November 2015).

7. Aman Sharma, 'Narendra Modi, Nitish Kumar, Rahul Gandhi Campaign Close to Each Other', *The Economic Times*, New Delhi, 3 November 2015. Available at http://articles.economictimes.indiatimes.com/2015-11-02/news/67953382_1_prime-minister-narendra-modi-rahul-gandhi-rallies

8. Sevanti Ninan, available at http://www.thehoot.org/media-watch/media-practice/one-step-forward-two-steps-backwards-9007 (accessed on 9 November 2015).

9. Available at http://www.hindustantimes.com/india/poll-did-rss-chief-mohan-bhagwats-comment-on-reservation-turn-the-tide-against-the-bjp-in-bihar/story-2zccfO-HaX36R4QPJ06MELN.html (accessed on 9 November 2015).

10. Muzamil Jaleel, available at http://indianexpress.com/article/india/india-news-india/big-picture-lets-talk-caste (accessed on 9 November 2015).

11. Muzamil Jaleel, available at http://indianexpress.com/article/india/india-news-india/big-picture-lets-talk-caste (accessed on 9 November 2015).

12. Muzamil Jaleel, available at http://indianexpress.com/article/india/india-news-india/big-picture-lets-talk-caste (accessed on 9 November 2015).

13. Muzamil Jaleel, available at http://indianexpress.com/article/india/india-news-india/big-picture-lets-talk-caste (accessed on 9 November 2015).

14. Chandan Mitra, available at http://www.ndtv.com/opinion/bihar-rejects-amit-shahs-high-pitched-campaign-1241426 (accessed on 9 November 2015).

15. Chandan Mitra, available at http://www.ndtv.com/opinion/bihar-rejects-amit-shahs-high-pitched-campaign-1241426 (accessed on 9 November 2015).

16. Chandan Mitra, available at http://www.ndtv.com/opinion/bihar-rejects-amit-shahs-high-pitched-campaign-1241426 (accessed on 9 November 2015).

17. Surajit Dasgupta, available at http://linkis.com/swarajyamag.com/poli/eKfBX (accessed on 9 November 2015).
18. Surajit Dasgupta, available at http://linkis.com/swarajyamag.com/poli/eKfBX (accessed on 9 November 2015).
19. In Dadri 50 km from the national capital Delhi, a lynching mob killed a Muslim on the suspicion of his storing beef for consumption. The incident though took place under the jurisdiction of Uttar Pradesh Government the responses of BJP were tardy. The incidence dented BJP's image badly even among its supporters.
20. Amit Shah's address in a public meeting at Raxaul on 29 October 2015, *The Hindustan Times*, New Delhi, 30 October 2015.
21. Interview to catch news by Surjit Bhalla, available at http://www.catchnews.com/politics-news/poll-forecast-spot-on-surjit-bhalla-says-the-verdict-start-of-campaign-2019-1447092984.html (accessed on 9 November 2015).
22. Suhas Palshikar, Sanjay Kumar and Sandeep Shashtri, 'Voters had better image of Bihar than PM painted', *The Indian Express, New Delhi,* 10 November 2015.
23. Interview to catch news by Surjit Bhalla, available at http://www.catchnews.com/politics-news/poll-forecast-spot-on-surjit-bhalla-says-the-verdict-start-of-campaign-2019-1447092984.html (accessed on 9 November 2015).
24. Arun Jaitley's press statement on 9 November, *The Hindu*, New Delhi, 10 November 2015.
25. Sagarika Ghose, 'Crumpled Kurta vs. the Suit', *The Times of India*, New Delhi, 11 November 2015.
26. Arati R. Jerath, 'Nitish and Lalu got both Math and Chemistry Right', *The Times of India,* New Delhi, 9 November 2015.
27. Ghose, 'Crumpled Kurta vs. the Suit'.
28. Pratap Bhanu Mehta, 'A Vote Against Hubris', *The Indian Express*, New Delhi, 9 November.

Select Bibliography

There is hardly a monograph-length-focussed study on election campaign in India. Nonetheless, there are texts, books and articles in peer-reviewed journals which have dwelled on this aspect as integrally linked with the changing nature of Indian politics. Just like the texture of Indian politics, election campaigns have undergone sea changes since the first national election in India, held in 1952. This is a very short bibliography because the literature on this theme is scanty. We have selected those texts which may not have dealt with the election campaign per se, but have referred to the campaign strategies that the parties have deployed to garner support during the election. Our main purpose is to acquaint the reader with those studies which are useful to understand the impact of election strategies on the poll outcome. In the context of Indian politics, election strategies, as these texts underline, provide critical inputs to comprehend the election verdict. This short bibliography is, thus, an endeavour to provide directions to those seeking to explore further the complex theme of election campaign in a specific socio-economic milieu on the basis of the dialectical interconnection between the context and what is considered to be the election strategies.

Adeney, Katharine and Lawrence Saez. *Coalition Politics and Hindu Nationalism.* Oxford: Routledge, 2005.

Advani, L.K. *My Country My Life.* New Delhi: Rupa, 2008.

Auerbach, Adam Michael. 'India's Urban Constituencies Revisited', *Contemporary South Asia* 23, no. 2 (2015).

Banerjee, Mukulika. *Why India Votes?* London: Routledge, 2014.

Basu, Dipankar and Kartik Misra. 'BJP's Youth Vote Dividend', *Economic Political Weekly* 17 January (2015).

Basur, Rajesh M., ed. *Challenges to Democracy in India.* New Delhi: Oxford University Press, 2009.

Bose, Sumantra. *Transforming India: Challenges to the World's Largest Democracy.* India: Picador, 2013.

Brass, Paul R. *The Politics of India since Independence.* Cambridge: Cambridge University Press, 1992.

Browne, Ray B., ed. *Lincoln in the Popular Mind.* Chicago: Brown and Howell, 2013.

Butler, David. Ashok Lahiri and Prannoy Roy. *India Decides: Elections, 1953–1991.* New Delhi: Living Media India, 1991.

Chakrabarty, Bidyut. *Communism in India.* New York: Oxford University Press, 2014.

Chakrabarty, Bidyut and Rajat Kujur. *Maoism in India.* London and New York: Routledge, 2010.

Chakrabarty, Dipesh. 'In the Name of Politics: Democracy and the Power of the Multitude in India'. In *From the Colonial to the Post-Colonial: India and Pakistan in Transition,* edited by Dipesh Chakrabarty and Rochona Majumdar. New Delhi: Oxford University Press, 2007.

Chandra, Bipan, Mridula Mukherjee and Aditya Mukherjee. *India after Independence, 1947–2000.* New Delhi: Penguin, 2000.

Chandra, Kanchan. *Why Ethnic Parties Succeed: Patronage and Ethnic Head Counts in India.* Cambridge: Cambridge University Press, 2004.

Chatterjee, Partha. 'Democracy and Economic Transformation in India', *Economic and Political Weekly* 43, no. 16 (April 2008): 19–25.

Chhibber, Pradeep and Rahul Verma. 'The BJP's 2014 Modi Wave: An Ideological Consolidation of the Right', *Economic and Political Weekly* 27 (September 2014).

Christophe, Jaffrelot. 'The Modi-centric BJP 2014 Election Campaign: New Techniques and Old Tactics', *Contemporary South Asia* 23, no. 2 (2015).

Corbridge, Stuart and John Harriss. *Reinventing India: Liberalization, Hindu Nationalism and Popular Democracy.* New Delhi: Oxford University Press, 2000.

Corbridge, Stuart, John Harriss and Craig Jeffrey. *India: Economy, Politics and Society.* New Delhi: Oxford University Press, 2014.

Dhavan, Rajeev. 'The Ayodhya Judgment: Encoding Secularism in the Law', *Economic and Political Weekly* 29, no. 48 (26 November 1994).

Dixit, Avinash K. *Landlessness and Economics: Alternative Modes of Governance.* New Delhi: Oxford University Press, 2006.

———— ed. *Nehru–Patel: Agreement within Differences.* New Delhi: National Book Trust, 2010.

———— *Ethnic Conflict and Civic Life: Hindus and Muslims in India.* New Haven: Yale University Press, 2002.

———— *Forging Power: Coalition Politics in India.* Delhi and New York: Oxford University Press, 2006.

Francine, Frankel. *India's Political Economy, 1947–2004: The Gradual Revolution,* Second edition. New Delhi: Oxford University Press, 2005.

Ganguly, Sumit, Larry Diamond and Marc F. Plattner. *The State of India's Democracy.* New Delhi: Oxford University Press, 2007.

Ghose, Sagarika. 'Crumpled Kurta vs. the Suit', *The Times of India,* New Delhi, 11 November 2015.

Gould, Harold A. and Sumit Ganguly, ed. *India Votes: Alliances, Politics and Minority Governments in the Ninth and Tenth General Elections.* Boulder: Westview Press, 1993.

Guha, Ramchandra. *India after Gandhi: The History of the World's Largest Democracy.* London: Picador, 2007.

Hasan, Zoya. *Congress after Indira: Policy, Power, Political Change (1984–2009).* New Delhi: Oxford University Press, 2012.

Heath, Oliver. 'The BJP's Return to Power: Mobilization, Conversion and Vote Swing in the 2014 Indian Election', *Contemporary South Asia* 23, no. 2 (2015).

———— *Indian Politics and Society since Independence.* London and New York: Routledge, 2008.

Jaffrelot, Christophe. *India's Silent Revolution: The Rise of Low Castes in North Indian Politics.* New Delhi: Permanent Black, 2003.

Jayal, Niraja Gopal, Amit Prakash and P.K. Sharma, ed. *Local Governance in India: Decentralization and Beyond.* New Delhi: Oxford University Press, 2006.

Jenkins, Rob, Loraine Kennedy and Partha Mukhopadhyay, ed. *Power, Policy and Protest: The Politics of India's Special Economic Zones.* New Delhi: Oxford University Press, 2014.

Jerath, Arati R. 'Nitish and Lalu got both Math and Chemistry Right', *The Times of India*, New Delhi, 9 November 2015.

Khare, Harish. *How Modi Won It: Notes from the 2014 Election*. New Delhi: Hachette, 2014.

Kishwar, Madhu Purnima, *Modi, Muslims and Media: Voices from Narendra Modi's Gujarat*. New Delhi: Manushi Publications, 2014.

King, Richard. *On Offence: The Politics of Indignation*. London: Scribe Publications, 2013.

Kohli, Atul. *Democracy and Discontent: India's Growing Crisis of Governability*. Cambridge: Cambridge University Press, 1990.

Kothari, Rajni. *Politics in India*. New Delhi: Orient Blackswan, 2005.

Kumar, Sanjay. *Changing Electoral Politics in Delhi: From Caste to Class*. New Delhi: SAGE, 2013.

Lieten, G.K. *Development, Devolution and Democracy: Village Discourse in West Bengal*. New Delhi: SAGE, 1996.

Lipset, S.M. 'Some Social Requisites of Democracy: Economic Development and Political Legitimacy', *American Political Science Review* 53, no. 1 (1959).

Macmillan, Alistair. *Standing at the Margins: Representation and Electoral Reservation in India*. New Delhi: Oxford University Press, 2005.

Menon, Nivedita and Aditya Nigam. *Power and Contestation: India since 1989*. New Delhi: Orient Longman, 2007.

Mehta, Pratap Bhanu. 'A Vote against Hubris', *The Indian Express*, New Delhi, 9 November.

Menon, Aditya. 'It's all go in Goa: Modi looks to BJP National meet to get PM nomination in the bag', *Daily Mail*. Available at: http://www.dailymail.co.uk/indiahome/indianews/article-2337097/Its-Goa-Modi-looks-BJP-National-meet-PM-nomination-bag.html#ixzz3cOSWdcec (Published: 20:49 GMT, 6 June 2013, Updated: 20:49 GMT, 6 June 2013).

Mill, J.S. *Considerations on Representative Government*, reprint. New York: Oxford University Press, 2008.

Mitra, Subrata K. and V.B. Singh. *Democracy and Social Change in India: A Cross-sectional Analysis of National Electorate*. New Delhi: SAGE, 1999.

Mitra, Subrata K. *Politics in India: Structure, Process and Policy*. London and New York: Routledge, 2011.

Mukherjee, Jhumpa. *Conflict Resolution in Multicultural Societies: The Indian Experience*. New Delhi: SAGE, 2014.

Mukherjee, Pranab. *The Dramatic Decade: The Indira Gandhi Years*. New Delhi: Rupa Publications, 2015.

Mukherji, Rahul. *Globalization and Deregulation: Ideas, Interests and Institutional Change in India*. New Delhi: Oxford University Press, 2014.

Narayan, Badri. 'Modi's Modus Operandi in the 2014 Elections', *Economic and Political Weekly* 39, no. 20 (17 May 2014).

———— *Politics of Inclusion: Castes, Minorities and Affirmative Action*. New Delhi: Oxford University Press, 2009.

———— *Poverty amid Plenty in the New India*. Cambridge: Cambridge University Press, 2012.

Palshikar, Suhas. 'Lalu, Nitish aur Woh', *Indian Express*, 10 June 2015.

Quintus Tullius Cicero and James Carville. 'Campaign Tips from Cicero. The Art of Politics, From the Tiber to the Potomac', *Foreign Affairs* May/June (2012).

Quintus Tullius Cicero. *How to Win an Election*. Princeton: Princeton University Press, 2012.

Rees, Laurence. *Selling Politics*. London: Random House, 1992.

Quintus Tullius Cicero. 'Regional Resilience and National Party System Change: India's 2014 General Election in Context', *Contemporary South Asia* 23, no. 2 (2015).

———— *Representing India: Ethnic Diversity and the Governance of Public Institutions.* London: Palgrave, 2006.

Roy, M.N. *Men I Met*, reprint. New Delhi: Ajanta Publications, 1981.

Roy, Ramashray and Paul Wallace, ed. *Indian Politics and the 1998 Election: Regionalism, Hindutva and State Politics.* New Delhi: SAGE, 1999.

Roy, Ramashray. *Democracy in India: Forms and Substance.* New Delhi: Shipra, 2005.

Rudolph, Lloyd I. and Susanne Hoeber Rudolph. *Explaining Indian Democracy*, three volumes. New Delhi: Oxford University Press, 2008.

Ruparelia, Sanjay, Sanjay Reddy, John Harriss and Stuart Corbridge, ed. *Understanding India's New Political Economy: A Great Transformation?* London and New York: Routledge, 2011.

Sardesai, Rajdeep. *The Election that Changed India 2014.* New Delhi: Viking, 2014.

Sengupta, Mitu. 'How the State Changed its Mind: Power, Politics and the Origins of India's Market Reforms', *Economic and Political Weekly* 30, no. 1 (7 January 2008).

Shastri, Sandeep and Reetika Syal. 'Leadership in Context: Impact of Leadership in the 2014 Election', *Economic and Political Weekly* 49, no. 39 (27 September 2014).

Shirky, Clay. 'The Political Power of Social Media: Technology, the Public Sphere, and Political Change', *Foreign Affairs*, January/February (2011).

Sinha, Aseema. *The Regional Roots of Developmental Politics in India: A Divided Leviathan.* New Delhi: Oxford University Press, 2005.

Singh, Neerja, ed. *Gandhi Patel Letters and Speeches: Differences within Consensus.* New Delhi: National Book Trust, 2009.

Tawa Lama-Rewal, Stephanie, ed. *Electoral Representations, Political Representation and Social Change in India: A Comparative Perspective.* New Delhi: Manohar, 2005.

Tillin, Louise. 'Indian Election, 2014: Explaining the Landslide', *Contemporary South Asia* 23, no. 2 (2015).

Trent, Judith S., Robert V. Friedenberg and Robert E. Denton, Jr., *Political Campaign Communication Principles and Practices,* Seventh edition. Plymouth, UK: Rowaman & Littlefield Publishers, 2011.

Varshney, Ashutosh. *Democracy, Development and the Countryside: Urban–rural Struggles in India.* Cambridge: Cambridge University Press, 1995.

Verma, Rahul and Shreyas Sardesai. 'Does Media Exposure Affect Voting Behaviour and Political Preferences in India?' *Economic and Political Weekly* 27 (September 2014).

Vora, Rajendra and Suhas Palshikar, ed. *Indian Democracy: Meanings and Practices.* New Delhi: SAGE, 2004.

Wallace, Paul and Ramashray Roy, ed. *India's 1999 Elections and 20th Century Politics.* New Delhi: SAGE, 2000.

Wallace, Paul. *India's 2014 Elections: A Modi-led BJP Sweep.* New Delhi: SAGE, 2015.

Westen, Drew. *The Political Brain—The Role of Emotion in Deciding the Fate of the Nation.* New York: Public Affairs, 2007.

Wilkinson, Steven. *Votes and Violence: Electoral Competition and Ethnic Riots.* New York: Cambridge University Press, 2004.

Wyatt, Andrew. 'Arvind Kejriwal's Leadership of the Aam Aadmi Party', *Contemporary South Asia* 23, no. 2 (2015).

Index

About the Authors

Bidyut Chakrabarty, PhD, is currently a faculty at the Department of Political Science at University of Delhi, India. He was also Dean of the Faculty of Social Sciences and Head of the Department of Political Science, University of Delhi. He has taught in some of the most prestigious educational institutions such as Hull University, UK; Indian Institute of Management (IIM) Calcutta, India; Monash University, Australia; National University of Singapore, Singapore; Hamburg University, Germany; and James Madison University, USA. Dr Chakrabarty has authored three textbooks for SAGE India: *Indian Government and Politics* (with Rajendra Kumar Pandey, 2008), *Modern Indian Political Thought* (with Rajendra Kumar Pandey, 2009) and *Public Administration in a Globalizing World* (with Prakash Chand, 2012).

Sugato Hazra, Senior Adviser, DTA Consulting, has a Master's in Economics and more than 30 years of experience in banking, government, Industry chamber and media. He has also worked with two large corporate groups on economic and policy issues.